A S O C

LIBR

W9-BDZ-014

Sud Ingle is Quality Control Manager for Mercury Marine, part of the Brunswick Corporation, in Fond du Lac, Wisconsin. He is also on the Board of Directors of the International Association of Quality Circles.

QUALITY CIRCLES MASTER GUIDE

INCREASING PRODUCTIVITY WITH PEOPLE POWER

Sud Ingle

A SPECTRUM BOOK

PRENTICE-HALL, INC.
Englewood Cliffs, New Jersey 07632

Library of Congress Cataloging in Publication Data

Ingle Sud.
    Quality circles master guide.

    (A Spectrum Book)
    Bibliography: p.
    Includes index.
    1. Quality circles.   I.   Title.
HD66.147   658.4′036   81-13874
                                 AACR2

ISBN 0-13-745018-4

ISBN 0-13-745000-1 {PBK.}

This Spectrum Book is available to businesses and organizations
at a special discount when ordered in large quantities. For
information, contact Prentice-Hall, Inc., General Publishing Division,
Special Sales, Englewood Cliffs, N. J. 07632.

© 1982 by Prentice-Hall, Inc., Englewood Cliffs, New Jersey 07632

A SPECTRUM BOOK

All rights reserved. No part of this book
may be reproduced in any form or by any means
without permission in writing from the publisher.

10   9   8   7   6   5   4   3   2   1

Printed in the United States of America

Editorial/production supervision and interior design by Frank Moorman
Cover design by Jeannette Jacobs
Manufacturing buyer: Barbara A. Frick

Prentice-Hall International, Inc., *London*
Prentice-Hall of Australia Pty. Limited, *Sydney*
Prentice-Hall of Canada, Ltd., *Toronto*
Prentice-Hall of India Private Limited, *New Delhi*
Prentice-Hall of Japan, Inc., *Tokyo*
Prentice-Hall of Southeast Asia Pte. Ltd., *Singapore*
Whitehall Books Limited, *Wellington, New Zealand*

CONTENTS

v

PREFACE

This book demonstrates that the Quality Circle concept can work anywhere in the world. Based on my experience with a Quality Circle program, I can say without any hesitation that cultural difference does not interfere with the basic philosophy of the program. This philosophy is valid for all cultures, and a program will succeed anywhere as long as the people involved show continued determination, will power, and commitment.

Quality Circles have been in operation for more than two years at Mercury Marine, a marine engines manufacturer in Wisconsin. Many people have contributed their ideas and expertise to the success of the program. A Quality Circle is an integrated system that involves recognition, training, participation, and many other aspects. Even with two years of experience, we are still modifying and improving the Mercury Marine program. With this book, others can share this valuable experience and understand the depth of the program.

During recent years, many articles have been written on this subject. However, it has been hard to find a book with systematic guidelines for implementing Quality Circles in industry. To fill this gap, this book develops a systematic approach to Quality Circles, including a history, some suggestions for operation, and much more information about such programs.

Emphasis on the practical implementation of a program is a unique feature of this book. As we enter a new space era, the world becomes smaller, and the fierce competition among nations has directed enormous importance to the quality and cost awareness features of any product. On one hand, this book can serve as a practical and handy guide to the industrial professional; on another, it can serve as a textbook for introductory courses on Quality Circles in schools and colleges. The book can also be a useful complement to consultants who want to develop Quality Circle programs for new clientele.

A historical review of various Quality Circle models shows the variety of forms that have developed. The operation of a model program is then reviewed in detail. The importance of the training phase and statistical training techniques, the heart of any successful program, are discussed in depth in Chapters 10 through 12. Peripheral aspects of Quality Circle programs are then reviewed to show why present management styles should be changed. We need to recognize the importance of participative management and its effective application in many industries.

The last three chapters briefly review the application of Quality Circles in service industries and future trends. In short, the book serves as a master guide to all theoretical and operational aspects of this people-building program.

The great success of the Mercury Marine program results from the efforts of the creative and dedicated people involved. Limited space prevents me from mentioning everyone who should be credited. However, the following people were helpful in putting togther and supporting this program: C. Alexander, president, Mercury Marine; R. V. Jordan, vice-president and general manager, Outboard Division; Dr. E. J. Morgan, V. P., Engineering; J. Anthony, V. P., Manufacturing; K. Frankenberry, V. P.; J. Stevenson, V. P.; H. E. Riordan, Director, Engineering Services; M. Hennings, L. Toriello, J. Hunt, D. Aylesworth, G. Hodkiewicz, G. Scott, D. Kind, R. Scheunemann, R. L. Oakland, A. Martin, J. Dietrich, B. Bergen, and many others at Mercury Marine. R. D. Diener, executive director of I.A.Q.C., R. Tate of Dover Electric, D. Dewar, J. Beardsley, W. Rieker, and the board members of I.A.Q.C. also provided support for the completion of this book at a time when it is badly needed in the industrial world. I would also like to thank my wife Neelima, my brothers Dr. T. R. Ingle and V. B. Deshpande, my niece Vasudha Deshpande, and my secretary Rosemary Warren, who coordinated all efforts during the writing of the manuscript. Finally, I cannot forget my daughters Geeta and Vinita, who had to give up many hours we might have spent together.

Sud Ingle

Dedication

To all the employees and the management
of Mercury Marine, a Brunswick Corporation,
who made this program successful,
and to my family, Ingle and Deshpande,
whose inspiration and encouragement made this book possible.

1

INTRODUCTION

Today our nation faces serious economic problems because of the high cost of production and keen foreign competition. Each of us has an important part to play in finding a solution to these problems—our jobs depend on it. American industry's loss of competitiveness over the past two decades has been nothing but an economic disaster. In the 1960s, the United States accounted for more than one fourth of the manufacturing exports of industrial nations, while supplying 98% of its domestic market. Since then, the United States not only has been losing market shares both at home and abroad, but the decline actually has been accelerating.

Business Week magazine has recently reported, "The decline in the U.S. position in the 1970s alone amounted to some $125 billion in lost production and a loss of at least two million industrial jobs." [1]

During the past 10 years, 19 nations surpassed the U.S. average annual productivity growth rate, which is less than 2.5%. Japan led the growth with an annual increase of nearly 10%. Since 1950 the United States has had one of the poorest growth rates of the industrialized nations. In 1977-1978, U.S. output per hour was 1.5 units of production, while Japan's output was 8.3 units—one of the world's highest. (See Fig. 1-1.)

Time magazine recently described the U.S. television industry as slowly dying while the Japanese companies were growing. Zenith laid off 5000 people in 1975 because of the high cost of manufacturing in the United States. It is well known that today the motorcycle business is also dominated by Japanese companies. Honda, Suzuki, Yamaha, and Kawasaki account for more than 80% of the world's production. Let us look at the small cars that were built in Japan, but sold in the United States. While the United States was laying off more than

FIGURE 1-1   (Reprinted by Prentice-Hall, Inc. from IRON AGE, February 2, 1981; Chilton Company.)

Japan Seizes Lead in Manufacturing Output Per Hour

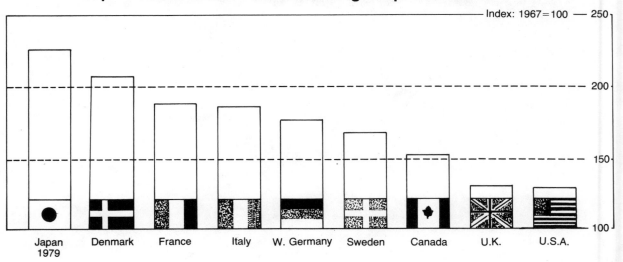

200,000 people, Japan's automobile companies were working overtime to satisfy the demand. During 1980, for the first time in history, Japan will have built more cars than the American companies. Cameras, watches, steel, and other industries are also slowly coming to be dominated by Japan. In short, the U.S. position of world leadership is now in question, and its status as a world power is also doubtful. Today Japan builds a variety of quality products at reasonable cost and can compete with any nation in the world.

It is interesting to review the history of quality workmanship in the world. During the 19th century and at the beginning of this century, the quality of material built in England and in Germany was considered number one. After World War II, the number one place was taken over by the United States. However, by the end of 1970 and clearly in 1980, the market was completely dominated by Japanese products. Today Japan is undoubtedly the leader in quality workmanship in the world.

During my visit to Japan in 1979, I visited the Japan Productivity Center in Tokyo. I discussed Japan's superiority in quality products with Yukio Suzuki and Junji Noguchi, Planning Manager of the Research and Development Department, Union of Japanese Scientists and Engineers, Tokyo. Mr. Noguchi made it clear that quality is not a dream that comes true with the wave of a magic wand. Japan has worked for the past three decades to get to the top, and it is going to be almost impossible for any other nation to reach that place now. What did Japan do to achieve this undisputed number one place?

Japan adopted a six-point program to maintain a quality image. The six-point program includes the following:

1. Quality audits
2. Nation-wide promotion for good quality
3. Quality training
4. Use of higher statistical methods
5. Nation-wide quality control activities
6. Quality Circles

Mr. Noguchi states that the spectacular performance of Quality Circles and the important role they play in improving quality and productivity is astonishing. It is estimated that in Japan between $20 and $25 billion is saved every year as a result of the creative activties of Quality Circles. Mr. Noguchi stressed that Japan has successfully harnessed people's brainpower through Quality Circles. It is extremely important that one respect human beings and their jobs, no matter how big or small they are. The Japanese believe that everyone contributes something to the betterment of the society and the world.

NBC televised a special program called "If Japan Can, Why Can't We?" in June 1980. The program reviewed Japan's successful story of productivity. This five-part program discussed three major problems that we face today:

1. U.S. strict Occupational Safety and Health Act (OSHA) standards
2. New equipment and modernization in Japan
3. Employee participation program, Quality Circles

Quality Circles involve people in solving problems and tap their brainpower effectively. The managing director of the Japanese tire manufacturer Bridgestone once said "Through everyone's participation, we will become the best." At present, it is estimated that more than ten million people have participated in this program and have helped to build a superior quality program in Japan. Japan has shown the rest of the world that productivity can be improved not only by using new equipment or more people, but also by tapping human brainpower and working together in companies.

People, and their brains, are the most precious resources we have. We want to improve our productivity, not at the expense of our people, but at the expense of wasted time, lost motion, unnecessary work, and products of poor quality. Our most valuable partner in cutting waste is people on the production floor who know their jobs better than anyone else. We want the involvement of their minds as well as their hands. When we can achieve this effectively we will have the greatest team in the world, one that no one will be able to compete with.

Nobody in this world uses the full capacity of people. There are also many times when we waste time. The point is that everyone has a great reserve of capabilities and time. If a person perceives that working harder is a threat to him, he will work less, thus using less of his brainpower. On the other hand, if a person sees working cooperatively can improve communications and quality, cut waste, and also eventually give more job satisfaction and enjoyment, he will work more effectively and will use more of his untapped brainpower. This is not just a theory to many of us. It has been a reality that has profited both the company and its people. It is the foundation of Quality Circles.

While underlying principles are stated simply, the key elements that make this program successful are complex and have to be practiced at all times throughout the program, so that they will be used properly for the benefit of the people. What are these key elements? The following paragraphs will describe the basic foundation of the Quality Circle program: [2]

1. *It's a People Building Philosophy:* Quality Circle programs will work only if there is a sincere desire on the part of management to help their employees to grow and develop through Quality Circles. We would advise any company whose only goals are for selfish gains for management not to bother to try Quality Circles. It will be seen just for what it would be—another management manipulation attempt.

2. *It's Voluntary:* This is the second most important element of the program and one which seems difficult for management to accept or at least deal with. This is the visible proof to the members that it is for their benefit—they are completely free to take or not take advantage of it.

3. *Everyone Participates:* Quality Circles are a participative program; therefore, the leader must see that the quiet, more introverted person also has a chance to say what is on his mind.

4. *Members Help Others to Develop:* Since all members will not be equally able to understand and use the techniques, it is important that all the members help in everyone's development. It is not only the leader's job to see that this happens, but every member must look out for the development and growth of the others.

5. *Projects Are Circle Efforts—Not Individual Efforts:* A Quality Circle is a group, a team effort. Everything a Circle does should be done as a team. The projects chosen to work on should be of interest and value to all of the members. The Circle as a whole should receive recognition for any achievements it has accomplished.

6. *Training Is Provided to Workers and Management:* It is not enough to turn the workers loose to find answers to their problems in an unstructured manner. They need to know effective techniques for doing this or they will become frustrated at their ineptitude. Management must also receive training in the role they are to play—one of support, not domination.

7. *Creativity Is Encouraged*: A non-threatening environment for ideas must be created. People will not risk suggesting a half-developed idea if they feel they may be ridiculed or rejected. From seemingly wild ideas often come practical solutions.

8. *Projects Are Related to Members' Work:* The projects which Circles undertake need to have something to do with their work—not the work of others or non-work-related subjects. Members are experts at what they do, but not at what other people do.

9. *Management Has to Be Supportive:* Unless someone in management is willing to give Quality Circles some time, some advice, and some commitment in the beginning, Quality Circles will not have the encouragement they need to grow and mature.

10. *Quality and Improvement-Conciousness Develop:* All of the above will be useless unless the steps result in an awareness on the part of members to be thinking always of procedures to improve quality and reduce errors.

11. *Reduction of the "We" and "They" Mentality:* Each of us strives to make his or her job more creative and meaningful. Quality Circles, when used correctly, help a company to reduce the "we" and "they" mentality of the employees. Since everyone (labor and management) is encouraged to participate in problem solving, the feeling develops that the employees are all in it together and that it is up to each of them to try to produce the best quality products.

We will discuss these policies in this book and show the important role each one plays in a successful Quality Circle program. Each chapter will show a different aspect of the Quality Circle program and is written in order to enhance your knowledge of the program and make you an expert in this field.

A member of one company's Quality Circle said:

Quality Circles are enjoyable for me.

Money or recognition for me means nothing. Seeing an idea I had a hand in developing, incorporated by the company is my satisfaction.

The Circle is the catalyst, the means by which the worker can bring about progress in spite of a minor official who has been standing in the way of progress for years.

I like to get together and rap with people who have different jobs than mine in our plant. Where thinking is stifled and politics is fostered in the work area, the Quality Circle is a breath of fresh air.

My ultimate goal is to try to get the company to incorporate an idea plan for the individual. The person who likes to work alone, constantly nurturing ideas, sometimes working on the idea for months. So far, there is no official effective central channel to convey a good idea.

We need such a program so ideas are not ignored, swiped, buried or ridiculed.

Notes

1. "The Decline of U.S. Industry," *Business Week*, June 30, 1980, p. 59.

2. W. S. Rieker, "Tapping the Creative Power of the Workforce," *Quality Control Circles*, W. S. Rieker, Inc., 1978.

2

HISTORY OF QUALITY CIRCLES

Informal Circles in America

America is the land of plenty. Many ingenious ideas were born here, and many great people have made the impossible possible in this country.

The basic idea of worker participation was effectively used by many people in America in the 1940s. One of the most famous users was Walt Disney. He used to call the wives and children of his employees weekly just to meet and talk with them. He would say, "I get good, useful ideas from children and mothers." It is even said that he got his best ideas from them.

Walt Disney encouraged worker participation all the time. Whenever a new attraction was built, he would call the employees together and ask for their suggestions for improvement. On one occasion, one of the key attractions was reviewed by several employees. A janitor did not like the setup, mainly the atmosphere. When asked why, he replied, "It does not resemble the actual conditions." He then went on to explain the differences. When asked how he knew so much about the place, he replied, "I was born there and lived there for twenty years; I should know something about the place." The attraction was modified immediately according to his suggestions. This practice was the reason Disney was able to maintain quality and near perfection in his work. Many other great entrepreneurs used the same techniques. Even

6

though there are no formal records, it is certain that, years ago, companies were small, communication was good, and employees were closer to their management.

Peter Drucker, in his book *Management*,[1] has also reported group activities that took place in Germany during 1890. Ernst Abbé of Zeiss Company, a famous German optical company, did a lot of problem solving with the help of his workers. He turned the responsibility for working out jobs to the work force itself. He called in the masters and journeymen from the plant, explained to them the new techniques and disciplines, and asked them to organize the jobs and do the work. To make optical glass in the quality and quantity needed required entirely new machinery and new tools. Abbé insisted that the skilled worker, with the assistance of scientists and engineers, develop the machinery. He also insisted on feedback and ideas from workers and respected craftsmen. Group problem solving helped the Zeiss Company become one of the well-known companies in the optical business.

Frank Squires recently reviewed in *Quality* magazine, the origin of statistical quality control techniques that were achieved through group participation.[2] In 1925 in New Jersey, A-T-&-T had just acquired Bell Laboratories. They promptly appealed to what was to become the "brains" of A-T-&-T for help in solving the massive inspection problem at Western Electric. At Bell Laboratories, Drs. Shewhart, Dodge, Romig, and others shares the honor for developing statistical quality control. The classic work on this subject is *The Control of Quality of the Manufactured Product* by W. A. Shewhart, which appeared in 1931.

IBM also used group solving techniques in the late forties. When one of the first electronic computers was being developed, demand for it was so great that production had to begin before the engineering work was fully completed. The final details were worked out on the floor by engineers collaborating with foremen and workers. The result was a superior design; the production engineering was significantly better, cheaper, and faster. As a result of participating in engineering the product and his work, each worker did a significantly better and more productive job.

After World War II, companies grew at a much faster rate and mass production caused too many management and worker problems. Unfortunately, communications and closeness of management and workers were lost.

In the late 1950s, Sidney Rubenstein started a program called Participative Management System. The basic idea was the same as that of Quality Circles. He implemented this program in many small companies. One was a glass factory which, as a result, achieved a higher production, better quality, and improved communication. Another company which made envelopes not only achieved higher production, but also reduced the cost of production and could therefore compete more successfully in the business world. Recently Rubenstein has worked with the Chrysler Company as well as General Motors plants.

Participative Management System indirectly taught techniques similar to those taught in Quality Circles. The philosophy that workers know their jobs best and have the knowledge needed to improve the quality is used effectively in this program. The planning and implementation of the system is similar. Some of the techniques that are taught are as follows:

1. Concepts of participative problem solving
2. Studying a problem as a group
3. Organizing information
4. Strategy for planning the process when the end product is well defined
5. Strategy for understanding and controlling the process
6. Strategy for solving goal-oriented problems
7. The general sequence of the problem solving cycle:
   a. identify the problem
   b. analyze the problem
   c. plan the solution
   d. implement the solution
   e. evaluate the solution
8. Case studies and examples

Quality Education in Japan

After World War II, when many industries in Japan had been destroyed, there was no production as such; people were trying to survive the calamity. The quality of the goods built was known to be shabby, the product seldom lasted for more than a day or so. People were not trained to build quality. The nation was without guidance.

At that time, General Douglas MacArthur felt that something should be done to improve the nation's image and asked that the U.S. government send someone to teach better quality control methods to the Japanese people. Dr. Edward Deming, a statistician for the government, was sent to train management people in Japan. During 1948 to 1950, he performed this job so successfully that he was called upon again and again to train more engineers and scientists in statistical methods. In 1951, the Japanese government honored his services by awarding the Deming Prize. Dr. Deming's philosophy is also known as the Deming Wheel. He professes that everyone should plan, collect data, analyze, and construct the work and keep the circle rotating. This is how quality is properly maintained in a company. (See Figure 2–1.)

During 1954 to 1955, another famous consultant, Dr. Juran, started visiting Japan. He lectured and preached what is known as Total Quality Control. Quality begins in the design stage and ends after satisfactory services are provided to the customer. It is not just the manufacturing quality one should be concerned with, but the total quality that counts for the success of the company. The Japanese government was also deeply involved in this service aspect for a quality improvement program. Later, many programs on quality control, statistics, and related subjects were broadcast on radio and television. The month of November was proclaimed Quality month. "Q" flags, quality slogans, seminars, and conventions were initiated during November to promote a quality drive.

FIGURE 2-1

THE DEMING WHEEL

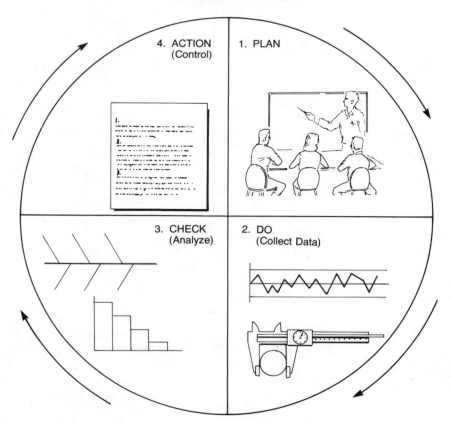

Slowly the Japanese image was changing. Special checks and additional requirements were added for the products that were to be exported. Exportation started slowly. By the 1970s the quality of Japanese products was no longer considered low. Today that quality in a number of different fields—cameras, electronics, motorcycles, television sets, and radios—is considered to be number one. This change in quality was not an overnight development. It took Japan thirty years of hardship and a constant striving for quality to become the third industrial power in the present world. The following is a brief review of the thirty-year history of quality progress in Japan.

History of Quality Progress in Japan

Pre 1940   Japan known worldwide for poor quality
1946-1950   Government declared better quality a national priority.

Dr. W. E. Deming gave lecture series on statistical control of quality for Union of Japanese Scientists and Engineers (JUSE).

JUSE offers six-month course to industry.

Goverment permits "JIS" symbol for high quality products.

Japanese standards association organized to promote Q.C.

1951	Deming awards established by JUSE
1953	Minister of International Trade and Industry (MITI) Awards.
1954	Dr. Juran's lectures of total Quality Circles. Quality is responsibility of all from top management to workers.
1956	Weekly radio series on quality—repeated annually.
1960	Government declares November of each year as "National Quality Month". Abundance of "Q" flags, seminars, posters, and so forth. Weekly television series on quality.
1962	Japan "invents" Quality Circles. Magazine "Q.C. for Foreman"
1963	Top management annual quality audits gain popularity.
1973	Fantastic growth in Quality Circles—½ million circles. 6 million members. Japanese image for high quality is achieved.
1974	Annual Quality Circle meetings on international basis. Top twenty Quality Circle leaders sent around the world in recognition of their contribution.
1980	Goal is to become undisputed world leader in quality.
MESSAGE:	The effort to improve quality begins long before the reputation for quality is achieved.

One of the key factors that helped Japan in this revolution was Quality Circles! Quality Circles are not only helping Japan to improve quality constantly, but are also saving billions of dollars in all types of industries.

Quality Circle Progress in Japan

The origin of Quality Circles in Japan was in the valuable training given to the Japanese people by Dr. Deming and Dr. Juran. Most of the foremen in industries, who received quality training, were wondering what to do with the knowledge they received. Someone asked, "Why not form small groups in the shop and teach the workers these techniques? Why not spread the knowledge and ask their help in solving daily problems? After all, who knows the job best?" That is how Quality Circles were born in 1962.

According to records kept by JUSE, there were approximately 2000 circles formed in Osaka. The Circles grew rapidly, and in 1974 the registered number of circles were approximately 700,000. Each circle involved approximately three to ten people. Not all circles are registered with JUSE, and today, it is estimated that one million circles are in operation and nine to ten million people are involved in these activities.

The following history of the Quality Circles shows the major impact on the United States and the rest of the world in the 1970s.

Quality Circle Progress

1962 JUSE published a quarterly magazine "Genba-To-QC" (Quality Control for Foremen) monthly since 1964. A Quality Circle headquarters was established.

1962 The first Quality Circle was registered with the Quality Circle headquarters (Matsuyama Carrier Equipment Circle of Japan Telephone and Telegraph Corporation).

1963 The first Quality Circle conference was held in Sendai, northern Japan.

1966 Dr. Juran observed Japanese Quality Circle activities. First Quality Circle session at the 10th conference of EOQC was held in Stockholm, Sweden.

1968 JUSE sent the first Quality Circle study team overseas.

1971 The first all Japan Quality Circle conference was held in Tokyo.

1974 A major U.S. firm started Quality Circles.

1977 IAQC (International Association of Quality Circles, U.S.) was created.
Mexican study team to Japan.

1978 The first International Quality Circle convention.

1979 100,000 registered Circles in Japan (Kanto Auto Works, Ltd.) Circle concept spreads internationally.

1980 More than 500 United States companies started Circles. Circle movement in Brazil, Mexico, Argentina, Taiwan, Korea, China and many other countries.

Most of the circles started working on problems concerned with quality. The foremen gathered the volunteers together and suggested they pick up a problem in their area and offer a solution that would improve the quality of their product. The objective also supported the nation's need for building good quality products. The nation was striving to improve its quality image, and the Quality Circle movement helped to get many people involved. Most of the people were supportive. They realized the need, and Quality Circles became a successful program to build a quality product. As quality problems became fewer, people turned their attention to other objectives. Some of the Circles began working on cost reduction problems while others attacked maintenance, tooling, and fixturing problems.

The Quality Circle program was absolutely voluntary from the beginning. Generally, people were asked to join a circle as they started working and went through the training during normal employment. In the beginning most of these people met on their own time. Today, meetings are generally held on company time or on paid overtime. At the same time, there are some companies who don't pay employees for attending. However, the lifetime employment concept helped most of the companies keep people interested in the program. Generally, the meetings are held once a week for thirty to sixty minutes. Some of the meetings are longer, but most are limited to an hour. People are given assignments, and most show tremendous cooperation and enthusiasm. The major thrust today lies in cost reduction along with quality improvement. Many of the companies realize that they have to be cost competitive to stay in business and at the same time offer better quality so that customer satisfaction is achieved.

Why Were Circles Successful?

When one sees the tremendous success that is achieved through the operation of Quality Circles, one wonders about the reasons behind this participative management style. The following cover most of the reasons behind the success:
1. Use of basic statistics
2. Group dynamics
3. Job satisfaction

When the problems are attacked in Quality Circles, the solutions or suggestions are not based on opinions or on imagination. Generally, the people involved use statistical techniques, such as cause and effect diagrams, Pareto diagrams, or checksheets. This helps to collect new data and analyze the problem logically and systematically. The workers like this, and management approves it since the facts are collected and the suggestions based on sound statistics.

Working together in a group also helps people make better decisions. They build a cooperative spirit. Communication improves and, as a result, the company works like a team with one goal in mind. Labor problems are generally minimized, and a healthy competitive force is created in the company. People help each other, waste is reduced, and self-inspection is automatically implemented throughout the organization.

Job satisfaction is also enlarged in the Circle operation. People feel they are part of the company and, since their views and suggestions are listened to and implemented, most of them enjoy the work. They look forward to coming to work and solving company problems. They enjoy the degree of authority and freedom that is given to them.

In short, the success of the Circles lies in the effective use of motivational principles that are discussed by Herzberg, Argyris, Mayo, and McGregor.

Quality Circle Progress
in the United States and the World

It is said that, once upon a time, God threw seeds on the earth. Some seeds fell on the stones, and some fell on busy streets in the cities. Fortunately, some also fell on fertile ground. All of the seeds got plenty of sunshine; however, the seeds on the stones were burned by too much sunshine. The seeds that fell on the streets were damaged by people. But nobody touched the seeds on the fertile ground. The rain came and fell on all of the seeds. As one can imagine, it did not do any good to the seeds on the stones or on the streets. However, the seeds that fell on the fertile ground grew rapidly, and soon flowers grew and radiated happiness and satisfaction.

The same thing can be said about Quality Circles. Although the basic idea originated in the United States, the right combination of factors existed only in Japan. The seeds planted by the Americans were accepted by the Japanese and nourished to the fullest extent. Dr. Deming felt that the combination of the people and their willingness to learn and their need to improve were so great that he predicted in the 1950s that in twenty years Japan would surpass other countries in quality and progress. As we can see today, Japan is undoubtedly building the number one quality product in the world.

The amazing productivity success in Japan has generated a lot of interest in this technique in the United States. In 1966, Dr. Juran visited Japan and was impressed by the work carried on by Circles. He wrote "Quality Circle Phenomena," which described his feelings and predictions regarding this program. Companies like Honeywell and Lockheed started similar pilot programs. Quality Circle programs in Honeywell have flourished impressively. In August 1980, a convention was held to honor the achievement. In 1973, quality programs in Lockheed were publicized in a number of magazines, but the Lockheed program was set back because of unforeseen difficulties in the company. During the past five years, companies like Mercury Marine, Northrup, Hughes Aircraft, Hewlett-Packard, Babcox and Willcox, Memorex, Tektronix, General Motors, Ford, Federal Gage, Chrysler Solar Turbine, and many more had developed similar programs, and a number of them have reported tremendous success. The majority of these Circles are mainly working on quality problems. However, some Circles also work on cost reduction problems to stay competitive in business.

A society called the International Association of Quality Circles (IAQC) was formed in 1977 and issues a quarterly magazine called *Quality Circle*. The magazine publishes many articles on Quality Circles and reviews recent developments in the field. IAQC also offers training courses and materials. The society is growing, and many companies are getting involved in implementing Quality Circle programs.

The American Society for Quality Control (ASQC) has created a separate subsection on Quality Circles, and a panel has been formed to collect more details on the subject. The success and growth thus far has been impressive, and future progress will depend on the cooperation between management and the workers.

13

Quality Circles in the United States have a bigger impact on management styles. Generally, companies are used to Taylorized type managements, in which top management makes the decisions and passes them to middle and lower management. The participative management style in Japan is unfamiliar in the United States. Quality Circles are based on participative management and allows the workers to make many decisions. Daily chronic problems are frequently solved through Quality Circles, and higher management has a chance to spend more time on difficult problems. Even though many companies are trying this program, the total percentage is small. If many more companies see that the system is successful then the program could spread rapidly throughout the United States. Many service industries have shown interest, and it is also possible that banks, hospitals, and other similar service industries will also attempt to implement some kind of **Quality** Circles in their respective areas. Therefore, the future for this program looks bright.

Interest has also been growing in the rest of the world. Countries close to Japan, like Taiwan and Korea, have already used this philosophy and have been reaping the benefits. Mexico, Brazil, Argentina, and China have also started Quality Circle programs. Similar movements can be seen in European and American countries. The impact seems to be worldwide. The basic philosophy behind Circle programs is that they are for the benefit of human begins, and no country or culture should be barred from using the program. One may not see the same degree of success or the same type of cooperation all over the world. However, there is no doubt that this People Building program will definitely help all people.

Notes

1. Abridged and adapted from p. 259 in *MANAGEMENT: TASKS, RESPONSIBLIITIES, PRACTICES* by Peter F. Drucker. Copyright © 1973, 1974 by Peter F. Drucker. Reprinted by permission of Harper & Row, Publishers, Inc., and William Heinemann Ltd., Publishers.

2. Frank Squires, "The Displaced Mecca," *Quality* (Hitchcock Publications, Wheaton, Ill.), February 1981, p. 57.

FIGURE 2–2

International Association of Quality Circles (IAQC)

P.O. Box 30635
Midwest City, Oklahoma 73140
Telephone: (405) 737-6450

WHAT IS THE INTERNATIONAL ASSOCIATION OF QUALITY CIRCLES?

It is an organization representing people involved with Quality Circles world-wide.

WHY AN IAQC - WHAT ARE ITS OBJECTIVES?

1. Serve the needs of members

2. Promote the recognition and spread of the Quality Circle concept.

3. Act as a central clearing house for Quality Circle information.

HOW DOES IAQC CARRY OUT ITS OBJECTIVES?

* Issuance of a quarterly publication, "Quality Circle Quarterly"

.. Technical articles written by qualified individuals

.. Up-to-date current events on Quality Circles

.. Reports of government legislation affecting worker participation

.. New techniques used successfully by others

.. Articles by Circle members

.. Special features of interest to:

- Management personnel   - Leaders

- Facilitators   - Members

* Publishing educational materials on the subject of Quality Circles.

* Sponsoring regional and area seminars.

* Sponsoring Annual International Conferences.

* IAQC Facilitator Development Program.

3
QUALITY CIRCLE MODELS: JAPAN VERSUS THE UNITED STATES

Quality Circles were originated in Japan in 1962. The intention was to use the knowledge that had earlier been transmitted to foremen. It was also apparent that there was a critical need for better quality in production. The environment was perfect; people were cooperative and were looking for a way to utilize their brainpower. Quality Circles were just the right answer for them.

Let us review in detail Quality Circles and the models that existed in Japan. In simple words, a *Quality Circle* is a participative management system in which workers make suggestions and improvements for the betterment of the company.

Some definitions of a Quality Circle follow:

1. It is a small group of people doing similar work, meeting to identify, analyze and solve product quality problems. They usually meet for one-half hour to one hour each week in or near their area. Membership is strictly voluntary and anyone who wishes to join is welcomed as a member. Each person is free to decline membership. An active Circle will attract more people in the long run.
2. It is a group of factory workers from the same area who usually meet for an hour each week to discuss their quality problems, investigate causes, recommend solutions, and take corrective actions when authority is in their purview (from IAQC).
3. It is not a "system," nor a "fad" or "program," it is a way of life, a change in the way one's mind is set. It will not change your man-

agement or organizational structure, but it will change the way you relate to people within the work environment (from General Electric).

Although it is recommended that people involved in a Circle be from the same area, some successful Circles are functioning with members from different areas who are working on a common part of the product. In some companies Circles are formed by the inspectors who work in different areas; in others Circles are formed in purchasing departments or data processing departments.

Usually Circles meet once a week for the specified one-half hour but the frequency of the meetings and the length of each meeting can vary in accordance with the company's requirements. The key points are:

1. Circles meet frequently and at scheduled times
2. Membership is voluntary
3. Problems are not just identified, but are also investigated and solved

Other time-tested characteristics of a successful Quality Circles program are:

1. People-building philosophy
2. Leader gets participation from everyone
3. Members help others to develop
4. Projects are Circle efforts, not individual efforts
5. Training is provided to workers and management
6. Creativity is encouraged
7. Projects are related to members' work
8. Management is supportive
9. A quality and improvement consciousness is promoted and developed

Why Quality Circles Work

Frequently, even the most competent employees are dissatisfied with their efforts to produce high-quality work. Some reasons for this dissatisfaction are poor communication, poor design, poor material, shortages, delays, and inadequate tooling. These conditions lead to disinterest in the job, poor quality, defective workmanship, waste and excessive absenteeism. People think that they are supposed to park their brains as well as their cars in the parking lot and use only their hands and sometimes their legs to perform routine tasks.

Quality Circles allow workers to participate, make suggestions, and solve quality problems. Most of their suggestions are implemented without much hassle. As the product quality improves, so does the company's reputation in the world, and as a result, sales generally increase. There are genuine reasons for having Quality Circles, and the effects are widespread. The impact of Quality Circle activities is felt by both the company and the community. People enjoy the work in Quality Circles since their suggestions are accepted; thus, more harmony is created within the company through Quality Circles. That is the secret of the success of this program.

Japanese System of Management

How do Japanese business executives explain their country's remarkable economic performance? To hear at first hand what some of the executives have to say, the assistant managing editor of *Fortune* magazine, William Bower, was sent to Tokyo in 1977 to conduct a round table discussion with Japanese business executives. The results were illuminating.

The article describing his experiences was published in *Fortune* magazine in November 1977 under the title "Japanese Managers Tell How Their System Works." *Harvard Business Review* also published an article called "Made in America (under) Japanese Management." Many other articles have also been published recently on Japanese management style.

The key elements of Japanese system of management are as follows:

1. Participation
2. Harmony—"Wa" Spirit
3. Cooperation
4. Jishu-Kanri-Principle—the process by which a team of workers get together and attack the problems of their own interest (J-K Group)

How the Japanese
Make Decisions

Peter Drucker, in his book on management, has described the Japanese decision-making system very well.[1] According to him, the Japanese are the only nation to have developed a systematic and standardized approach to a decision-making process. Their decisions are highly effective. In most cases a proposed decision is debated until an agreement is reached, and only then is a decision made. This process takes a long time. Drucker, however, points out the following key advantages in this method:

1. The focus is on deciding what the decision is all about.
2. The Japanese bring about dissenting opinion. There is no discussion on an answer until there is a consensus. Many approaches to a problem are explored.

3. The focus is on alternatives rather than on the "right solution."
4. It eliminates selling a decision. It builds effective execution into the decision making process.

Quality Circle Model
in Japan

Two key features of the Japanese management system (participation and decision making from the bottom up) are also predominant in Quality Circle operations. Quality Circles, which are also known as "small group" activities in Japan, are generally an inherent part of the company and there is no separate organization that exists for this work. Most of the work is shared by a number of different departments. Committees are formed to carry out the decisions that are approved at different levels.

The general arrangement of Quality Circles in any company can be outlined briefly in Figure 3–1.

FIGURE 3–1

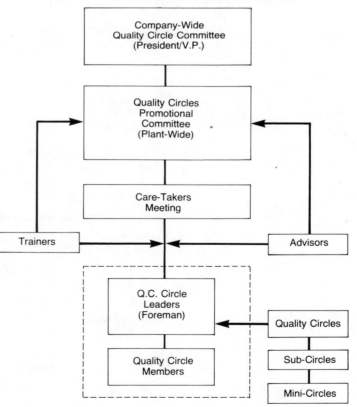

As you will notice from the figure, the system is well organized, and even though it is informal, each one knows his or her job. The commitment and participation flows right from the top down to all levels in the company. Some of the major functions and key features of the system are as follows:

Major Functions

Company-Wide Quality Circle Committee
1. Establishment of company policy
2. Promotion of executive committee
3. Overall planning of activities (instruction and training)

Promotion Committee
1. Promotion of group leader meeting, and study of problems
2. Promotion of presentations (twice a year)

Caretakers Meeting
1. Promotion of group meetings and study of problems
2. Work with leaders

Trainers
1. Develop and implement the Quality Circle training materials and techniques

Advisors
1. Help to promote program. Help in case of difficulties. Help in facility arrangements, interdepartmental communications.

Leaders
1. Leader of the Circle

Members
1. Backbone of the Quality Circle program. Voluntarily work to solve problems in the company.

Key Features of the Quality Circle Model
1. Well organized system
2. Systematic education and training programs
3. Circle leader's conferences
4. Plant-wide meetings
5. Company-wide meeting (annual)
6. Outside visits
7. Annual awards for best projects
8. Good publicity through pictures and posters
9. Clean, nice meeting areas on the floor
10. Well organized recognition program throughout the plants

Quality Circle models in two Japanese companies are reviewed briefly here.

Typical Quality Control Circles

1. Organization
The Quality Circle organization is shown in Figure 3–2.

2. Key Features
—Emphasis on cost reduction
—Once-a-week meeting after work for one-half hour
—Meeting attendance: $1.00 payment
—Committee to analyze improvements
—Book published every six months to inform members of improvements
—Pictures, data, charts in the shop to inform and remind personnel of the program

FIGURE 3–2

QUALITY CIRCLES AT TYPICAL JAPANESE COMPANY

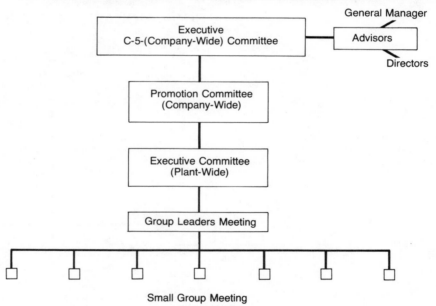

Quality Circles at Showa

1. General
Showa Company's headquarters are located in Tokyo. There are six plants in five various locations in Japan. The company manufactures various kinds of shock absorbers for automobiles, motorcycles and for other industries. Quality Circle programs are part of the company-wide program called "S.C.O.P." (Showa Creative Operation Plan). The S.C.O.P. program involves T.Q.C. (Total Quality Control), Q.C.C. (Quality Control Circles), I.E. (Industrial Engineering), and office efficiency improvement. There are 1800 Showa employees at present and there are 300 Quality Circles operating in the company.

2. Organization

Figure 3–3 shows the Quality Circle organization in the company.

3. Key Features

—Circles meet after hours without pay
—Annual company-wide meeting. (Best three circles get rewards from the president of the company
—95% of the employers are involved in the Quality Circle program
—Products are developed based on the customer's need and are thoroughly tested before being put into production
—Production and engineering departments work together
—Total integrated manufacturing system
—Precise production control
—Technology to create improved society

FIGURE 3–3

SHOWA QUALITY CIRCLE ORGANIZATION

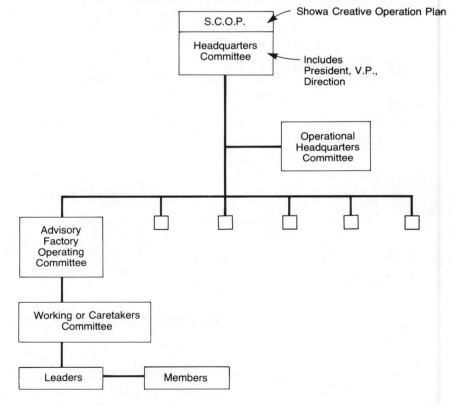

**Quality Circle Model
in the United States**

The general arrangement seen in the United States is shown in Figure 3–4.

Key Features

—Circle program is in infant stage
—Programs need refinement
—Training needs improvement
—Management committee is required
—Union cooperation is required

Actual arrangements in three American companies are shown in Figures 3–5, 3–6, and 3–7. Quality Circles are in an early stage in the United States and it is not easy to predict the future developments and changes that will take place in the next thirty years.

The key difference that one sees in the American version is the role that the facilitator plays in promoting the Quality Circle program and the training requirements needed for its implementation.

FIGURE 3–4

QUALITY CIRCLE MODEL IN U.S.A.

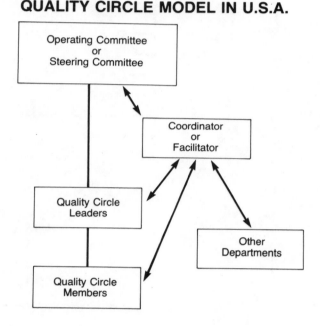

The facilitator's role in American industry is critical. As discussed before. Quality Circles represent a new management style in American industry and it will not be easy to sell this idea in any company. Facilitators, mini-coordinators, or program chairmen must work hard to convince both management and workers of the long range benefits of Quality Circles. People resist change and this change in style will pose many problems and erect many hurdles. However, we should not give up easily. We should expand the program "slowly but steadily" within the company.

Details of the operation and functions of each group in a Quality Circle are described in Chapters 5 and 6.

FIGURE 3–5

QUALITY CIRCLE ORGANIZATION
(Company on East Coast)

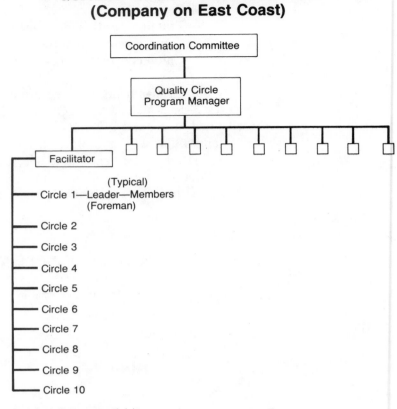

Note: One facilitator manages 10 circles.

FIGURE 3–6

QUALITY CIRCLE ORGANIZATION
(Mid-West Company)

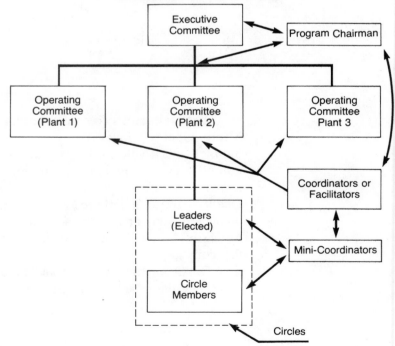

FIGURE 3–7 (From J. Hunley, "Our Experience with Quality Circles," *Quality Progress.* Copyright 1980, American Society for Quality Control, Inc. Reprinted by permission.)

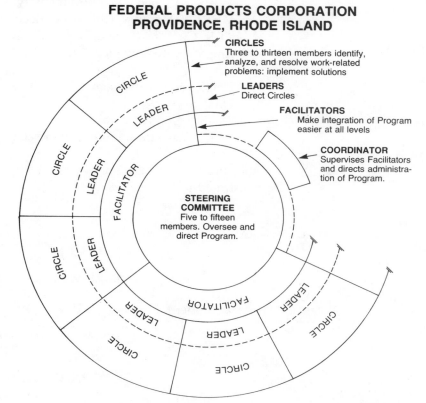

**FEDERAL PRODUCTS CORPORATION
PROVIDENCE, RHODE ISLAND**

Specialized training is needed to prepare personnel for the Quality Circle program. There is a key difference between the ways in which the United States and Japan address these needs. In Japan companies constantly carry out many valuable and effective training programs for workers and management. United States companies need to start similar programs and to educate all levels in the company in statistical quality control techniques. Facilitators and training departments need to cooperate in developing educational material and programs. Leaders, circle members, and various levels of management need training. The success or failure of the Quality Circle program in the company will depend on meeting these educational needs.

Even though at present most United States companies concentrate on productivity, many of them are also looking for improvement in the quality of their product. Still others are primarily interested in improving communication in the company. On the other hand, large automobile company plants are mainly interested in reducing grievances. Hence, it is clear that management will have to adapt Quality Circle programs to satisfy the various needs of the company.

The following list will show how companies personalize the program to meet individual needs.

Quality Circle Program Names in U.S.
—TAS—The American Spirit

—VIPS—Volunteers Interested in Perfection
—PPS—Participative Problem Solving Groups
—TOPS—Turned Onto Productivity and Savings
—MERC—Mercury Employee Recognition Circles
—TEK Circles—Tektronix Circles
—Employee Recognition Circles
—Gators Aids
—Employee Involvement Circles
—Quality Circles
—Quality Control Circles
—IP Circles—International Paper Circles

Finally, the two management styles, Japanese and Western, are briefly demonstrated in Figure 3–8.

FIGURE 3–8

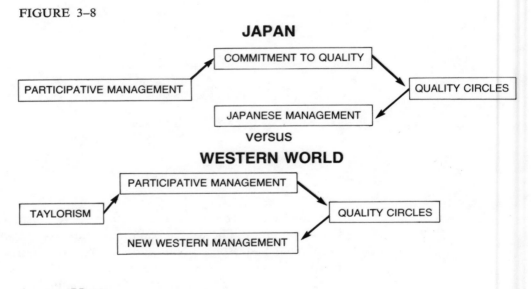

Notes

1. Abridged and adapted from p. 470 in *MANAGEMENT: TASKS, RESPONSIBILITIES, PRACTICES* by Peter F. Drucker. Copyright © 1973, 1974 by Peter F. Drucker. Reprinted by permission of Harper & Row, Publishers, Inc., and William Heinemann, Ltd., Publishers.

4

OBJECTIVES: THE SECRET TO SUCCESS

In order to achieve success in the Quality Circle program it is extremely important to lay down objectives or goals. Well-defined objectives help management to direct various activities and efforts, and to plan personnel and funding for future growth. Hence, it is essential to define objectives clearly and to relay them throughout the company. The objectives can consist of many goals, major and minor, short-range and long-range. As time goes on, the goals should be constantly reviewed and updated so that everyone is fully aware of the current program, and goals are kept compatible with the conditions that presently exist in the company.

There are a number of objectives that can be accomplished in the Quality Circle program. The following examples will give some ideas of the accomplishments that one can work towards:

1. Self-development
2. Mutual development
3. Improvement in quality
4. Improvement in communications and attitude
5. Waste reduction
6. Job satisfaction
7. Cost reduction
8. Improvement in productivity

9. Safety improvement
10. Problem solving opportunities
11. Team building
12. Link all levels of management and workers together to achieve success
13. Get people more involved and interested in their work
14. Improve participation
15. Reduce absenteeism and grievances

FIGURE 4-1

QUALITY CIRCLE OBJECTIVES

1. *Self-Development:* One of the key elements in a Quality Circle program is training. Every person who joins the circle gets eight to ten hours of training and, as time goes on, gets more training to enhance their knowledge. Training helps them understand the company's needs while educating them so that their abilities are sharpened. The knowledge acquired through training and working with people helps to promote success in other areas of life, at home as well as in the society. Problem solving techniques such as Pareto diagrams, cause and effect analysis, and Check-Sheets, are so simple that they can be used anywhere to analyze and solve problems. In a broader sense, Quality Circles help people improve their abilities and develop themselves to the fullest extent.

2. *Mutual Development:* After the basic training is completed, Quality Circles are formed in areas where people work in a group. Working in a group is something different than working alone on the job. It is like playing football as opposed to playing tennis. Each player has to be at the right place and has to carry out given tasks properly to win the football game. The same is true in Quality Circles. Once the project is selected, the efforts of all members of the group are

crucial. Without cooperation and mutual understanding a project can go on forever.

In Quality Circles you learn how to work with others, how to cope with personal differences, how to understand another's views, and how to work cooperatively towards a common goal. Mutual cooperation and understanding not only help to solve company problems but also can be used to solve problems in church or school.

3. *Improvement in Quality:* Improving quality is a never-ending job. Consumers constantly demand better quality, and if a company wishes to stay in business, it must try to satisfy those consumer demands at all times. One of the reasons people today like to buy Honda, Toyota, and other small Japanese-built cars is for the quality of the machine and for the satisfaction they get for their money. Very few service problems are reported on these foreign cars. It has been reported that Detroit recalled millions of cars for mechanical problems in the 1970's, but Toyota did not recall one car during that same five-year period. Quality Circles in Japan started in 1962 to solve quality problems and even today more than 20% of the Circle activities are involved in solving quality problems. As long as we deal with people, process, machines, and material, there will always be the variation in the manufacturing of what constitutes good quality. A Quality Circle is one of the best answers for solving problems and improving the quality image.

4. *Improvement in Communication and Attitude:* One cannot deny the importance of good communications and attitudes in our work life. Many times we face misunderstandings and confusion due to a different interpretation of the messages heard and because of delays that occur between the sender and the receiver. Poor communications also cause dissatisfaction and undue tension. Quality Circles help improve communication through group activities which take place frequently. People become more open-minded, too. In some companies people will talk about the problems even during breaks and over lunch. One company observed a change in the working atmosphere and the development of a more helpful attitude.

5. *Waste Reduction:* Waste can be found all around. People have to think "quality" and see how it can be achieved by cutting down the waste in material, rework, and time. Often many operations are added by different people in an effort to solve temporary problems without getting at the cause. Similarly, a lot of material is wasted because nobody has paid attention to the cost. For example, you will see the windows and doors of the plant open in winter; this will waste heat (energy). However, if we decide to work together and help each other, these wastes can be avoided. Many Quality Circle projects have proved that we can do this.

6. *Job Satisfaction:* People have to feel happy and enthusiastic at work and take pride in it to do a good job. However, they cannot achieve this sense of pride unless the opportunities are given to them to use their ideas and their brainpower. Quality Circles help promote more job satisfaction since people are aware that their ideas will be considered. This helps to satisfy their "achievement" need.

7. *Cost Reduction:* Cost reduction is another area which is of great

concern. With today's inflationary conditions the cost of material, wages, and so on, are rapidly increasing and it is necessary to find ways to reduce costs as much as possible. Today, many companies in Japan concentrate on cost reduction. It is possible to present costly items to the Quality Circles and ask them to reduce the cost without a reduction in quality. But simply, this is really nothing but "value analysis."

8. *Improvement in Productivity:* Productivity in the United States today is lagging behind Japan, Germany, France, and many other countries—practically, behind all other industrial nations. The recent statistics show the growth in this country is almost nil, while Japan, Germany, and France are growing at a rate of more than 4%.

    Reducing costs and eliminating rejects help to improve productivity of the industry. Genesco Company, a garment manufacturer, reported a 5% improvement in productivity by reducing rejects. In the same manner, Nashuo Company improved productivity in its paper products.

9. *Improvement in Safety:* Every company is interested in improving the safety of the employees. However, it is hard to know all of the hazards and problem areas that should be watched and improved to eliminate accidents. Quality Circles have done an excellent job even in this area. One of the Quality Circle members interviewed approximately 200 workers and collected data on safety problems. The Circle also analyzed the data and prepared the list of major safety changes that were requested by the people. Many of these changes were implemented and thereby helped to improve safety of the employees.

10. *Problem Solving Opportunities:* Quality Circle programs provide an excellent opportunity to solve many problems that people face daily and can do something about collectively. It gives the people a chance to get together and think about the problem and then to try their ideas to get it solved. As long as companies have to make use of men, machines, and materials to build a product, variations in the process are going to exist. Brainpower is unmatched as a means of solving problems.

    Quality Circles in general offer members unlimited opportunity to solve these problems and at the same time make them feel they are a part of their company.

11. *Team Building:* Once members start working in the Circle, slowly but surely team spirit is created in the group. People get to know each other, they start liking to see each other, and, thus, the feeling of "togetherness" is created in the group. Circles create new friendships. People start talking about business as well as other problems. They help each other. These teams become a strong force in the company to combat growing competition and inflation problems.

12. *Linking All Levels in the Company:* Typically, an organiztion is structured in a traditional way with a president on the top and various levels below. Many times, if the company is large, people on the floor really don't know who is who. Floor workers hardly ever get to see the plant manager or engineers. However, this prob-

lem can be solved to some extent. Start Quality Circles! This writer's experience has shown that this is one of the ways to link all people in a company no matter what their formal position in the company. The Quality Circles' operational procedure can call anyone in the company to their meetings and ask for help or for details needed to solve a problem. People in the shop get to know many more functions and people, and this indirectly helps to link all levels of the company. Management presentations that take place at the completion of the project also help to make known to others a number of people who work in the company. When one links all these people, old water-tight compartments are opened and people mix together; this is a measure of the success of the program.

13. *Getting People Involved:* This writer's experience has shown that after a certain time people come to work to earn a living, but the job has become boring and monotonous. Tightening the same nut on the same part does not provide challenge enough for some workers who like to work. Many companies have proven statistically that people engaged in Quality Circle activities get more interested in their jobs. They enjoy coming to work, they look forward to Circle activities, and at meeting times they feel more "involved." Statistics also show that productivity is greater because of the Circle program.

14. *Improve Participation:* Participation in the program can be slow but sure if the operating committee determines to offer help and to work closely with the people. Getting more people involved in this program helps to create cohesiveness and unity in the company. It helps to eliminate the "we" and "they" feeling that generally exists between the management and the union. Many people stop participating but come back later because they miss that participation.

   The same thing is true in Circle operations. The number of different ideas that you can generate in the Circle is unbelievable. It can only happen if you get good participation in a Circle. People are generally shy in the beginning, but once they see that it is going to help them in the long run, there will be no limit to the cooperation that you will get with the help of the Circle activities. However, you should be careful and realize that this path is not always smooth—you have to expect hills and valleys.

15. *Reducing Absenteeism and Grievances:* Quality Circles have also helped many companies in two key areas, reduction of absenteeism and grievances. The human resources research department in one major company compared the absenteeism rate in the department where Quality Circles existed with that in an area where there were none. A six months' study showed a remarkable reduction in absenteeism in the QC department. Many members commented that the Circle program helped them to enjoy the work and made them come to work instead of staying home for minor reasons.

   Many companies have also seen reduction in grievances. One major auto company reported that it used to get between two to three thousand grievances every year. After the implementation of a similar program, the number of grievances dropped to less than

500. The Circles link all kinds of people together, which leads to the solution of many problems, before they become part of a grievance. There is no reason to spend time and money and energy in this area. America today needs higher productivity, better quality, and products that can compete in the world. The only way to do this is to work together and face the challenge. We must set aside minor differences and work for the betterment of the society.

The list of objectives can be extended to modify the program to fulfill individual needs. The sky is the limit in setting the objectives.

FIGURE 4–2

Objections to Quality Circles

You should not get the impression that implementation of the Quality Circle program is smooth and easy. There are a number of old customs and traditions that have to be overcome. Many people have to be convinced to try managing business the new way. Some of the frequently heard objections are described here: [1]

1. *Resistance:* Many companies feel that this program will change the organization or add many people and put more of a financial burden on the organization. People in the company also resist change fearing they might have to treat people differently or listen to them more carefully, and that they cannot neglect or cover up mistakes anymore. In reality, there is very little change in the organization. Once people understand the basic principles and learn the techniques, most of the operation is smoother.
2. *No Time for Quality Circles:* Many people feel that they really don't have the time for Quality Circle work. They are already busy for

eight hours and they don't have time to work harder for the company. They are not "workaholics" like the Japanese. One should remember a quick retort given by the latter, "What's wrong with hard work? It got us where we are." Once again Quality Circle work may look like extra work at the start, but in the long range it saves money, avoids wasted energy, and improves quality.

3. *Loss of Management Authority:* This is another invalid objection. Participation of management does not mean the loss of authority. Management still has the final say in the solution of a problem. What happens is that people from all levels get involved in solving the problems. Some of the problems solved could be the ones that were never tackled before. With more input, better decisions are made.

4. *Members Feel "Used":* Some Quality Circle members get the feeling of being "used". However, everyone has to remember that the company is not made up of management only. Members make the company and there is nothing wrong in helping the company build better quality and cut down on waste. There is no reason to park the brain with the car outside the fence when one comes to work. Today everyone needs help, and only those companies who are going to build good quality products at a reasonable cost will survive. If there are no sales, there is no need for any workers in a company. Therefore, there is no reason to believe that one is being used.

5. *Why Should I Help My Company:* This is an objection that needs the special attention of the facilitator. Many people feel that the company is something apart. In reality, workers make the company. No one closes the doors if a few management people quit, but many companies have to shut down when workers go on strike. Hence, in real life the members are helping themselves by building better quality and building it cheaper, too. A facilitator and other managers have convinced people and lead them to understand these concepts.

6. *It Is a Quality Control Work:* Many members feel that because the company maintains a quality control department the people in that department should take care of all the qualiy problems. However, it is practically impossible to employ one inspector per operator. People have to realize the need for building better quality all the time. Detection of defective goods comes too late and does not make money for the company. At the same time, quality control is always busy on major problems. Quality Circles can also extend help to other Circles and thus solve minor problems that annoy the workers daily.

7. *N.I.H.:* "Not invented here" is another reason that people use to stop Quality Circle programs. Many companies and people feel that this technique was invented in Japan and so it only works in Japan because their customs and culture are different from ours. It is true that the culture is different, but the philosophy behind the program is universal and so it can work anywhere at any time.

8. *It Won't Work Here:* This is another frequently heard objection. Many people will say "Well, we tried these kinds of ventures ten years ago. It won't work here. We are different. Our operation is different. Let's not disrupt the good thing that is going on here." Such comments make you realize that hard work lies ahead in

33

convincing those people. People dislike change and hesitate to try something new. This is common. You have to convince top key people first and then just keep trying until you gain the confidence of all the people. Later on things become much smoother.

These are just a few objections that will arise. But again, the list is not complete. What is important is to try to cope with such objections and meet them with a proper answer.

Cautionary Notes

The objections that have been discussed will give you a general idea about the problems you can expect. Before we reveal the secrets of a successful program, there are some precautions that you should take while trying to implement this program. We will discuss a few here for your information:

1. *Right Conditions Must Be Created:* As previously discussed, this is a new style of managing people and it will not happen if the conditions in the company are not right. Management has to change slowly, see the benefits, and at the same time members have to extend their cooperation also. This takes time. But it can be done, it has been done. It might take a few days, months, or even years in some cases. Be patient and avoid starting this program prematurely.
2. *Unforeseen Risks:* Management's support for this type of program is a must. However, mere "lip service" will not serve the purpose. Poor management will create poor Quality Circle programs which might last for three to four months. This program cannot be treated lightly, and people have to make a part of their time available for consultation.
3. *Appropriate Actions:* One of the key factors will be to take appropriate action at the right time. On many occasions you will notice a person will not give up his or her rights. It could be a member, a foreman, or an engineer. What you will need is a third party coordinator who should watch out for the company's interests and effect compromises when necessary. Similarly, if it is a problem of personal differences, those should be settled immediately but carefully so that nobody's feelings are hurt. Appropriate action at the right time is essential to prevent things from getting too far out of hand.
4. *Union Reaction:* Many unions today see the benefits of the program. Douglas Fraser, United Automobile Workers president, has talked on several occasions on television about the need for such participative programs. People in these programs enjoy working together and see the benefits when they realize that the quality race is never ending. However, the picture is not all that rosy yet. Not all union leaders are convinced. It is going to be a gradual change. Constant work in this area is needed so that union confidence can be gained in the early stages.

34

5. *Middle Management Feelings:* Dr. R. Cole, a professor at the University of Michigan, has many times expressed a great concern for the middle management. He thinks that if the program is not treated properly that there is a strong possibility that the middle management will kill it. The feeling of participation does not exist yet, and the middle management sometimes feels that there is a loss of authority when you ask people to solve problems and implement solutions accordingly. Once again the facilitator has to watch this area carefully and make sure that it will not adversely affect the program.

6. *Overpublicity:* Many companies get carried away and rush into extended publicity all over the organization. Sometimes this might hinder the program instead of helping the cause. Many people, if not properly informed, will make decisions about the program which will be hard to change later. Similarly, if in the beginning of the program, a few projects that are presented or followed through in a wrong manner get publicized, everyone will get to know the problems only. This situation will not create a healthy atmosphere in the company.

7. *People Building Philosophy:* It is important to remember this objective all the time. It is easy to lose sight of this key philosophy and to neglect to watch the people. People make the program work and it is for their benefit as well as for the benefit of the company that this objective should be constantly remembered so that wrong actions can be avoided.

8. *Too Much Paperwork:* This is another aspect of the program that needs everyone's attention. It is necessary and important that Circles make impressive presentations to the management. A well-organized report always helps to demonstrate achievements to management. Many times, however, it takes too much time and many Circle members, especially those in the shop, do not like to spend that much time and energy in a final presentation. You should look into this area soon. Once the program is well established in the company, much of this paperwork should be streamlined as early as possible.

Secrets to Establishing a Successful Quality Circle Program

In order to start a successful Quality Circle program you should understand the secrets of a successful program.[1] When everybody in the company understands the principles thoroughly and implements them properly, then you can rest assured that success is close at hand. There are many ways you can achieve success. Some of the important aspects are described here:

1. *Establish a Suitable Atmosphere:* It is necessary that the company create a proper atmosphere for the Quality Circle program. Various management levels in the organization need to accept the idea of participative management. The program chairman has the responsibility for spreading the good word about it. Meetings are arranged so that many people can get to know the basic philosophy of the

program. Top management, middle management, as well as union leaders, should be introduced to the program properly. This will help to acquire necessary funding, time, and space to initiate the Quality Circle. A pilot study can be publicized to create a warm atmosphere in the company. In general, the first secret is to generate warmth and an acceptable atmosphere in the company.

2. *Obtain Commitment from Top Management:* Commitment of top management is essential to this type of program. Reports on other companies where such a program exists should be prepared and presented to the top management. Once the basic concept is sold, acceptance and formal commitment can be achieved very easily. It is not advisable to start this type of program without such formal commitment from the top.

3. *Select the Right People and the Right Area:* One of the slogans used commonly in this program is "There is no limit to what we can do together." It indicates that success comes from the co-operative efforts of many people. The program chairman or manager has to be enthusiastic, persistent, and hardworking. A facilitator is the key to the program. He must be energetic, people-loving, and cooperative. The details of these jobs are discussed in Chapter 5.

   Care must be taken in selecting the proper areas. The first trial-run should be one in which cooperation and enthusiasm can be expected from the people. You should try to dig where the ground is soft.

4. *Select Objectives:* Quality Circles are not a panacea for everything. Companies have to select objectives for the program and make them clear. A Hughes Aircraft Company plant decided to improve communications for the company. Mercury Marine Corporation's major thrust lies in improving quality. There are a number of objectives that you can choose for the program, but the objectives should be made clear to the people so that there is neither confusion nor unrealistic expectations for this program.

5. *Expose People to the Program:* New ideas like Quality Circles need to be clearly understood by all those concerned. The idea of participation and sharing authority is new to the American society and needs incubation before such a program can be started. Even if there is no change in the organizational structure, there is a major change in the basic philosophy. Some people feel that their authority is lost, whereas others don't like the idea of participation. One of the best ways to lessen this tension is to introduce Quality Circles by newsletters, articles, and by visits to other companies who have already employed this type of program.

6. *Inform and Communicate:* Once the program is started, information has to be disseminated throughout the company. Timely communication is important. If it is neglected, grave consequences for expanding the program may result. Rumors fly quickly, people get mistaken ideas and sometimes get discouraged if they do not get involved formally. As soon as the program is accepted, try to inform as many people as possible of the program and its objectives. Better communication will always result in less resistance.

7. *Keep the Program Voluntary:* This is one of the key elements of

the Quality Circle program. Forcing people to participate will not work to motivate them. As they say, "You can lead a horse to water, but you can't make him drink." The same is true here. People should realize the need and should understand the advantages that can be derived from such a program. The basic philosophy and operation of the Circle is for the benefit of the society and once people accept this concept participation becomes easy.

8. *Training is Crucial:* Training is another important feature of the program. In Japan, this type of training is formally offered in the schools or by the companies (employers) as a usual practice. However, the same is not true in the United States. Many U.S. companies do not have good formal training programs. It is of the utmost importance that workers as well as management are properly prepared for the program so that all of them know what is involved. Without the proper training input this program will be phased out quickly.

9. *Start Slowly, Grow Slowly:* Whenever a new concept is initiated, care has to be exercised that it does not become too much of a burden to others. So, in order to achieve success, it is better to go slowly but steadily. This helps you to foresee the future problem areas and plan corrective actions. Careful and concise introduction helps to expose people to new concepts and helps to eliminate many unnecessary doubts about the program. On the other hand, if you start big—publicized all over—you may not get the necessary support, and may have to face the consequences of that. There will be little chance of getting something similar started again in the future.

10. *Be Open and Positive:* Quality Circle programs need to be open. Everyone in the program has the right to know what is happening in the program. All the information should be available to the people and if they need assistance, it should be provided as soon as possible. Management should also be positive in thoughts and in actions at all times. There are always ups and downs in this type of program. Therefore, one has to keep a warm spirit, high aspirations and try to reach the SKY. As it is said, "not failure, but low aim is the crime."

   If we don't try, we cannot expect to achieve anything in life. The same is true here. We have to be open and positive while trying to convince people.

11. *Monitor Progress and Changes:* Quality Circle programs have been working in Japan for the last eighteen years and are still working. They will work in any country as long as they are properly nourished and supervised by the facilitator. It is based on sound people-building philosophy. There are elements of trust and mutual cooperation.

   The program also combines the use of statistics, group dynamics, and job satisfaction. It is going to stay in the company as long as it is monitored and guided by a committee made up of management and employees, both union and non-union. Such a committee should always encourage and support constructive action. It should also be alert to dangers and take corrective measures immediately.

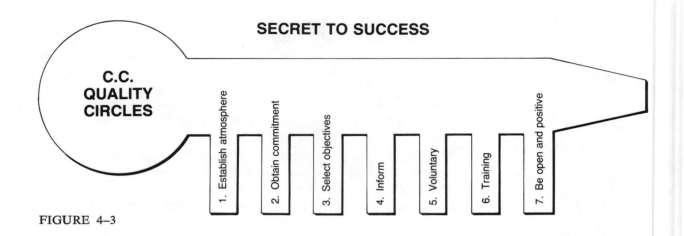

FIGURE 4–3

How to Sell
Quality Circle Programs

Quality Circles are excellent but how can one sell the idea to the top management?

Kathleen Terry from Hughes Aircraft Company gave a significant talk in the 2nd Annual IAQC meeting, which was held in February 1980 at San Francisco.[2] She emphasized the need for careful planning and systematic approaches to this program. Many key points have already been discussed. It is important to plan and follow through the following steps as the need arises:

1. Expose key personnel to the concept
2. Obtain key personnel's commitment
3. Clarify objectives and expectations
4. Assess the needs
5. Develop the program-plan and present it to management

The details for each point mentioned have already been discussed in this chapter. Anyone who is interested in starting this program can review all the material, prepare a five-point outline, and then can present it to the top management.

If you do your homework right there is very little chance that top management will object to this people-building philosophy.

Advantages of Establishing
a Quality Circle

The objectives that are discussed in detail at the beginning of the chapter explain various advantages of the program.

One or more of the following advantages can be accomplished simultaneously.

1. Quality improvement
2. Waste reduction
3. Attitude change
4. Cost reduction
5. Safety improvement
6. Improved communications
7. Higher productivity
8. Increased job satisfaction
9. Team building
10. Improvement in skills

Finally, the ten principles of successful Quality Circle operation as reported by the Japan Productivity Center in the introductory film entitled "Quality Circle Operation" [3] are as follows:

FIGURE 4-4

A QUALITY CIRCLE PROGRAM IS NOT

SOMETHING MANAGEMENT NEED FEAR

ONLY A MANAGEMENT PROGRAM

A "CURE-ALL"

GUARANTEED TO SUCCEED

ALWAYS GOING TO SURFACE WHAT WE WANT TO HEAR . . . . . .

FIGURE 4-5

A QUALITY CIRCLE PROGRAM IS

ONE EFFECTIVE METHOD FOR INVOLVING AN ORGANIZATION'S EMPLOYEES IN ASSUMING RESPONSIBILITY FOR "QUALITY" ....THE "QUALITY" OF THEIR WORK, THEIR WORK ENVIRONMENT, THEIR PROFESSIONAL GROWTH, AND THEIR PERSONAL DEVELOPMENT.

1. Participation and cooperation
2. Enthusiasm, spirit, and quality consciousness
3. Intensified daily quality control work
4. Discussing the improvement of work method
5. Creativity and resourcefulness
6. Planning ahead
7. Constant inquisitiveness
8. Self-control
9. Self-inspection
10. Education and training

Notes

1. Much of the information in this list and subsequent parts of this chapter was gathered from workshops and discussions at the Second Annual IAQC International Conference (February, 1980) in San Francisco and from various IAQC publications.

2. Kathleen Terry, "Quality Circles—an Exciting Proposition," talk given at Second Annual IAQC International Conference (San Francisco, 1980).

3. "How to Operate a Quality Circle," Japan Productivity Center, Tokyo.

5

ROLES AND FUNCTIONS OF QUALITY CIRCLE ORGANIZATION

As stated in Chapter 4, there is no separate organization that exists in Quality Circle work. It should also be noted that there is no need to form a separate organization for this purpose. Most of the Quality Circle functions are considered the normal work of the company and should be carried out through normal channels of the organization. There are more advantages to working with the same people under the same chain of command than to creating new positions or forming a new department or area. This might create friction, and the company might, as a result, gain very little from the Quality Circle program.

Even though there is no formal organization, the Quality Circle program does create indirectly an informal organization which helps to carry out many functions of the program. Management, as well as shop people, get involved in different segments of the program and play different roles in the projects. Figure 5–1 will show you the informal organization that can exist in any company. Let us review each element in detail.

Executive Committee

The executive committee is, in actuality, the top management of the company which establishes and approves Quality Circle policies and programs. The executive committee also gives the approval to start the program and offers basic guide lines so that Quality Circles can operate within the company's administrative policy. Once the top management

FIGURE 5–1

INFORMAL QUALITY CIRCLE ORGANIZATION

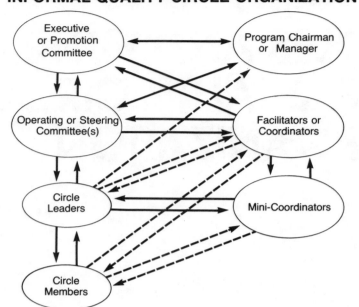

(executive committee) approves the program, Quality Circle policy should be established so that guide lines can be set for the rest of the organization. Later on it will be simpler to get approval from the executive committee on major issues, such as pay policy and recognition issues. Generally the operating committee handles most of the Circle program. However, the executive committee performs the following functions:

1. Attends Quality Circle meetings frequently
2. Understands principles and techniques of Quality Circles
3. Suggests problems from time to time
4. Promotes Quality Circle programs in levels of top and middle management
5. Promotes benefits and advantages of Quality Circles

Operating Committee(s)

Once the Quality Circle program is approved and the training is started, it is wise to form an operating committee. The operating committee is also known as the "steering committee" in many companies. The operating committee consists of the plant manager, quality control manager, an industrial engineer, manufacturing manager, the personnel manager, plant superintendent, the facilitator and one of the Circle leaders. The operating committee is really another informal Quality Circle which oversees the Quality Circle program to insure proper implementation of Circle projects and to promote Quality Circle activities.

If there is more than one plant, each plant should have its own operating committee and all of them should work closely with one another. This will ensure harmony and togetherness in the program, rather than independent action.

The operating committee should also maintain records on cost savings, implementation costs, project costs and general Circle program progress. Operating committee members should also attend all Circle presentations. They should invite senior management personnel who are instrumental in supporting and implementing the Quality Circle program to attend, too.

The operating committee in each plant should meet on a weekly basis to review and discuss such items as training, publicity, program improvement, progress of the Circles, planning and implementation of completed projects, cost analysis, and other related subjects. As discussed before, training is a vital part of the Quality Circle program. It is essential to review the progress weekly and also to plan for future expansion. It is not easy to carry out this function, because of the number of different types of problems. Some of these may look simple but can cause disturbances. The problems must be reviewed and the proper means taken to prevent them. Inconvenient timing and poor location of the training, faulty pay policy, are some of the problems that should be avoided. The operating committee also maintains publicity functions for the plant. Effective and timely publicity on the program helps to expand it. Maintenance of the Quality Circle activity board or proper presentation of a successfully completed Quality Circle project also helps to promote the program.

The operating committee's function is to keep Quality Circles effective and on target. The committee ensures that the company does and will continue to support all Circle activities and solutions.

Most importantly, it opens the door for better communications between management and those people actually doing the work. It gives the employee an opportunity to see how the management operates and to help in the decision-making and the problem-solving process within the organization.

In short, the following key functions are performed by the operating committee:

1. Is responsible for preparing objectives for the plant
2. Meets with facilitator
3. Promotes Quality Circles throughout the organization
4. Attends meetings and constantly reviews the progress
5. Keeps program interesting and fun for members
6. Publicizes the program
7. Reviews training material
8. Follows up the completed projects
9. Reviews training program
10. Obtains training material and adds new material to enhance the knowledge of the members

Quality Circle Leader

The Quality Circle leader is elected by the Circle members. He is responsible for the operation of his Circle and is therefore responsible for the Circle's activities. The facilitator is responsible for a number of Circles, the leader is responsible for one Circle. The leader works closely with the facilitator, and receives much the same training as the facilitator.[1]

The leader may be the supervisor, if that is the desire of the group. Otherwise, the supervisor can be a member of the Circle or may act as an aide to the group. The foreman should be kept informed of all activities at all times. Quality Circles utilize the existing organizational structure, chain of command, and authority. Employees must sell their ideas to management. The advantage in the Quality Circle lies in the fact that all members learn to work as a team, analyzing and solving problems, and presenting their solutions as a team to the management.

The very heart of the Quality Circle concept is one of full participation by all members. Quality Circle leaders are not expected to do all the work, everyone shares in the task of getting things accomplished.

Quality Circle leaders should be careful not to monopolize the activities of the Circle or the members will view Quality Circles as the same method of operation that they have worked under in the past. They may feel Quality Circles do not provide them with the opportunities to influence new ways of performing as they had been led to believe. Quality Circle leaders, together with the facilitator, help keep the Circle meetings on the right track applying Quality Circle techniques in developing a cohesive team approach to solving quality problems. The more positive and constructive the leader's attitude is, the more responsive the members will be.

Although it has been emphasized that leaders are not to do all the work and that leaders have a facilitator to help them, leaders should not lose sight of the fact that the Circle members are also people with ideas. But the leaders should remain responsible for the operation of the Circle. Circle leaders are taught how to maintain necessary records. Also, if the Circle doesn't seem to be making progress, the Circle leaders are the ones who should discuss the problem with the facilitator or mini-coordinators to see what corrective steps can be taken.

When the Quality Circle program becomes well established in the plant, it is a good idea to set up, on a regular basis, a series of meetings involving all Circle leaders. At these meetings many new ideas can be exchanged with other leaders. The Circle program is strengthened by this additional communication between Circles.

Most of the Quality Circle training is done by the facilitator or mini-coordinator. However, it is not a bad idea to involve members or Circle leaders in teaching part of the course work. Leaders enjoy the participation and feel proud of their involvement. Sometimes leaders can be sent to other plants or companies to promote the Circle program. However, it is important that Circle leaders have gained sufficient knowledge and understanding of a technique before they attempt to teach it, since it is vital that the members learn the techniques correctly.

Some of the major functions that the leader should perform are listed in the following:

Quality Circle Leader's Functions

1. Generate enthusiasm for Circle activities
2. Take care of operation of Circle
3. Meet with the Circle once a week
4. Use facilitator for assistance
5. Be responsible for Circle records
6. Create coordination and harmony in the Circle
7. Be key link between members and management
8. Attend leadership training
9. Work closely with the foreman
10. Seek advice and help if required
11. Keep the meeting on track
12. Enforce code of conduct
13. Maintain a good attitude above Circles
14. Give assignments
15. Start and end meetings on time
16. Help get new members for the Circle
17. Promote Quality Circle program
18. Visit other companies
19. Attend quality programs
20. Teach others useful material to better the society and surroundings

Sometimes initial enthusiasm may fade because of a lack of new ideas. The leader must keep this from happening. The Circle techniques, especially brainstorming, can be used to encourage suggestions and ideas from Circle members. If that fails, ask others, the management, quality personnel, or facilitator for suggestions.

When a member dominates the discussion and doesn't give others a chance to talk, the leader should be firm and ask for other viewpoints. Turn some point made by the dominant member into a question you can direct at another member who is competent to speak on the point. If necessary, ask the facilitator for the ground rules of discussion.

In most groups, one or two people hold back. Leaders should engage those silent members in private conversation before or after the session, and encourage their participation. Asking for their ideas during the meeting may also help. Sometimes, however, the silent member wants to sit and listen. He or she may talk with the leader later and offer help. Leaders should treat these cases as they occur and use tactful methods to involve such people.

Some people in the Circle may not know exactly how to express their ideas. The leader has to help them without hurting their feelings. Expressions like "are you saying that . . . ?" or "do you mean . . . ?" may help them to organize their thoughts and help them communicate their ideas to the rest of the group. Without the leader's timely assistance, many good ideas may not be brought up in the meetings.

The leader will sometimes have to deal with persons who like to argue all the time. It is extremely important that these persons be watched carefully, and handled tactfully, so that the whole group does not become disenchanted because of unnecessary arguments. Arguments or disagreements should be looked on as an asset and not a problem. However, there should be a limit to the discussion, and the leader should use expressions such as, "that really poses a challenge to the way we have been talking," or "now, that is another way of looking at the situation," or "that's an interesting point of view; I wonder if we can think along those lines for awhile?" These expressions will make the group see the value of the dissenting opinions and still keep unity and harmony in the group.

It is highly recommended that the leaders take time to discuss a code of conduct with Circle members at the time the Circle is first organized. Everyone should know from the beginning the ground rules of the Circle operation. Some items to include in a code of conduct are suggested in the following:

Code of Conduct
—Each member should participate
—Criticize ideas, not persons
—Each one teach one
—Each member is free to express his or her ideas
—Each member must listen respectfully to other suggestions
—Circle work on the project is a group project
—Start Circle meetings on time and end on time

The leader should always ask members to keep open minds and ask for new ideas. Everyone's knowledge and experience is important. The leader should encourage them to participate. Papers can be posted in work areas, and leaders can ask members to write down ideas that occur to them while they are working. No idea or question should be ridiculed or underestimated by anyone.

A successful Quality Circle program requires hard work and cooperation from many people. The leader is the one who has to keep encouraging his group all the time. Tackling the first project is hard and needs the attention and understanding of the leader. Once the members see the value of the group decision, the job of the leaders becomes easier. Many times middle management and other groups try to stop the progress or cold-shoulder the new ideas. The leader has to keep promoting and keep trying out his group's ideas. It often helps to invite outside people. Those in the group who are reluctant to listen, when they are confronted with someone from outside may change their minds.

Quality Circle leaders can use some of the following tips to enable Circles to work more efficiently.

Tips for Quality Circle Leaders
—Plan for meetings
—Summarize action items for next meeting
—Use an agenda
—Critique group
—Work on members' problems

—Document meetings—keep records on status of projects
—Ask questions—refer to code of conduct
—Be open-minded and objective
—Budget time
—Be aware of members' non-verbal communication
—Make things visible (flip chart)
—Experiment
—Stay on track
—Start and end on time
—Listen for "messages" and clarify
—Have visitors
—Show sincerity and interest in Circle process (know material)
—Limit "air" time

Quality Circle Member

The Quality Circle member is most important, for without members there are no Circles and no program at all. Hence, the members are the heart of the program, and proper use of their untapped brainpower is the key to its success. Membership is strictly voluntary, and anyone who wishes to join should be welcomed. Each person must also feel free to decline membership. An active Circle will attract this person later. Experience has also shown that some members who join the Circle and decide to leave for awhile, frequently return at a later date.[1]

Quality Circles can be formed in various areas. In Japan, the original Circles started in the manufacturing areas and then expanded into others. Even today, the majority of Quality Circles function in manufacturing. However, there is no reason why this philosophy cannot be expanded into other areas as well. Interest has been shown by some service industries. Banks, hospitals, insurance companies and large retail stores are also considering starting Quality Circles to improve services to their customers. At present few Circles have been formed in industries like engineering, maintenance, data processing, and finance.

Members for Quality Circles can come from all parts of a society. There is no restriction on the membership. Although the original Circles were formed mainly in one work area, there are different ways to group the people in Circles to solve daily problems. In the future there will be many changes in the way Circles are formed.

One of the key elements for Circle members to remember is training. In Japan, basic quality control techniques and statistical training is given in schools and colleges. Once the worker joins the company, he or she is also trained thoroughly here. However, in other countries this is neglected. To implement a Quality Circle program, training has to be properly planned and managed.

Suitable training material should be developed. All members must go through training so that they will understand the basic concept, and become familiar with the techniques. Without the training there will be less cohesiveness in the group, and members may soon lose interest in the project as a result of lack of good guidance and understanding.

In general, Quality Circle members perform the following functions:

1. Attend all meetings
2. Learn statistical techniques
3. Attend meetings (on time)
4. Follow the code of conduct
5. Stay within all Quality Circle policy rules
6. Promote Quality Circle program
7. Enjoy the work
8. Help recruit new members for the Circle
9. Participate in solving problems

In short, Quality Circle members are the backbone of the program and their active participation makes the Quality Circle program successful.

The role of the facilitator and mini-coordinator is the last segment of the Quality Circle organization. This vitally important function of the successful Quality Circle is discussed in detail in the next chapter.

Notes

1. This material is drawn from Donald L. Dewar, *The Quality Circle Handbook* (Red Bluff, Calif.: Quality Circle Institute, 1980) and from *IAQC Quality Circle Quaterly* (Second and Third Quarters, 1979).

6

MANAGEMENT OF THE CIRCLES: THE FACILITATOR'S ROLE

The facilitator or coordinator is the person who really makes the program work in the United States. Originally, in Japan, some companies established this as a separate position, but many companies promoted the program through the industrial relations department sharing various responsibilities among departments.

Education and training is sometimes handled by outside training institutions, and committees are generally formed in the company to follow the various activities. However, in the United States and in some other countries, the Quality Circle program is new and it is, therefore, essential to the success of the program that one person be responsible for coordinating the program. Everyone's work becomes no one's work and without proper planning by one responsible person this type of program becomes one of the many programs that companies start every year. Once the decision is made to start a Quality Circle program, it is important that a company look for a facilitator immediately so that he or she can take over the program and begin working on implementation plans.

Generally, a company begins the program with one part-time or full-time facilitator. Even though 100 percent attention is required at the start, some companies may not be willing to appoint a full-time facilitator for this work. It is better to start with a part-time facilitator, and when the company is convinced of the benefits of the program a full-time facilitator can be appointed. The facilitator should report to someone in a high level position in the company so that he or she can seek high level support when necessary. This reporting arrangement also helps to get cooperation from various departments. There is another part-time position in a Quality Circle program that has been used in some companies—a mini-coordinator. Mini-coordinators mainly attend meetings, help solve problems, and follow-up on completed projects. Mini-coordinators can be co-opted from quality control, manufacturing, engineering, or industrial engineering departments. Facilitators generally work with mini-coordinators and keep track of the overall program. Good coordination and effective communications are the keys to a successful program, and facilitators and mini-coordinators have to carry this responsibility all the time.

The facilitator's position is very important in the Quality Circle program. How do you select the person for this job and what kind of qualities do you look for in a candidate? Let us discuss some of those qualities. It should be realized that these are only recommendations. It may not be possible to find all of these qualities in one person—a facilitator may look like a unique individual—but anyone who possesses many of the recommended qualities may be qualified for the job.

Facilitator

A facilitator should have a good educational background, preferably a college degree. Such an educational background helps to train people to plan and organize work properly and to function effectively. A facilitator also needs a good working knowledge of manufacturing, quality control, statistics, and engineering work. A facilitator works with a variety of people and problems, and is the one who has to help Circles in case of difficulties.[1]

Since he is also the one who must effect improved communication and cooperation, another key quality a facilitator should possess is the knack for getting along with people. He or she has to be people-oriented. Most of the work that is carried out by the facilitator is concerned with people, and if he knows how to handle them many problems are easily solved. As you will see later on, this program will face many problems in human relations. Some people get upset very easily, become unhappy over remarks that are passed, and it is the facilitator who investigates and resolves these types of differences. The facilitator, in general, should be a dynamic human being who is interested in people's growth.

Public speaking is another skill that a facilitator should have, or try to acquire. This is essential since he or she has to speak in meetings and has to train people on a periodic basis. Skill in public speaking is an aid to implementing effective training. Without good training—getting the proper message across—Circle programs will grow very slowly or be lost completely.

The facilitator should also know different styles of speech. When he works on the floor, he should use the language of the people on the floor; when he works with office people he may have to change his style to convince them. The two areas are different and in order to achieve success and coordination the facilitator has to work closely with both of them. This can be achieved only through being sensitive to the people and talking their language so that they will accept the facilitator as an insider.

The facilitator should be bold, but tactful. The solutions of many problems may depend on help and coordination from manufacturing, engineering, and other related areas. Since many people from these areas feel that Quality Circles interfere with their work, getting cooperation may sometimes be difficult. A facilitator has to find a way, talk with people, and even contact management, to keep the projects alive. This is not an easy task. There is often frustration, even unhappiness. However, as long as a variety of personalities are involved it is bound to happen. Patience and coolness are needed to guide the people right.

In general, a facilitator should be pleasant at all times. He should carry the full responsibility of the Circle program and should thoroughly understand the basic philosophy of Quality Circles. He should, however, be willing to share with others credit for the success of the program so that expansion can be achieved smoothly and effectively.

The facilitator has to carry a number of different responsibilities. These responsibilities vary daily. Sometimes he might have to act as a teacher and train people, while at other times he might work as a consultant and have to help a Circle in their projects. He also has to act as a counselor, promoter, mediator, and public speaker. His duties are never-ending and cannot be fully described.

If the company cannot easily find a suitable person for this position, it is possible to train such a person with the help of training courses and pertinent materials. The brief outline of such material is shown in the following lists.

General Information on Quality Circle Program
Sources
1. JUSE (Union of Japanese Scientists and Engineers), Tokyo, Japan
2. IAQC (International Association of Quality Control) Midwest City, Okla.
3. ASQC (American Society of Quality Control) Milwaukee, Wis.
4. Companies in Japan
5. Companies in the United States (partial list can be obtained from IAQC)
6. Books
7. Articles in a number of magazines such as *Quality, Quality Progress, HRD, Quality Circles Quarterly, Production, Harvard Business Review, Iron Age, Business Week,* and others
8. Telephone Contacts
9. Consulting Services
10. Visits to companies in your area

Requirements for the Job of Quality Circle Facilitator

Thorough Knowledge of the Quality Circle Program

1. History
2. Communications
3. Group dynamics
4. Objectives and goal setting
5. Roles and functions of committees, leaders and members
6. Statistical techniques and their uses
7. Progress evaluation systems
8. Problems in managing program
9. Leadership
10. Training techniques
11. Public speaking

Working Knowledge

1. Operation of the company
2. Statistics
3. Product service
4. Purchasing/vendor relations
5. Mathematics
6. Business management (accounting and budgeting)
7. Manufacturing processes
8. Quality control
9. Speech
10. Behavioral science

Education: B.S. in Education or Engineering
Experience: Three to five years in a related industry with manufacturing exposure

The following is a list of the major duties that a facilitator should carry:

1. Support Circles in Various Stages: Each Quality Circle goes through five different stages, as follows: [2]
   a. Initiation
   b. Training
   c. Development
   d. Maturation
   e. Closure

   A facilitator has to play a different role in each of these stages and in all try to support the Circle as much as possible. During the initiation stage the facilitator has to do a lot of campaigning in order to convince people to listen to the program and attract them to it. Sometimes it takes a lot of time to convince hardliners. However, with good strategy, this author's experience has shown that it is possible to change people's minds. During the training phase the facilitator is mainly involved in instructing, coaching, and helping people to form Circles.

Duties of the Facilitator
1. Sits as an active member of the steering committee
2. Serves as Quality Circle program coordinator
3. Trains members, leaders, management
4. Coordinates Circles
5. Maintains Circle records
6. Arranges meetings with outsiders
7. Attends in-Circle meetings
8. Solves personal problems
9. Searches for new members
10. Works in the shop daily
11. Searches for new ideas
12. Publicizes the program
13. Spreads a good word about the program
14. Links all people in the organization
15. Prepares for presentation—invitations, papers, visual aids
16. Prepares new training material
17. Follows up on completed projects
18. Attends conferences
19. Reads outside materials
20. Organizes informal gatherings—invites outside speakers

The development stage is crucial, and the facilitator or the mini-coordinator has to monitor the Circle closely at least at the beginning so that people will not give up easily. The facilitator performs a number of different functions here, watching, counseling, coordinating, disciplining, monitoring, evaluating, and cheerleading, and finally he makes it happen!

Success is achieved when the Circle members make their first Project presentation to the management.

The problems in the maturation phase are different. Many times, the Circle will keep working on its own; however, it is advisable that the facilitator continue to monitor and consult the Circles as necessary. The closure of a Quality Circle is a hard experience, but is a part of reality. Some Circles may stop meeting because of layoffs, differences in opinions, or for other personal reasons. It is always beneficial for the facilitator to gather all Circle members and, through the plant manager or the Operating Committee, thank them for their contribution.

2. *Keep Track of Progress:* This is an important function of the facilitator in the Circle program. There are a number of ways to follow the group's progress. Graphs and Circle meeting schedules are good ways to check out what is happening.

The facilitator should keep track of a number of Circles in his or her plant, their meeting time, and their project progress. He or she should attend as many meetings as possible, and help or guide them as required. Generally, most of the Circles are enthusiastic and like to rush the project. Sometimes they do not collect sufficient data.

The facilitator should watch them and convince them of the need for careful work so that the project will be accepted.

3. *Help to Put on Management Presentation:* Helping to put on a management presentation is the next key function that needs to be performed by the facilitator. Without his timely help and keen interest, these presentations might fail. The Circle may have done an excellent job in solving problems; however, if the data is not presented properly, it may be hard to convince management to go the new way. The facilitator should assist the Circle in putting on good presentations. He might ask them to rehearse a number of times so that everyone knows what to say, and how to say it. He knows the acceptance of the project depends on the presentation for which he is also partly responsible.

4. *Follow-Up on Projects Started:* The facilitator's work does not end with the presentations made to the management. The Circle has then finished its part of the work. It is recommended that the operating committee review the presentation in the following meeting and come up with the plan of acceptance. The facilitator can then prepare an "action plan."

Once the project is completed, a notice to that effect can be put on the bulletin board. This helps to improve communication, and gets more people involved in the Quality Circle program. Outsiders see that ideas are accepted and implemented, and this helps to attract more people to the program.

5. *Training:* Last but not least is the training function that is carried on constantly in the company. The facilitator is always busy training various groups of people. It may be formal or informal training. It may be in classrooms or elsewhere. Training is essential and must be carried out. The facilitator is also involved in finding new material or revising old material so that interest is kept high throughout the training period. As the need arises, he might have to create his own material. Remember that there is always an opportunity to start something new.

There are certain precautions that the facilitator should take to prevent major setbacks to the program. Some of these are as follows:

1. Do not impose your decisions or feelings on others all the time
2. Do not work alone
3. Do not avoid people
4. Always try to explain management decisions (good or bad) to the members
5. Never forget promises regarding meetings or work
6. Do not argue in the group
7. Do not complain in public
8. Do not talk improperly behind someone's back
9. Do not waste time unnecessarily
10. Do not try to agitate anyone
11. Never deny help to the Circle
12. Never talk about old problems or arguments

Problems That the Facilitator Faces

The work and the job of the facilitator are not always rosy. There are problems and obstacles that have to be overcome to achieve the goal, that is, to have a successful Quality Circle program. Sometimes it is hard to realize why people will not all see things in the same way. But that will happen as long as each has a different personality. Some of the problems the facilitator faces can be briefly reviewed here.

1. *Task versus Growth Orientation:* Sometimes the facilitator gets stuck between two different personalities. The Quality Control manager might want to see fast growth in the program so that he can see the involvement of more people building better quality. On the other hand, the manufacturing manager might want to evaluate progress with return on investment or by savings. It seems difficult to decide which path to follow.

2. *Ownership Problem:* The Quality Circle program belongs to everyone. However, sometimes the manufacturing manager wants to see the Circle under his or her control, but the personnel manager will show willingness to cooperate only if it is under his control. This problem needs to be addressed early in the game, and the resolution of it should be approved by the president and accepted by all top management.

3. *Responsibility:* Even though the facilitator is responsible for the success of the program his job carries very little authority. He has to seek help from all the departments. Sometimes it is difficult to achieve the desired cooperation. Hence, the facilitator has to play a tactful role, try to compromise, and devise solutions that he thinks best for the company.

4. *Loss of Enthusiasm:* The Quality Circle program is spreading rapidly and enthusiasm is generally high at the beginning. It is like a honeymoon. Once the first effect is over, people sometimes feel dragged. The facilitator has to watch these Circles and offer suggestions to effect a change of attitude to generate renewed enthusiasm for tackling new problems and difficulties.

5. *Stale Condition:* Sometimes Circles pick up a project but then go on for a long time without doing any constructive work on it. Some members miss meetings, some keep interrupting the meetings by introducing unrelated topics. Here again the facilitator is the one who should watch for such a condition, find out the reasons, and then apply positive thinking and actions to modify the moods of the meetings.

6. *Administration:* Administering a number of Circles can become a problem. In the beginning when there are only one or two Circles, there may not be much pressure. However, as the program grows the facilitator has to take one or more Circles, and it can become hectic. One Circle might just start operating, another might need help from outside, and at the same time, a third Circle might be

getting ready for management presentations. It is the facilitator's duty to monitor activities of all the Circles effectively. He cannot afford to lose any of them. An efficient facilitator will work on his job in such a way as to keep everyone happy.

7. *Wrong Approach:* Sometimes the facilitator faces very difficult tasks steering the Circles in the proper direction. The Circle might pick up the project and, because of old animosities or ignorance about future plans, might spend time on the project but work in the wrong direction. Then the difficult task comes for the facilitator—to change their minds. However, he should be realistic and steer the Circle in the proper direction as soon as possible. Something else he or she should watch for is misunderstanding between the management and the Circle members. Such cases do occur and the sooner they are resolved the better.

Mini-Coordinators

Mini-coordinators are helpful in expanding the Quality Circle program a little faster without affecting the enthusiasm. As mentioned before, mini-coordinators can be selected, requested, or volunteered from various departments.

One mini-coordinator is generally responsible for only one or two Circles. In Japan this type of work is carried out by foremen or other department heads. Mini-coordinators do not have to spend 100 percent of their time on Quality Circle activities. This is generally part of their routine work. However, it is a tremendous help to the company since it serves a twofold purpose. During the initial stage, the company can use this method without investing too much in the program. It also helps in the long range to develop additional facilitators for the company.

A mini-coordinator performs the following key functions:

1. Attends assigned Circle meetings
2. Contacts outside people if required
3. Works closely with facilitator and conveys members' messages or needs that are necessary for the success of the Circle's project
4. Guides the Circles in their project if required
5. Reviews training material with assigned Circles if required
6. Keeps unity in the assigned Circle operation
7. Watches for problems, and calls for help
8. Reminds members to follow the code of conduct
9. Passes on interesting informative material, keeps the Circle rolling
10. Provides feedback on the projects that are presented to the management.

The idea of a mini-coordinator in the United States is new, and it will take some time to spread in the industry. This writer's experience has shown that there is no harm in adopting this system in a company.

Middle Management Support

As shown in Figure 5–1, the Quality Circle organization does not show middle management as a separate group. Their participation is in operating committees and promotional committees. Middle management support is essential, but is not easy to gain in the United States. There are a number of reasons for this, for example:

1. NIH principle—Quality Circles are not invented here
2. Lack of understanding of the concept
3. Lack of knowledge of Quality Circle techniques
4. Feeling that the Circles are a waste of time
5. No time to get involved
6. Threat of losing authority
7. "Nothing in it for me" attitude
8. Poor job of convincing done by the facilitator
9. Late introduction to the middle management
10. Loss of management control

Companies in Japan have done an excellent job in solving this problem. Most of the companies hire qualified people in this area who have already mastered the techniques. Newcomers are also given three to six months of special training, and this automatically helps them to learn Quality Circle techniques. Support from Quality Circles is achieved without any problem. Once the people understand the system, the middle management becomes a part of the "informal" Quality Circle organization.

The Quality Circle concept is still new in companies in the United States, and the problem of middle management support is difficult. One of the ways to solve this problem is by getting middle management involved in the Circle activities right from the beginning. Once the top management accepts the concept, or the pilot program is successful, the middle management should be invited to participate, and should be given a thorough explanation of the program. Managers and engineers should be invited to the classes and schools and be encouraged to start Circles in their areas. Periodically, successful projects should be presented to middle management. In this way they will come to appreciate the value of Quality Circles and to understand the Circles' need for their support.

Middle management can serve in five major functions.

1. Support Quality Circle activities
2. Participate in the Circle
3. Promote the Quality Circle
4. Serve as mini-coordinators
5. Form Quality Circles in each area

Top Management's Support

As shown in Figure 5–1, top management involvement in the Quality Circle program is essential in setting up the policy and guidelines. In the informal organization, the top management acts as the executive committee.

Top management should be informed periodically about the progress of the program. Annual or biannual gatherings are one of the best ways to communictae Circle activities. The program chairman or the facilitator should invite top management to the program and present the best completed projects. This helps to show the Circle achievements to the top management, and at the same time helps to gain top management support.

Sometimes top management should be invited to address the leader's periodic conferences. This indirectly forces top management to get involved in the program more effectively and to understand the basic principles thoroughly.

Top management support can also be obtained by getting them to write articles or messages for the company paper or magazines. This helps to promote more funding, participation, guidance, and cooperation throughout the company.

Finally, it is important to obtain top management's support for the program from the beginning so that many obstacles can be avoided. This allows the pilot program to be expanded very easily in the future. In companies where unions exist, it is essential that top management know the participative approach so that any union-management disagreement can be ironed out easily without long disputes.

Program Chairperson or Program Manager

In order to maintain a successful program in the United States, it is essential that a company appoint somoene as a Quality Circle chairperson or program manager. It is not necessary that this be a full-time job. On the contrary, many companies, as in Japan, appoint someone as a chairperson on a part-time basis, making this assignment a part of his routine work. Some successful companies have used Quality Control managers, personnel managers, or manufacturing managers for this position. This informal position links the executive committee and the operating committee together and promotes a Circle program uniformly throughout the organization.

Among the major functions that a program chairperson should carry on are:

1. Constantly reviews the overall program and its progress
2. Helps to establish company-wide policies regarding Quality Circle operations
3. Promotes Circles in middle management
4. Attends operating committee meetings

5. Helps the facilitator or mini-coordinators in case of difficulties
6. Thinks of new ideas to expand the Circle program
7. Helps to arrange conferences, visits, or training programs
8. Helps to publicize the program throughout the company
9. Prepares new training material
10. Contacts other companies or institutions and obtains new information on recent developments in the Quality Circle movement

In conclusion, this is a people-building program and it belongs to all of the people in a company. The success of the Quality Circle program depends on good cooperation, effective communication, and maintaining harmony in the groups. The objectives of the program should be clear and should be agreed upon by all. Finally to get the most out of a membership follow these suggestions.

1. Don't expect perfection from everyone
2. Participate effectively
3. Enjoy yourself
4. Appreciate the people
5. Request feedback from everyone
6. Establish objectives of the program
7. Follow the principle, "Each one teach one"
8. Use the statistical knowledge
9. Promote group activities
10. Insist on people-building philosophy

Notes

1. This material is adapted from Donald L. Dewar, *The Quality Circle Handbook* (Red Bluff, Calif.: Quality Circle Institute, 1980).

2. Notes taken at Second Annual IAQC International Conference (San Francisco, 1980).

7

OPERATION OF A QUALITY CIRCLE

Real operation of a Quality Circle begins after the Circle members' graduation. If a large group is trained at one time it should be divided into smaller groups. However, the decision as to the formation of smaller groups should be left entirely up to the members. The facilitator should help in preparing members for their work. Some groups will be large, some might be small. However, it doesn't make any real difference. It is recommended that the groups be formed by the members who generally work in one area, but that is not necessary. A key aspect of the formation of a Circle is to let members decide the membership for the Circle.

1. *Members Bring Potential Problems:* At the first meeting, the facilitator or coordinator generally provides the necessary organization kit describing the Circle's activities. This kit contains such basic tools as pens, pencils, paper, notebook, calendar, folders, and other small useful things that the Circle members will need while working on a problem. The group then chooses a name for their Circle, and a leader and secretary. The secretary is to take care of the paper work and other assignments.

   When these formalities are completed, the Circle generally decides to prepare a list of all the problems that members wish to tackle. Once the list is prepared it is necessary to devise a method to quantify or evaluate the severity of those problems. One way is to collect data by frequency of occurrence, by scrap or rework, by rejects, or in any other way that the Circle can use to assess the depth of the problem.

The following diagram will give an overall picture of Circle operation.[1]

FIGURE 7–1

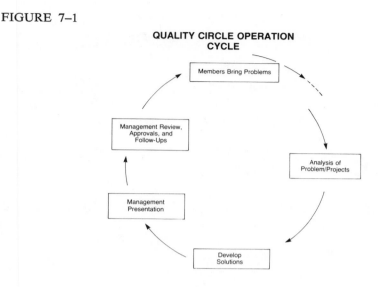

QUALITY CIRCLE OPERATION CYCLE

The next step will be to make assignments to various members for the collection of data. The statistical techniques called checksheets or graphs are handy at this time. The time period and collection of fresh data is very important since some of the problems may already be solved, or a solution might be in process. This type of analysis is also helpful to eliminate beliefs, which are meaningless without sound data, that there are many problems. Even though the data collected is crude and covers a short period of time, it can help to prepare a Pareto diagram. A Pareto diagram will generally point out the important few and the trivial many. Based on this analysis, members can decide which of the problems should be worked on collectively. Although it is useful to follow the democratic way, through the use of Pareto diagrams the problem becomes so obvious that everyone generally agrees to tackle the number one or number two problem shown by a Pareto diagram. In some cases the problems might be obvious and Circles may not wish to spend so much time in collecting and analyzing data. That should not stop the Circle from tackling any problem if most of the members agree to work on that particular problem. However, it is necessary to take precautions so that the Circle may not fall into a trap and waste its time on minor problems or on projects where solutions are already in process.

2. *Analysis of Problem/Projects:* Once the problem has been selected, the Circle can start analyzing the problem with the help of two important statistical tools—brainstorming and cause and effect diagrams (see Chapter 10). Generally a cause and effect diagram is developed where effect is noted at the end and where four or five major areas for causes are marked on the right-hand side. The idea-generating brainstorming techniques help get all members involved so that various causes can be listed on a sheet. The leader generally asks members for their opinions regarding causes and lists the possible causes

Figure 7–2 shows a sample form that can be used for recording purposes.

FIGURE 7–2

QUALITY CIRCLE MEETING REPORT

CIRCLE NAME _____ Plt. #_____

DATE: _____ TIME:_____

PROJECT: _____

_____

a. REVIEW OF LAST MEETING'S MINUTES:

_____

_____

b. KEY NOTES:

_____

_____

c. ASSIGNMENTS:

_____

_____

d. ATTENDANCE:

_____

_____

given on the sheet. With group consent, the key cause is picked for analysis, and another set of data is collected to verify the cause. If it proves that the Circle has picked up the key cause, they can generally proceed further to seek the solution to the cause. However, if the data does not show sufficient evidence, then the Circle will have to search for another problem cause and collect new data for verification. Sometimes this process might have to be repeated two or three times until the true cause is found. Once the major cause is found the Circle will generally proceed to develop a solution.

3. *Development of Solution:* Once the cause is verified Circle members have to get together and put their brainpower to work and start pro-

posing solutions. One member might think of a change in a fixture, another might suggest a change in material, and similarly other Circle members may make different suggestions to eliminate the cause. Since most of the members face these problems every day their suggested solutions are generally reliable. Not only that, but one of those solutions generally remedies the problem permanently, provided any other necessary changes that will affect the solution take place at the same time.

Once the Circle arrives at a method to fix the problem, a plan should be prepared for implementation. Approval to test the solution on a small scale should be obtained through the foreman or facilitator. This test helps to verify the solution. A small scale pilot run, rather than a full scale implementation of the wrong solution, saves time, money, and the energy of the Circle. This early stage is an important phase of the Circle operation and it might vary from two or three weeks to two to three months. One should not insist that the Circle finish the project within a certain time period, nor should one rush the Circle to finish the project. That type of pressure generally discourages Circle activities and is not fruitful. On the contrary, management should extend outside help without interfering in the daily operation of the Circle. In order to maintain an effective Circle it is recommended that weekly meetings be held ranging from thirty to forty-five minutes depending on the need. This helps to maintain good communication, create new solutions, and keep harmony in the Circle. Solutions that are suggested can be tested on a small scale through the Circle work also. A preventive system should be devised to make sure the problem remains solved in the future. Without a good preventive program the solutions are effective for only a short period of time. Circle members should also review all other aspects of the problem and see if the solution can be implemented in other areas where similar problems exist. This helps to avoid duplicate efforts, and eliminates waste quickly. After a certain period, when the Circle arrives at an effective solution, the facilitator has to arrange the next phase—show management the results of the work.

4. *Management Presentation:* A presentation for management is an important form of recognition for the Circle. The conscientious endeavors of the Circle members need to be recognized by management to sustain Circle members' morale. It is most important that the facilitator arrange for such a presentation for each project, whether it is successful or not. It is possible that the new information might show up in the middle of a Circle project which would indicate that there is no further need to continue to work on the project. The facilitator or mini-coordinator should review the situation at that time and should suggest that a member of the Circle present an interim report to management. This helps both sides. Circle members feel that their work is not in vain, while management gets to hear some aspect of a project that they might otherwise have neglected. Through such a presentation, one of the Circles at Mercury Marine Company helped avoid repetition of an old mistake.

There is a lot of hard work in preparing a presentation. However, it is enjoyable for most of the members who must prepare short talks, short reports, visual aids, and in some cases even prepare small samples to prove their point. Each presentation is different and is always interesting, never dull. Quality Circle members may have to learn to operate a slide projector, movie projector, and other visual aid equipment to put on an effective presentation. The Circle works as a team of professionals as they prepare and present evidence of their achievements.

Quesetions are always asked about arrangements for management presentations. First, the facilitator or mini-coordinator reviews the project with all Circle members present. Once an agreement is reached on the presentation, a rehearsal is arranged with all necessary equipment on hand. It may take more than one rehearsal to be certain that everyone knows his part.

A management presentation helps Circle members to become assertive and to learn how to talk in front of others. A facilitator has to make arrangements for the place, date, and time of the presentation. He should make sure that all of these things are suitable for management as well as for the Circle members. A meeting room should be large enough so that everyone can be comfortable. It should be quiet enough for people to be able to hear the talk easily. These are small matters, but they do count in the evaluation and effectiveness of the program. Another important aspect of the presentation is the invitation. Facilitators should review the project and make certain all of the concerned parties are invited. This will include the plant manager, industrial engineers, manufacturing engineers, quality control, and various other people. It should be remembered that good communications help build a successful company, and the more people who know what is going on the better the results. (The details about management presentations are given in Chapter 10.)

5. *Management Review and Follow-Up:* After the Circle members have presented the solution to management, it is management's duty to review the suggestions and solutions thoroughly. People from engineering, quality control, industrial engineering, and manufacturing engineering should be asked to evaluate the impact of the work, or to provide help that might be needed to complete the project. Generally, when the management presentations are given, the advantages are also discussed at that time. Most of the work is already completed by then unless a large amount of financial help or additional manpower is required to complete it. Management has to review these aspects as well as time factors in certain cases. The steering committee has to assume this responsibility in each plant.

After the presentation, a discussion should take place for approvals or disapprovals of the suggestions. The follow-up program should be prepared for future use. Figure 7–3 shows a sample form that can be used in such a case. The Circle should be informed about the decisions so that the communication is completed and members know the outcome of their efforts.

At a later time the steering committee should see that the work is completed and the facilitator should make sure that Circles are informed about the program.[1]

FIGURE 7–3

```
                  QUALITY CIRCLE PROJECT FOLLOW-UP


PROJECT _____

CIRCLE NAME: _____

PRESENTATION DATE:_____

- - - - - - - - - - - - - - - - - - - - - - - - - - - - - -

A.  MANAGEMENT REVIEW OF THE PROJECT:  DATE:_____


B.  IMPLEMENTATION PHASE:
```

Proposed Suggestions	Approved (if not, why)	Person Responsible	Tentative Completion Date	Follow-Up

Remember the key factors to a successful Circle.

1. Work closely with the facilitator
2. Always work through the chain of command
3. Keep everyone informed—Circle as well as management
4. Use all resources available (people, computers, daily reports, and so on)

The following case study demonstrates how a Quality Circle operates.

Case Study

A Story of Barb Fitting Breakage [2]
Circle: Quest Quenchers

<pre>
Members: Dick Birkholz, Leader and Secretary
            Dave Miller
            Don Ferry
            Ed Miller
            Steve Brusius
            Paul Mehleis, foreman and adviser
Project: Breaking and leaking of barb fittings
</pre>

BACKGROUND

After an initial eight hours of training, the Circle picked a name—"Quest Quenchers." Using brainstorming techniques and a democratic system, the Circle picked its first project and successfully completed it in three months. The project involved people from die cast, engineering, and machining plants. Later on, with great enthusiasm, the Circle decided to work on the second project. The following are details of the procedure used in solving the second project.

MEETING ONE

After the management presentation on the first project, Quest Quenchers decided to review the various other quality problems that most of them felt should be solved. A list was again prepared by using brainstorming sessions.

MEETINGS TWO AND THREE

All of the problems were discussed for everyone's information. More input was encouraged. After considerable discussion the group took a vote and decided to work on the breakage and leakage of barb fittings on cylinder blocks.

MEETINGS FOUR AND FIVE

The Quest Quenchers then decided to collect the data on the problems. Line repair reports were collected by Francis Roberts and Dick Birkholz. Quality Control reports indicated breakage and leakers ran about 5% to 8% in 1979, and in 1980 the percentage was 5% to 6%. These fittings were made by one of the vendors. Hence, the Quest Quenchers contacted the vendor through the proper channels and requested information about the breakage. The vendor informed them that the breakage ran around 10% to 12%. With all this information, the Circle decided to analyze the problem using another Quality Circle technique called the cause and effect diagram.

FIGURE 7-4

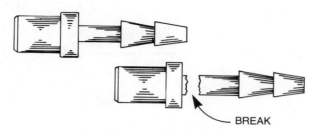

BREAK

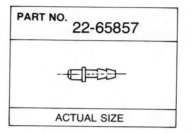

PART NO.
22-65857

ACTUAL SIZE

MEETING SIX

The cause and effect diagram shown in Figure 7-5 was constructed by the Quest Quenchers.

MEETING SEVEN

The Circle requested a blue print to gain understanding of the construction of the part and to use for tolerance analysis. The drawing immediately revealed a thin section at the neck which could cause breakage and leakage. The following three suggestions for eliminating the thin section were discussed.

1. *Change to Heavier Fitting:* This was easy and a very good idea. However, this change required revision in other fittings and mating hoses.
2. *Use of Plastic Fitting:* This was another excellent idea that was discussed by the members. However, this also necessitated the collection of more information on cost and the possibility of getting some samples, since no one could predict the results without tests.
3. *Change Machining of Fitting:* The genius Circle, "Quest Quenchers," came up with the idea of redesigning the barb fittings. Two simple changes were asked in machining of the fittings. One was to cut generous radius where neck met base and the second was to move transition point back under heavy base.

FIGURE 7–5

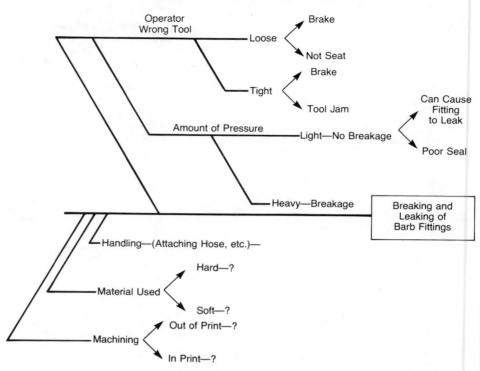

CAUSE AND EFFECT DIAGRAM

MEETING EIGHT

Meeting number eight was held with an engineer who was responsible for approval of these kinds of changes. The last two changes were immediately approved for final run. The vendor was requested to make changes accordingly. The engineer was helpful in obtaining some plastic fittings. However, more attention was given to change number three, since everyone felt it was cheaper and should do the job satisfactorily.

MEETING NINE

After two or three weeks of rest because of a normal shutdown of the plant the Quest Quenchers came back to work. The quality control manager reported enthusiastically the results of changes at the vendor's plant. The Circle was told that 7000 barb fittings were machined without any breakage. Besides that, the change also helped the vendor in other areas. In the old process, the fittings were breaking at a 10% to 12% reject rate, and required the vendor to change drills three to four times daily. With the new procedure there was not a single breakage and drills were changed only once a day. Hurrah! Tremendous success.

MEETING TEN

A sample batch of fifty of the new pieces was provided to the assembly line. The operator felt the new fittings were firmer, could be bent at least

45 degrees without breaking, and could also take more pressure during installation. There was not a single breakage in installing those fifty pieces.

MEETING ELEVEN

The Quest Quenchers were happy that they had again achieved their goal of improving the quality of the product. In this case the help also extended to the vendor. The word was spread in the vendor's company about the Circle's work.

The Quest Quenchers also discussed the other similar fittings that are used at the other points in the company and decided to review all others for possible change.

MEETINGS TWELVE AND THIRTEEN

A preliminary trial run was performed for the management presentation. Sample parts, visual aids, good graphs, and typed material were prepared for the final rally.

FIGURE 7–6

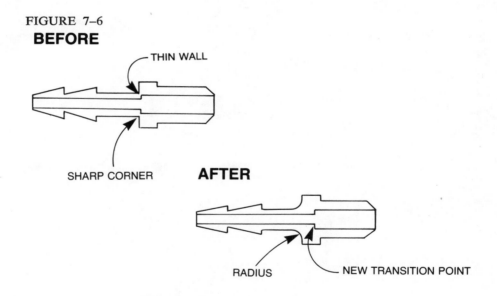

MEETING FOURTEEN

Management Presentation. The Quest Quenchers invited the plant managers to tell them the story of the barb fittings. Most of the project was already implemented. There was no problem of getting approval. The management was impressed by the Circle work and congratulated all of the members for their good work.

MEETING FIFTEEN

The Quest Quenchers met again the next week and decided to quench their problem-solving thirst by attacking their next problem.

And so the cycle of work goes on. This is the story of achievements of Quality Circle members!

Notes

1. This information was prepared by D. Aylesworth, Quality Control Engineer, Mercury Marine, Fond du Lac, Wisconsin.

2. This information is drawn from the experience of the Quest Quenchers Quality Circle, Mercury Marine.

8

IMPLEMENTATION PLAN

It is said that many good ideas are spoiled because of poor planning. This is equally true in a Quality Circle program. The basic ideas of Quality Circles or worker participation programs are exciting and appealing; however, they will be fruitless without good implementation plans. Quality Circles involve various aspects of human behavior as well as a change in the management style. The complex nature of the program requires careful and systematic planning so that no one in the organization gets disturbed and the "people-building philosophy" can be implemented slowly and successfully. People resist change, and to see this type of change in the operation, one should try to avoid hasty and quick planning.

One suggested step-by-step plan involves the following:

1. Select a two-man team; one quality control and one industrial relations
2. Research and learn as much as you can
3. Attend a one-day seminar
4. Witness a Quality Circle in action
5. Decide to start
6. Select a facilitator/coordinator
7. Form a steering committee
8. Develop plans and goals
9. Present your plan to management and union people
10. Develop training materials
11. Present concept to the groups

12. Start training
13. Form Circles
14. Review monthly progress

The implementation procedure requires more details than might be expected. Each step needs careful analysis and necessary adjustments to form a suitable plan. Let us review the details of these steps.

1. *Select a Two-Man Team:* It is recommended that this kind of program begin with good research because of its complexity in terms of human management and because of the statistical techniques used in the program. A two-man team approach has proved successful. A person from quality control or manufacturing and a person from industrial relations make an excellent combination, and this helps to form a healthy Quality Circle program. Two people supplement each other in work as well as in times of sickness or vacation. This way the Quality Circle work does not stop because of insufficient manpower. As the program grows more personnel might be added to carry out various functions in the program more effectively—training, publicity, meeting attendance to name a few.

FIGURE 8–1

2. *Research and Learn:* Even though formal Quality Circles were introduced in Japan in 1962 very little attention was paid to them until 1966. Dr. Juran then wrote the major article on this subject, which generated more interest in the western world. There was very

little material available on the subject for several years. Now, many papers have been published which cover various aspects of Quality Circles. You should research and study as much material as possible on this subject, and then form a suitable plan for your company. Today, the International Association of Quality Circles (IAQC) and the American Society for Quality Circles (ASQC) supply detailed information on this subject. However, remember that most of the information is of a general nature and needs refinement before application.

FIGURE 8–2

3. *Attend a Seminar:* Sometimes it is helpful to attend a seminar on Quality Circles offered by outside experts. In Japan, Japan's Union of Scientists and Engineers (JUSE) fulfills this need. Several courses are offered to top management as well as to workers. In other countries, especially in the United States, many experts have started to offer seminars ranging from one to five days in length. Attending this type of seminar will help to reinforce the material that the team has already studied. However, many companies might not need this step if the management has committed itself to this type of program.

4. *See Quality Circles in Action:* It is said that a picture is worth a thousand words. This is true in a Quality Circle program. The best proof of the program is to see a circle in operation. Many companies

in Japan welcome visitors to observe their Quality Circles. In fact, most of them are proud of their progress and achievements. Some companies do the same in other countries. Those who need to view the actual operation of the Quality Circles should visit such companies. This experience is extremely helpful in planning, organizing, and coordinating a program.

5. *Decide to Start:* Once the two-man team has gathered all the information, a formal presentation should be made to top management before any decision is made regarding introduction of the Quality Circle into the company. Presentations should include at least the following major aspects:

a. Advantages and disadvantages of Quality Circles
b. Problems in running the Quality Circle
c. Planning for Quality Circles
d. Training requirements
e. Funding requirements for the program
f. Objectives of the program

The presentation should follow a discussion on specific problems that may be foreseen, and then a decision should be made regarding introduction of the Quality Circle program. Experience has shown that it takes more than one meeting to reach a final decision. Once top management's approval is obtained, the program should be intro-

FIGURE 8–3

duced through normal channels of the organization. There is very little need, if any, to announce big changes or create new departments. A team should be given further responsibilities to continue the detailed work. The material that is collected during the research period should help in planning future steps.

6. *Select a Facilitator:* As discussed before, this program needs a facilitator or a coordinator to plan, organize, train and follow-up these phases. That is the key position in a Circle program. He must be enthusiastic and cooperative in nature. Chapter 6 describes, in detail, the responsibilities and functions of the facilitator. The selection for this position needs careful consideration. One of the persons in the two-man team can become the facilitator. The facilitator gets involved with the program from the beginning and his responsibilities never end as far as the Circle program is concerned. Once the person is selected for the position, a formal announcement of the appointment should be made to management and workers. The sooner he becomes involved with the organization the better for the organization.

7. *Form a Steering Committee:* Questions are always being asked about the need for and importance of the steering committee.[1] The steering committee can be called an advisory committee. It is made up of representatives from various departments in the company. It is really an informal Quality Circle which makes sure that the Quality Circle program is progressing well, and in case of difficulties, guides the Circles in the right direction. Once the facilitator is selected, he should contact the various departments in the company to form the steering committee; but his major job at the start is to convince department heads of the benefits of a Quality Circle program and to try to get active participation from them. Representatives from each major department, for example, industrial engineering, manufacturing, engineering, and quality control, should be included in the formation of the steering committee. Experience shows it takes from one to two months to form a steering committee and have it become effective. Various functions and responsibilities of the steering committee are described in detail in Chapter 5.

8. *Develop Plans and Goals:* Once the steering committee is formed and begins to function, the committee should concentrate on formulating the plans and goals. Of course, the two-man team approach previously described should offer a basic plan and goals. However, it is necessary for the steering committee to understand and review the plan, and develop alternative courses of action in case of difficulties in the sequence and timing of major steps. Some possible goals are to train 30 people in crank shaft department, start four circles within three months, or prepare training material for middle management within six months.

The planning phase involves planning for training, planning for developing material, planning for area or departments that should be involved in this program. A good facilitator should spend at least 20% of his time in planning and preparation.

9. *Present the Plan to Management and the Union:* Once the detailed plan is developed, it is essential that the plan be discussed with the middle management and the union leaders. The discussion should be held as an information session to make them familiar with the program. The people-building philosophy should be insisted upon, and a request be made that the information be disseminated among all the people in the company. With this procedure, more people know about the program and become aware of what is going on. In many companies in Japan, the union is neither for nor against the program. The same is true in the United States. Douglas Fraser, President of the United Auto Workers, appearing on "Good Morning America," expressed his views regarding workers' cooperation in building good quality. He referred indirectly to Quality Circles in Japan and praised the work that has been achieved there. He insisted that American workers follow this exmaple in order to do a better job on quality and to be able to meet the competition. Experience in various companies in the United States shows we are slowly realizing that our position in the world is in jeopardy, and we need to forget the "we" and "they" feeling in the company and try to work together to build a good quality product.

10. *Develop Training Material:* This is another big hurdle in starting and implementing a Quality Circle program. Although many books and visual aids have been developed in Japan, there is very little training material available in English. Therefore, the best thing a company here can do is to develop its own training material. Recently, many papers and a few books have been published on Quality Circles. A good facilitator or a two-man team can collect this information and prepare a training manual for the company. Basic statistical techniques such as Pareto analysis and cause and effect diagrams are described here, as well as in many other statistical books. A facilitator should add other material that he feels is necessary for the members. Having your own material gives you independence. As far as material content is concerned, it provides guidelines and techniques to get people working together in harmony. People make the program work, and effective use of their untapped brainpower makes the program a success.

11. *Present the Concept to the Group:* Once the plan is developed and the training material is prepared by the facilitator, he should discuss the next step—selecting the area—with the steering committee. He should seek approval for the area or department when the company takes the first bold step of initiating a Quality Circle. The area can be selected in a number of ways. Some companies like to start the program where more than the usual number of quality problems exist. Some start where scrap and rework is excessive, while others start where there are a lot of communications problems. There are no hard and fast rules. In general, one should pick areas where reasonably good cooperation can be expected, and where people are receptive to new ideas.

Once the area is selected, people should be informed and requested to attend the first meeting, which should be held on compnay time. Experience shows that most well-planned meetings are successful, and more than 90% cooperation and participation is not

FIGURE 8–4

unusual. In the meeting, the voluntary aspect of the program should be emphasized, and it should be stressed that people are free to join or quit the program at any time.

Names of the people who are interested—volunteers—in training should be distributed to the prospective members.

12. *Start Training:* Once the list of those who wish to undergo training is prepared, the facilitator should prepare the training plan. A good training place, which is quiet and pleasant, should be selected so that people will not be disturbed during training sessions. Various visual aids can be used during training. The facilitator should try to get most of the members involved in the training through question and answer periods or through small talks. The training should continue for the next eight weeks. A graduation ceremony should be held to make people feel more important and respected. The details regarding training are discussed in Chapter 14.

13. *Form Circles:* During the training period (in the sixth or seventh session) the facilitator should review the progress of the group and the procedure for the formation of the Quality Circles. If the group is too big, he should recommend dividing it into more manageable units with a membership of from three to ten each. The recommended Quality Circle size is five or six members. However, the decision of a Circle formation is entirely up to the Circle members. They may also select the name of the Circle and their leader. It is advisable to start two or three Circles at the beginning and then slowly expand the program. Also, a starting kit should be provided to each Circle member.

14. *Review Monthly Progress:* This is an extremely important step in the implementation process. The steering committee must meet every week to review the problems and/or training. At last once a month a progress report of all the projects should be reviewed to locate difficulties. In some cases outside help from vendors or engineering may be needed. In other cases, samples may be required after the project report is presented to management.

FIGURE 8–5

FIGURE 8–6

In short, these fourteen steps should give a basic idea about the implementation plan. If they are followed properly, a company should be able to achieve success in the Quality Circle program. All these steps may not be required; they can be combined in different ways depending on the type of company.

Notes

1. J. Beardsley, "The Quality Circle Steering Committee," *IAQC Quality Circle Quarterly,* Fourth Quarter, 1978.

FIGURE 8–7

```
                    ┌─────────┐
                    │  C.C.   │
                    │ QUALITY │
                    │ CIRCLES │
                    └─────────┘

         MONTHLY QUALITY CIRCLES REVIEW


DATE:_____    PLACE: _____    PLANT #_____

AGENDA:

        1.   TRAINING

        2.   GRADUATION

        3.   PUBLICITY

        4.   MANAGEMENT PRESENTATIONS

        5.   CIRCLE PROGRESS

        6.   FOLLOW-UP

        7.   SPECIAL EVENTS

        8.   NEW BUSINESS
```

9

QUALITY CIRCLE POLICY

Need for Policy

Company policies provide a guide to the proper courses of action both present and future. They give a better understanding of the limits and regulations to which people should conform. Without a strong policy, the program can lack direction and continuity. Well-defined and properly-constructed policies help managers to delegate responsibilities to subordinates. It also permits people at different levels of the organization to make appropriate decisions as long as those decisions fall within the limits of the published policy. Thus the policy encourages uniformity of action and follow-up within the company.

However, it must be remembered that policies need to be reviewed periodically to maintain their effectiveness and must be updated constantly to reflect changes in the company. Even though it is recommended that companies have a policy for a Quality Circle program, it is not necessary to cover each and every detail. That will make the policy too tight, and there will be less chance to improve the program. Policies need to be flexible enough for the betterment of the program.

The Quality Circle program is just gaining acceptance in many companies in the United States. The idea is new and there are very few guidelines available for management. Since this type of program deals with human management it is essential for the survival of the program that top management take a keen interest in establishing a good effective policy. The well-defined policy eliminates a lot of confusion and mis-

81

understanding. However, it is not easy to write such a policy within a short period of time. One of the first duties of the steering committee should be to formalize a policy and submit it to the top management for review and for approval. It should be possible to establish a working policy within six to eight months.

How to Write the Quality Circle Policy

People always like to see a well-defined policy established by the top management. However, there are many times when the top management does not know the details and requirements essential to the formation of a good policy. Middle management in this case can help to prepare a draft proposal that is acceptable to the subordinates and submit that to the top management for approval. The Quality Circle program is one of those programs in which middle management has to take the initiative and formalize the rough draft of the policy. Many sources, articles, and other references can be used to prepare the policy. But the rules and limitations of the company should not be forgotten. The facilitator should then review the policy with the personnel department and with other related departments to establish a workable policy. The revised policy should be submitted to the steering (operating) committee once again for review. Once agreement is reached the final proposal should be submitted to the top management for approval.

Within two to three months one should be able to achieve approval for the final format. Once the approval is given, the policy should be open to everyone in the company. This openness will help to build people's confidence and stimulate cooperation. The policy should define the duties and activities of the steering committee, facilitator, members, leaders, and other related functions in the program.

The steering committee should then review the approved policy periodically and suggest any changes that are needed to render the program more effective. Remember that the program is based on the people-building philosophy and the policy should be focused on this basic premise. Cooperation is needed from everyone and the only way to get it is to be open and demonstrate the people-oriented aspects of the program.

SAMPLE POLICY

The following example is a suggestion for preparing a Quality Circle policy for your company.[1]

Purpose
This procedure will define the objectives, policy, and organization of Quality Circles within the company.

FIGURE 9–1

Objectives
Quality Circles are aimed at the following objectives:
—Improve quality
—Improve communications
—Promote team work
—Reduce waste
—Further employee satisfaction and education

Executive Committee
Representatives are chosen from higher management levels. The committee is responsible for establishing the program's policies and procedures for the total organization. The committee also provides guidance and direction to the program and approves any major changes needed to improve the effectiveness of the program.

Policy
A. All employees are free to
—Join, or not join, to drop out or return to a Circle in their work area
—Suggest problems to Circles as potentials for investigation

B. Management will support Circles by
—Encouraging Circle members to attend scheduled Circle functions
—Providing adequate meeting places for Circles to conduct meetings
—Providing space, materials, and so on to publicize Circle activities
C. Management will participate in Circle actions by
—Replying to Circle requests and, when necessary, give detailed explanations of denied requests
—Implementing approved Circle solutions
—Providing training assistance
D. Management may suggest problems to Circles and suggest departments where new Circles may be formed.
E. Circles will
—Be totally voluntary
—Follow techniques as described in members' manual
—Set up schedules for meeting and presentations within the framework of known company workloads
—Collaborate on any work-related problem pertaining to quality of product or service in the Circle area
—Have the right to accept or refuse problems submitted from any source
—Identify, analyze, and implement, when possible, solutions to problems.
—Circle will present the problems and its requested solution to management for acceptance
—Present periodic reviews to management on the progress of the Circle
—Attempt to improve communications between all employees
F. Circles will not address the following subjects:
—Employee complaints
—Hiring, firing policies
—Pay policies
—Personalities

Organization
A. Quality Circles are small groups of people, usually four to ten in size, who do similar work voluntarily, meet regularly to identify and analyze causes of problems in their area, recommend their solutions to management and, where possible, implement the solutions approved by the management.
B. Role of Manufacturing Foreman
—Be primarily a staff adviser to his department Circle
—Be active and helpful if the group wants him or her involved, back off but keep informed and show interest if not directly involved
—Constantly promote and encourage the Circle concept
—Provide liaison contacts and feedback on requests in a timely manner

—Does not appear to "run" or take the leadership role unless specifically elected to do so by the group

—Encourages new employees in the department to join the Circle in his area.

C. Quality Circle leader is the chosen leader of the Circle, having been selected by the Circle members. He or she is responsible for the operation of the Circle and for teaching Circle members proper use of Quality Circle techniques

D. Quality Circle Facilitator or Coordinator

—Is responsible for the overall Quality Circle program

—Trains leaders and members

—Maintains records

—Coordinates Circle operations

—Interfaces between Circles and company organizations and departments

—Works closely with the steering committee

—Attends Circle meetings and organizes leaders' meetings

E. Quality Circle mini-coordinator

F. In-plant steering committee representatives are chosen by management from volunteers from the major functions of the plant. The committee is responsible for establishing program policies, procedures, objectives, and resources. They provide guidance and direction to the Quality Circle program within the plant. The committee publicizes Circle activities within and outside of the company. They incorporate Quality Circles throughout the plant. They also show their visibility by meeting regularly with the facilitators and by attending management presentations.

Notes

1. J. Beardsley, "The Quality Circle Steering Committee," *IAQC Quality Circle Quarterly*, Fourth Quarter 1978.

10

QUALITY CIRCLE TECHNIQUES: DATA COLLECTION

We have discussed so far the details of the history and operation of the Quality Circle. However, tools and training are needed if we are to use the brainpower of the participants. Most people are creative and intelligent, and it is important to use their brainpower effectively to achieve the goals of the company and the society. An understanding of basic statistical techniques has been a great help to many people. In the next two chapters we will discuss in detail the key statistical techniques that should be used in training Quality Circle members.

What Is Statistics?

Many people fear the word "statistics." But everyone of us uses statistics daily, in our work as well as at home. When we listen to the news on radio or TV we hear a lot of statistical data, average temperature for the month or number of cars manufactured last month, for example. Computers also generate a volume of statistical data that is read every day. Statistics is a part of our life that can be applied in problem solving.

"Statistics" in simple language can be described as a systematic way of collecting and analyzing any given quantitative data. In order to make effective use of quantitative data in making decisions, it is necessary to have a systematic method of organizing, summarizing, and analyzing the individual facts. These methods of analysis can be called statistical methods.

The following five basic steps are generally used in applying statistical methods:

1. Defining the problem
2. Collecting relevant information
3. Investigation
4. Analyzing the data
5. Presentation of the findings

There are many versions of this basic methodology in various applications.

Why Develop Quality Circle Techniques?

Is there any need for elaborate training on Quality Circle techniques? Why not start a program the right way? If employees were just called into a large meeting and told that the company would start Quality Circles tomorrow and that they were expected to join the group and participate in solving problems, what do you think would happen?

Many programs in the past may have been started in this way and many have worked effectively. However, this writer has experience that shows this old method does not always work. One has to be careful and go about this slowly when introducing Quality Circle programs in a company for the first time.

Training is a very important phase because we in the United States have not taken care of this for a long time. People need more information. The more they know about the product or costs, the wiser the decisions they will reach. Similarly, statistics has been considered useful only in offices or in colleges but nobody has taken the time to demonstrate how simple statistics can work for shop areas. Hence, most of our work force is ignorant in this area. In the absence of training, confusion about and dislike of the Quality Circle program may easily be created among its members. Therefore, it is important to teach the techniques to all members and show them their use. Once the members grasp the basic concept, there is no problem getting them to use the techniques effectively while they collect and analyze data.

Problem Solving Methods

A number of different types of problems exist in our society today. No one method will solve them all, nor are there known best solutions to all of our problems. We need to keep trying and keep searching for better ways to do our jobs and to improve the world in which we live.

87

Table 10–1 shows briefly the various problem solving methods that can be applied to problems in your organization.

Table 10–1   Problem Solving Methods (Partial List)

	Type	People	Suggested Approach
A.	High level (Design type) (when cause is not obvious)	Eng. Mfg. Eng.	Variation Research Creativity Designed Exp.
B.	Classical (When historical data available) Scrap, rework, eng. spec.	Eng. Q.C. Mfg.	Cost Avoidance Team Task Force Value Analysis K & T Method
C.	Daily shop problems, rejects, maintenance, people-oriented problems	All	Q.C. Circles Foreman involvement

Types of Quality Circle Statistical Techniques

Quality Circle Statistical Techniques can be divided into three groups:

1. Techniques Used for Data Collection
2. Techniques Used for Data Analysis
3. Advanced Techniques for Later Use

This division of techniques is mainly for convenience, there is no hard and fast rule for dividing the techniques in this way. Many of them, in fact, overlap, so I have considered the major objective of the techniques when inserting one into any of the groups.

1. *Techniques Used for Data Collection:* One of the key areas in which Circle members have to concentrate is on data collection. Once the problem or project is selected, it is necessary that members collect data to discover the magnitude of the problem. Historical information is useful, but sometimes it is confusing or nonexistent. It is always beneficial to collect new fresh data and to analyze it properly. There are a number of ways to collect data. The techniques described here will serve as guidelines. There is always room for improvement in techniques and we should always try to invent newer and better ways to do a job.
2. *Techniques Used for Data Analysis:* Once the data is collected, Circle members need to analyze it properly so that creativity and brainpower is encouraged and used effectively, and so solutions(s) can be found to eliminate the problems. Simple analytical techniques that are discussed here help to direct brainpower in the proper direction. Many times Circle members find solutions without going into too much elaborate analysis. However, when the problems become complex it is better to take time, digest all information, discuss the solutions with a number of personnel, and then propose the final recommendations.

3. *Advanced Techniques:* These techniques are mainly useful in analyzing more complex problems in management areas. Some of them are helpful in analyzing new investments, others are useful to attack assembly or field problems.

Teaching Statistical Techniques

Quality Circle members are mainly from the shops and offices. They are people from working areas whose ages range from 18 to 70 years. It is not easy to train people in this wide age range, and so it is necessary to use a different technique than is generally used in a company.

People generally retain between 10% and 20% of the information that is presented the first time. Also, it is hard to keep them interested on a continuous basis for more than 2 to 3 hours. Hence, it is recommended that the training should be stretched out over 6 to 8 weeks for convenience and effectiveness.

Table 10–2 shows the recommended class procedure. Of course the details can always be modified to make them more suitable for the specific organization.

Table 10–2   How to Teach Statistical Techniques

Class Duration—One Hour
Subject: Statistical Techniques (Pareto analysis)

1. Theory ....15 minutes
2. Step by step procedure by using examples ....15 minutes
                    Break (five minutes)
3. Simple exerecise for all class members ....15 minutes
4. Review answers and open discussion ....10 minutes

Data Collection Techniques

The following techniques are effective in collecting data in the Quality Circle program:

1. Check sheets [1]
2. Graphs [1]
3. Histograms [2]
4. Control Charts [3]
5. Sampling

1. *Check Sheets:* Many activities of Circles involve taking samples and data. Hence, it is important that Circle members know how to collect data and develop the check sheets for future use. The use of check sheets makes the collection of data easier and more systematic. Also anyone can use them and collect the same data without creating confusion.

FIGURE 10–1

CHECK DRAWING
GEARCASE M-100

Date: _____

Shift: _____

BUBBLES OR LAMINATED ALUMINUM

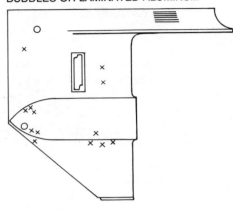

FIGURE 10–2

CHECK LIST

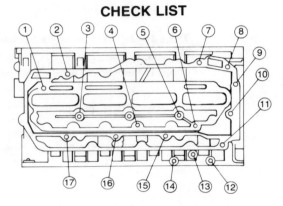

ITEM	8/20/80	9/15/80	9/16/80	9/17/80	9/18/80
1	4	1	1		
2		9	2	1	2
3	5				
4	1	9	5		
5	2			4	6
6	9		3	-	3
7	6	4	2	6	1
8					
9					7
10		9	7	2	
11	3				
12					

FIGURE 10–3

HYDRAULIC MACHINE INSPECTION RECORD

Contract No. _____ Machine No. _____

Date:_____ Inspected by: _____

Test NO. _____

Alignment of Manifold	acc_____	rej_____
Alignment of Motor	acc_____	rej_____
Leak Check on Pipe	acc_____	rej_____
Leak Check on Tank	acc_____	rej_____
Leak Check on Valves	acc_____	rej_____
Tension Check on Belts	acc_____	rej_____
Data Plate Info per Drawing	acc_____	rej_____
Wiring Tested	acc_____	rej_____
Muffler Type	acc_____	rej_____
Heater Specified _____Installed_____	Loose_____	
Erection Drawings Included	Yes _____	No_____

REMARKS:

FIGURE 10–4

ATTENDANCE CHECK LIST

NAME	M	T	W	T	F	S
Dick	✓	✓	✓	✓	✓	
Sud	✓	✓	✓	✓	✓	✓
Andy		✓	✓	✓	✓	✓
Gerry	✓		✓	✓		✓
Sue	✓	✓	✓	✓	✓	
Mimi	✓	✓	✓	✓	✓	
Mike	✓	✓	✓	✓	✓	
Donald	✓	✓	✓		✓	✓

Check sheets are divided into the following groups:

a. Check Drawings—Drawings or pictorial views can be employed to mark the locations of defects to find out problem areas (Figure 10–1).

b. Check List—A list can be made to make sure all of the critical items are checked. It can be used frequently in the future (Figure 10–2).

FIGURE 10–5

PLUNGER/CYLINDER INSPECTION RECORD

Contract No. _____ Type _____

Date _____ Inspected by _____

Plunger	Cylinder
Length comp to data _____	Length comp. to data _____
Size _____	Size _____
Finished O.D. (1) _____ (see sketch for location (2) _____ below.) (3) _____ (4) _____	Check I.D. _____ Support plate square ____ acc ____ rej ____ cyl. plu. Buffer wells type and loc. _____
Surface Finish ____ acc ____ rej ____	Seal Welding _____
Arrow ____ acc ____ rej ____	Sleeve as required _____
Type of "O" ring ____ acc ____ rej ____	Leak list ____ acc ____ rej ____
Splice condition ____ acc ____ rej ____	Inside of cyl. clean ____ acc ____ rej ____
Chamfer _____	reservation ____ acc ____ rej ____
Shipping "O" ring _____	

LOCATION OF FINISH OD CHECK

① ② ③ ④
|← 6″ →|← 6′ →| |← 6′ →|← 6″ →|

TELESCOPIC PLUNGER	SUNDRIES
Length _____	Material lists no. _____
I.D. _____	Complete check of parts ____ acc ____ rej ____
O.D. _____	
Stop ring _____	ASSEMBLY
Location of stop ring _____	
Chamfer _____	Pipe Plugs _____ Banding _____
REMARKS:	Contract No. Stamped _____

92

c. Check Sheet—A bowling score sheet is a simple check sheet after you have completed filling it out.

d. Other Types—Many other check sheets can be found in a company. Some examples are given on the next pages.

FIGURE 10-6

CHECK SHEET SYMBOLS
OR
"NUMBERS"

GEARCASES	Date:	STANDARD DEFECT CODES	
	Shift:	Defect Code:	Description
1647-7350	01, 03, 03, 03, 24		
1647-7350	0, 0, 0, 0,	01	Scored
		02	Burned
		03	Cracked
		04	Open Seam
		05	Chipped
		06	Inventory Adjustment
		07	Electrical Failure
		08	Excess Stock/Metal
		09	Leaking
		10	Material-Wrong/Out of Spec.
		11	Porosity
		12	Color of Material
		13	Misaligned
		14	Does Not Seat
		15	Short of Stock
		16	Damaged—Vendor
		17	Out of Round
		18	Out of Balance
		19	Stuck in Die
		20	Tool Reset
		21	Foreign Material Present
		22	Durometer
		23	Blisters
		24	Insert

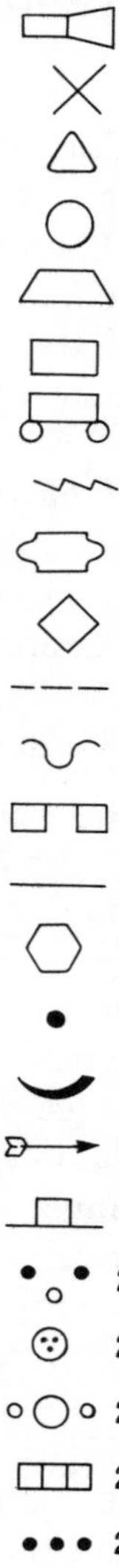

It is important that Quality Circle members understand the use and the need of good paperwork. Check sheets should be simple and useful. All members should have input when a new check sheet is prepared.

2. *Graphs:* Graphs, in simple terms, are a system of connections or interrelations among two or more things signified by a number of distinctive dots, lines or bars that tells a story without any further explanation.

There are many types of graphs used in a company. Some of them are as shown here:

1. Line Graphs are the most common of all graphs. They are used to plot things as they happen.
2. Column Graphs are just what the name implies. Vertical columns show the information desired.
3. Bar Graphs are just like column graphs, except that they run horizontally.
4. Pie Graphs are commonly used to show how much money is spent and where or what percentage of sales they represent.
5. Record Graphs are used to show temperature, roundness and surface finish. Many other types of records are also kept in graphic forms.
6. Pareto Graphs, Histograms, Cause and Effect Diagrams and other pictorial graphs, as well as many other forms, also exist today. Individual need and imagination will produce additional new forms of graphs in the future.

Remember

1. Graphs should be simple and should be meaningful
2. Graphs should be on graph paper or on grids
3. Graphs should have a title, data, and other pertinent information
4. Make use of color coding if required
5. Graphs should be as large as possible so that they are easy to read

3. *Histograms:* A histogram is a form of column graph which displays the distribution of values obtained whenever numerical data is collected. Although a histogram is constructed from sample data, the object is to suggest the probable distribution of the population from which the samples were taken. In a histogram, values of a continuous variable are represented by the horizontal axis, which is divided into classes or cells of equal size. Generally, there is one column for each cell, and the height of that column represents the number of occurrences of data values in the range represented by the cell.

For example, suppose 6.00, 6.50, 7.00, and 7.50 are selected as cell boundaries for a set of data. By convention this means that the first cell contains all numbers from 6.00 up to, but not including, 6.50; the second cell contains 6.50 and all larger numbers up to, but not including, 7.00. Likewise, the third and final cell contains numbers from 7.00 up to, but not including, 7.50, so 7.50, the largest cell boundary, must be larger than any value found in the data collected. Let the data consist of the numbers 6.91, 6.50, 7.49,

FIGURE 10–7

PIE GRAPHS

Using this formula, 3.6 × the percentage = the angle. This is clearly shown in this graph. It is very important that we keep a pie graph to scale.

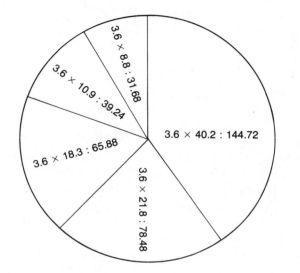

FIGURE 10–8

LINE GRAPHS

This is how it might look after one day. It is very plain to see when things get out of control.

PART No. 1643-6673
Gearcase bore 2.750 ± .005   DATE: _____

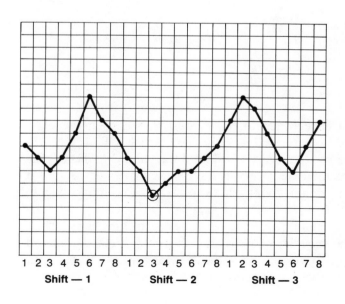

FIGURE 10–9

BAR GRAPHS

NUMBER OF PIECES

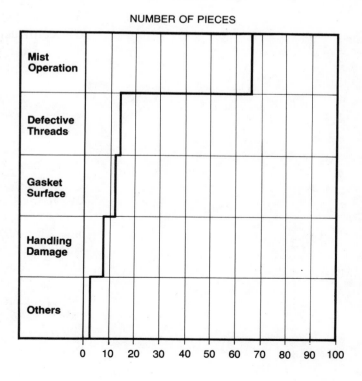

95

6.32, 6.74, and 7.00. Then 6.32 belongs in the first cell, 6.50, 6.74, and 6.91 in the second, 7.00, and 7.49 in the third. The histogram is shown in Figure 10–10.

FIGURE 10–10

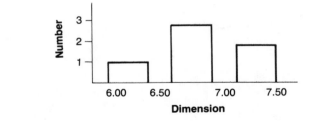

Next best is half or twice a power of ten: 0.0002, 50, 0.5, 200, 2, 0.2 or 0.05. Occasionally one fourth of a power of ten is used; the cell size might be 0.25, 250, or 0.025 for example.

STEP 5: Determine the cell boundaries. They are consecutive multiples of the cell size. The smallest one is less than or equal to the smallest sample value, but the largest one must be larger than the largest sample value. Suppose the data ranges from 0.750 to 2.125. If a cell size of 0.25 has been selected, then the cell boundaries are 0.75, 1.00, 1.25, 1.50, 1.75, 2.00, 2.25. On the other hand, if 0.5 has been chosen as the cell size then the cell boundaries should be 0.5, 1.0, 1.5, 2.0, and 2.5, rather than 0.75, 1.25, 1.75, 2.25 because the numbers in the former set are multiples of 0.5, whereas those in the latter are not.

STEP 6: Construct a tally sheet showing the range of each cell in such a way that there is no ambiguity as to which cell should contain a particular data value. For an example refer to the cell boundaries 0.5, 1.0, 1.5, 2.0, and 2.5 from the preceding paragraph. The construction of the tally sheet depends slightly on the precision of the sample data. If the data is recorded to the nearest 0.005, then the tally sheet might look like this:

Class Number	Class Interval	Tally of Data
1	0.5–0.995	
2	1.0–1.495	
3	1.5–1.995	
4	2.0–2.495	

But if the data is recorded to the nearest 0.001, then the class intervals should be expressed as 0.5-0.999, 1.0-1.499, 1.5-1.999, and 2.0-2.499, so that every possible data value has been provided for. Once the class intervals have been expressed as shown here, there is no doubt about where to assign a boundary value, such as 0.5 or 2.0.

STEP 7: Transfer the data from the data sheet to the tally sheet. Don't make the mistake of searching the data sheet to find all values belonging to class 1, then those belonging to class 2, and so on. Instead, proceed sequentially through the data sheet, examining each value in turn, assigning it to the appropriate class by making a tally mark. In case of an interruption it is possible to count the number of tally marks to determine where to resume the process. This tally sheet shows that seventeen values have been transferred from the data sheet.

Class Number	Class Inetrval	Tally of Data
1	0.5–0.995	11
2	1.0–1.495	1111 11
3	1.5–1.995	1111 11
4	2.0–2.495	111

STEP 8: Draw horizontal and vertical axis on a piece of graph paper. On the horizontal axis, indicate all cell boundaries with equally-spaced numbered tick marks.

0.5   1.0   1.5   2.0   2.5

Examine the tally sheet to find the largest number of tally marks in a single class; scale the vertical axis accordingly.

STEP 9: Transfer the data from the tally sheet to the graph paper by drawing in each cell a column, the height of which is proportional to the number of tally marks in that cell. The appearance of the histogram is enhanced by separating the columns slightly. If a cell contains no tally marks, leave a space on the histogram, so that all columns are properly positioned along the horizontal axis.

STEP 10: Add a legend. Indicate who collected the data and when and where, and include whatever additional information is necessary to identify the data. Give the date of preparation of the histogram and the name of the person or group responsible for its preparation.

How Is a Histogram Used?

There are two principal ways of using a histogram. One is to study the shape of the distribution shown on the histogram. The other is to compare the limits of the distribution with the limits required for the population from which the samples were drawn. Of course, these approaches can be varied in many ways. Sometimes an observation of the shape of the graph indicates a bias toward one extreme or the other. Other times it suggests that the data really comes from two different populations, such as parts produced from well-adjusted and poorly-adjusted machines. Sometimes the limits of the distribution are sufficiently close together, but both are larger or smaller than the corresponding required limits; the distribution is shifted from where it ought to be. At other times the distribution is too wide for the requirements, or it may be too wide and shifted. In any case specific types of corrective action are indicated.

Figure 10–11 shows the complete construction of one of the histograms.

FIGURE 10–11

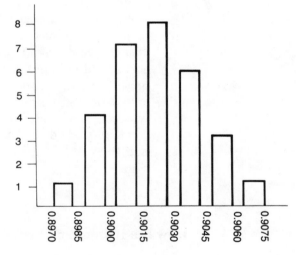

MEASUREMENT OF HOLE SIZES

Cell No.	Cell Boundaries	Tally of Samples
1	0.8970–0.8984	I
2	0.8985–0.8999	IIII
3	0.9000–0.9014	THL II
4	0.9015–0.9029	THL III
5	0.9030–0.9044	THL I
6	0.9045–0.9059	III
7	0.9060–0.9074	I

Name _____
Date _____
Source _____
Time _____
Covered _____

4. *Control Charts:* Control charts provide the user with an indication of stability in the process. The statistical analysis is done on a mathematical basis to arrive at control limits. The ultimate objective of a manufacturing process is to make parts or products which confirm print specifications. Once the process is known to be "in control" it is the role of management to get the most out of the process by running it at well-aimed and uniform levels of performance. By "in control" we mean that the process is capable of holding certain specifications as long as no "assignable" cause forced it outside the process control limits. By "assignable" cause we mean something that is specific, or findable, and can be pinpointed. For example, the reason the hunter missed the deer was because of the tree that came in between the deer and the hunter. This is an assignable cause. Process itself has also "random" variations but those will not cause

the process to exceed control limits. Random causes are those due solely to chance. The mathematics behind control charts uses ± 3 standard deviations while developing the upper and lower control limits.

Some of the steps to follow in setting up control charts are as follows:

1. Choose the dimension to be charted based on defective parts or based on Circle members' as well as management's decision.
2. Choose the type of control charts.
3. Decide what "center line" and what "limits" you plan.
4. Choose the size of the samples to be checked. Use equal quantities over regular intervals of time.
5. Provide a system for collecting data. Measurements must be simple and free of error.
6. Calculate the control units, provide specific instructions on the interpretations of the results, and the actions which are to be taken by the management.

There are many kinds of control charts used in industry. They can be divided into two groups in the following way:

1. Variable charts for controlling:
   central tendency—x chart
   variability—R chart
2. Attribute charts for controlling:
   fraction defective—p chart
   defects per unit—c chart

Figures 10–12 and 10–13 show an example of each.

The details regarding control charts can be found in these two books: *Quality Control* training manual, a publication of State University of Iowa, Iowa City; and *Control Chart Method of Controlling Quality During Production,* American National Standard Institute publication ASQC Standard B3-1958.

More references are given at the end of this chapter.

How a Histogram Is Constructed

Although the foregoing example serves to illustrate what a histogram is, it does not completely demonstrate how to construct one in a practical situation.

TEN VITAL STEPS

STEP 1: Collect the data, at least 30 to 50 items and preferably more. The more data there is the more confidence in the conclusions suggested by the data. Some thought should be given to the type of data sheet used. Lined paper is almost always desirable, but if the data must be recorded very, very quickly, the lines might prove a hindrance.

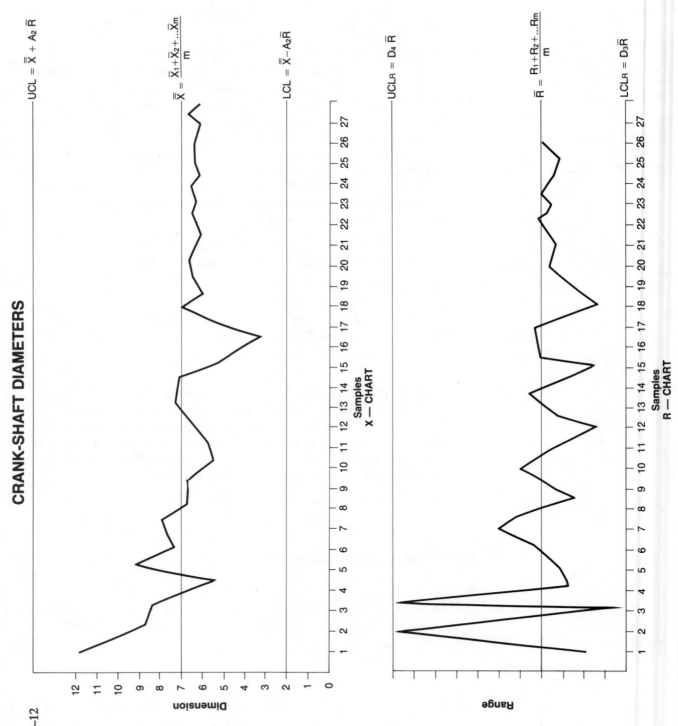

CRANK-SHAFT DIAMETERS

FIGURE 10–12

$UCL = \overline{\overline{X}} + A_2 \overline{R}$

$\overline{\overline{X}} = \dfrac{\overline{X}_1 + \overline{X}_2 + ... \overline{X}_m}{m}$

$LCL = \overline{\overline{X}} - A_2 \overline{R}$

Dimension

Samples
X — CHART

$UCL_R = D_4 \overline{R}$

$\overline{R} = \dfrac{R_1 + R_2 + ... R_m}{m}$

$LCL_R = D_3 \overline{R}$

Range

Samples
R — CHART

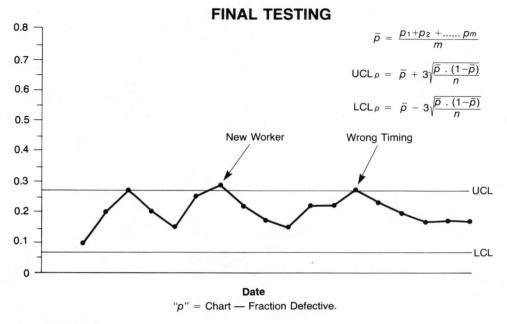

FINAL TESTING

$$\bar{p} = \frac{p_1 + p_2 + \ldots\ldots\, p_m}{m}$$

$$UCL_p = \bar{p} + 3\sqrt{\frac{\bar{p} \cdot (1-\bar{p})}{n}}$$

$$LCL_p = \bar{p} - 3\sqrt{\frac{\bar{p} \cdot (1-\bar{p})}{n}}$$

"p" = Chart — Fraction Defective.

FIGURE 10–13

STEP 2: Find the largest and smallest values and subtract to find the range.

$Range = Largest — Smallest$

STEP 3: Decide approximately how many cells or classes of data should be used. The simplest rule of thumb is to consider having ten cells. However, it's best to use fewer cells, say five or six, when the number of samples is under fifty, and more cells, even up to twenty, when more than two hundred observations have been made.

Consider the extreme cases of too few or too many cells. If all of the values are contained in one cell, the distribution of values is not shown at all. This extreme may be approached, although never actually reached, when the number of observations is so small that the distribution of sample values cannot accurately reflect the distribution of the population from which the samples were drawn. After all, chance plays a part in the values obtained by sampling.

At the opposite extreme, it is possible to have so many cells that there is no grouping of data at all; every distinct value is placed in a different cell. The result is an excellent display of the *sample* distribution in all its detail, including chance details peculiar to that sample. If the entire population could be contained in the sample, then this approach would be valid (but time-consuming), since the idea of a histogram is to approximate the distribution of the population. In reality, however, most populations may be considered infinite. For example, an entire production run produces only a sample from the population of parts that could have been produced.

STEP 4: To obtain the class interval or cell size, first divide the range by the chosen number of cells, then round the result so that it is convenient to work with. Notice that rounding upward might reduce the number of cells, while rounding downward might increase the number of cells. Keep in mind the reasoning of step 3 when determining the class interval. How should the rounding be done? A power of ten is ideal, say 0.0001, 100, 1, or 0.1.

Sampling

Many times people feel sampling is not accurate and that 100% inspection is the only way to do a good job. However, that is not true. Fatigue, monotony, and inherent inspector limitations prevent 100% inspection from being 100% effective. It is also costly and in some cases not possible, for example in destructive testing. On the contrary, sampling gives a better look at the lot and helps to analyze the lot quality more effectively.

There are a number of ways samples can be obtained from the lots. During election time we see the effective use of sampling on TV networks when, based on one percent or two percent sampling, NBC, ABC or CBS predict elections winners within a few hours after the polls are closed. Presidential popularity, or many other results, can be judged based on the results of similar samples.

The three samples found most useful in industrial applications are random samples, stratified samples, and consecutive samples.

1. *Random Samples:* To inspect the overall quality of a lot or shipment it is of the utmost importance that samples be selected randomly. The samples should not be picked from the tops of the boxes or all from one box. All parts should be treated equally, and then samples should be chosen for evaluation. Select random numbers from tables or use any similar simple procedure to avoid biased results. If the randomization is not observed, one might obtain false results and the decisions made, based on the results, would be completely erroneous.

2. *Stratified Samples:* "Stratification" means dividing data into two or more groups so that each group can be evaluated separately. Many times it is hard to examine mixed samples and to find the problem. Sorting the data in small groups based on certain characteristics helps to pinpoint problem areas.

Suppose the ABC Company is manufacturing compression springs and the total rejects for the month's run is about 10%. To analyze this data further for problem areas, divide the data by types of springs, by length, or by any other important characteristics. Samples to analyze further can then be obtained based on the problem area.

Stratified sampling can be used in the same product based on different lot sizes, different production quantity, and different days when it is manufactured.

3. *Consecutive Samples:* Multi-vari charts, to be discussed in Chapter 12, will explain this method in more detail.

Quality Control personnel should help in providing training in basic sampling theory.

The key points to stress are as follows:

1. Why sampling
2. Different types of sampling methods
3. How to get random sampling
4. How to check the parts
5. How to analyze sampling results

So far we have discussed some of the major data collection methods. However, one can expand on these methods in each industry, and depending on the need, can even invent many more for future use. The key point to remember is the basic way of collecting good, reliable data since the analysis and solutions depend on the data one collects.

Notes

1. This information was prepared by A. Martin, Quality Control Analyst, Mercury Marine, Fond du Lac, Wisconsin.

2. This information was prepared by R. Oakland, Quality Control Engineer, Mercury Marine.

3. This information was prepared by L. Stam, Quality Control Analyst, Mercury Marine.

11

QUALITY CIRCLE TECHNIQUES: DATA ANALYSIS

The Quality Circle techniques that are described here are mainly used in analyzing a problem or data. The data or problem can be single, multiple, or just for informal group discussion. These techniques should be applied properly and should be based on the problem and data. Once again there is no hard and fast rule for calling these techniques "data analysis." It is for convenience, and on the basis of the writer's judgment and experience this is being used in this division.

The main data analysis techniques are brainstorming, Pareto analysis, cause and effect analysis, and presentation skills.

Brainstorming

Brainstorming[1] is a technique for generating the greatest possible number of solutions to a problem for evaluation and development.

Characteristically certain things occur during brainstorming. The problem to be addressed is clearly stated and understood by all the members of the group. All suggestions are recorded. Each member of the group is given an equal opportunity to express his or her ideas. All suggestions, good or bad, are encouraged. At no time are any suggestions or possible solutions criticized.

WHY USE BRAINSTORMING?

Brainstorming is used because it is a proven effective step in generating a maximum number of solutions to problems.

Most employees are aware of problems affecting the quality of their work, and usually think about the solutions. With this general assumption, why does the best solution to a problem lie dormant in the minds of people? Often you will hear, "Well, if you knew how to solve the problem, why didn't you tell us?" Answer—"No one asked me!"

It is easy to say, if you apply the right solution to the right problem you can correct anything. In brainstorming, we are asking for your ideas so that we can apply the right solution to the right problems with a minimum of effort and time so that we can reduce scrap, improve quality, and enhance overall working conditions.

Brainstorming brings out the ideas trapped in people's minds. It recognizes that certain conditions exist, and that people can participate in a creative process that is self-fulfilling and makes use of the company's most valuable asset, the ideas and minds of the employees—those people actually doing the work day in and day out.

WHO USES BRAINSTORMING?

Everyone uses brainstorming for a variety of reasons—the Pentagon, the President and his Cabinet, scientists, and unions just to name a few.

Quality Circle members attempt to use brainstorming in analyzing a problem and looking for possible solutions to it.

Constant attention must be given to the essentials. Everyone must be thinking about the same problem. All ideas, good or bad, directly or indirectly related, are encouraged. This Is Not the Time to Criticize! All ideas are recorded. All members must be given an equal chance to participate. If these conditions are not satisfied, it is not a brainstorming session.

Brainstorming is not a "bull" session or a coffee klatch to get you away from work. It is one step in an organized approach to problem solving.

WHEN TO BRAINSTORM

There are times when people are faced with an unusual or different situation, one which cannot be solved through experience, a given formula, a normal procedure, or some other known method. Brainstorming is used then to broaden and diversify thinking with the production of as many ideas as possible. It is never used to produce a single line of thought, nor is it the answer to a problem that has only one solution. It is mainly a creative technique used when individual efforts do not yield satisfactory results.

105

HOW TO PREPARE FOR A SESSION

Brainstorming is worthwhile only if the problem to be solved is first identified. All members must be informed of the problem and must see all data relating to it. Afterward, a suitable meeting place must be found. A relaxed atmosphere which can readily accommodate laughter is usually the best for a creative, productive session. This will allow the participants to express themselves in their own way. All ideas should be listed and, whenever possible, kept open during an incubation period of one or two weeks.

RULES FOR BRAINSTORMING SESSIONS

Four basic rules prevail in a brainstorming session. We will examine and explain each of them.

1. *Criticism Is Ruled Out:* Judgment is suspended for a later session when all ideas will be evaluated. In the brainstorming session, being critical and creative at the same time is like trying to walk and run at the same time.
2. *Free-wheeling Is Welcomed:* The wilder the ideas, the better. The more fun you have, the more creative the session. Offbeat, impractical suggestions may trigger another member to make a solid, practical suggestion which otherwise might not occur to him or her.
3. *Quantity Is Wanted:* The more suggestions, the better. The greater the number of ideas, the greater the likelihod of success in your project.
4. *Combination and Improvements Are Sought:* In addition to contributing ideas, members are encouraged to combine suggestions made by others which can be turned into even better suggestions. Remember, this is a team effort and expanding on each other's ideas or combining them is not stealing someone else's thunder.

    Circle leaders are reminded to keep these "teams" on target. This is NOT a bull session.

    One should remember two key aspects of brainstorming: participation from all, and incubation period.

The following lists show two examples of brainstorming sessions.

How to Get Rid of Fleas on Dog
1. cut hair
2. flea collar
3. bathe more often
4. try to keep out of dirt
5. take to veterinarian
6. prescription shampoo
7. flea shampoo
8. flea powder
9. quarantine
10. clean sleeping quarters
11. keep away from landfill

12. foods/possibility
13. brush every day
14. get shots
15. get lots of exercise
16. have him scratch himself
17. move to different area
18. keep out of tall grass
19. take him swimming
20. if none of these work—shoot the dog

Improve Communication (in Company)

1. Improved intercom system
2. Improved telephone system
3. Use bulletin boards better
4. Company newsletter
5. More communication between foreman and workers
6. Memos
7. Better employee suggestion system
8. Better new employee indoctrination
9. Meetings (more frequent)
10. Charts and displays
11. New employee handbook
12. Picture book of employees
13. Group activities
14. Quality Circles
15. Office arrangements
16. Work stations
17. Reduced noise levels
18. Posters
19. Management encouragement of better communication
20. Formalized grapevine (management meetings and production people)
21. Training sessions
22. Cafeterias
23. Company related clubs
24. Company library (books and cassettes, for example)
25. Management information systems

Pareto Diagrams

A Pareto diagram [2] combines two of the common forms of graphs, a column graph and a line graph. The column graph is characterized by the arrangement of the columns in descending order of length. The horizontal axis does not contain the numerical scale; it is simply a base line for the columns, one column for each of a set of independent categories, and occasionally an "other" column for a group of the least significant categories.

The length of the columns is in proportion to the size, cost, or population associated with the categories, and a numerical scale along the vertical axis indicates the actual magnitudes. The line graph portion of a Pareto diagram plots the accumulation or summation of column length from left to right. It begins at the lower left corner of the graph and ends at the upper right corner at a height which is the sum of the heights of all the columns.

Vilfredo Pareto was an Italian engineer-sociologist who, in the nineteenth century, studied the numbers of people in various income classes and diagrammed his findings in the manner described above. Present-day applications of the technique compare frequencies of different forms of violent crimes, demonstrate the relative amounts of time office workers spend on various tasks, organize defective-part data according to type of defect, or indicate which of several similar machines produce the largest numbers of defective parts. In every case, the most important classes are identified so that corrective action can be directed where it will do the most good. When Pareto diagrams are constructed for the same kind of information for two different time periods, the effect of the corrective action can be demonstrated.

Notice that the categories used in constructing a Pareto diagram may be causes—different operators or different machines—or they may be effects such as rough, bent, cracked, unthreaded, dirty, or porous cylinder covers. Oftentimes a Pareto diagram of effects will be constructed first, then a cause and effect diagram will be used to lead from the principal effect to the most probable cause, which is then analyzed with another Pareto diagram.

The construction of a Pareto diagram follows these eight steps:

STEP 1: Decide how the data should be classified—by shift, by type of defect, by operation, or by part number, for example.

STEP 2: Choose a time period for your study, construct a check sheet to cover that time period and provide for all possible classes of data, and then collect the data. Whenever possible, try to translate quantities into monetary terms; the two are not always proportional.

STEP 3: For each category, count the data for the entire time period, and record the totals. If there are more than five to ten categories, consider grouping some of those with the smallest totals into a group called "others."

STEP 4: Draw horizontal and vertical axes on a piece of graph paper. Divide the horizontal axis into equal segments, one for each category. Scale the vertical axis in such a way that the top of the axis represents a number equal to the sum of the totals for all of the categories.

STEP 5: Plot the data in the form of columns. Begin at the left-hand side of the graph with the largest category, then the next largest, and so on. If there is a category called "others," plot it last, after the smallest category shown individually. The appearance of the graph is enhanced by separating the columns very slightly.

STEP 6: Plot the cumulative line. Begin by drawing a diagonal line across the first column, beginning at the lower left corner. From the upper right corner of the first column, continue in a new direction by moving to the right a distance equal to the width of a column and upward a distance equal to the height of the second column. From that point, draw another straight line segment, proceeding to the right a distance equal to the width of a column and upward a distance equal to the height of the third column. Repeat until the upper right corner of the graph is reached. The height of the cumulative line at this point should be such as to represent the total of all data collected.

STEP 7: Construct another vertical axis on the right-hand side of the graph and scale it from 0 to 100%. The termination of the cumulative line should be at the point marked 100%.

STEP 8: Add a legend. Tell who collected the data and when and where, and include whatever additional information is necessary to identify the data. Give the date of preparation of the Pareto diagram, and the name of the person or group responsible for its preparation.

Figure 11-1 shows the application of Pareto diagrams.

FIGURE 11-1

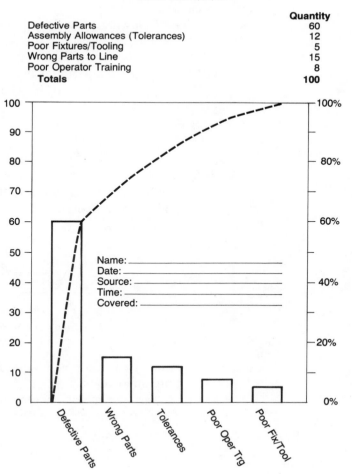

CAUSES FOR DEFECTS

Month End: 3/31/78

	Quantity
Defective Parts	60
Assembly Allowances (Tolerances)	12
Poor Fixtures/Tooling	5
Wrong Parts to Line	15
Poor Operator Training	8
Totals	**100**

Cause and Effect Diagrams

Cause and effect analysis was first developed by Professor Kaoru Ishikawa of the University of Tokyo in the early 1950s. His first application of this technique was in the Fulsai iron works in 1953. Since the final form looked like a fish, some people called it the "Fishbone Diagram." Others, to honor Professor Ishikawa, call this technique the "Ishikawa Diagram."

Three types of cause and effect diagrams are used today. They are as follows:

1. *The Cause Enumeration Type:* This is the type most commonly used. It is also called the "basic cause and effect diagram."
2. *The Dispersion Analysis Type:* The complete diagram looks like the enumeration type except that the approach in constructing it is different.
3. *Process Analysis:* The production process is written down step by step, and then minor causes are analyzed in each step. This is also known as a flow diagram.

Cause and effect diagrams are a picture of lines and symbols designed to represent a meaningful relationship between an effect and its causes.

The following procedure is used in constructing cause and effect diagrams.

STEP 1: Draw a horizontal line with an arrow at the right-hand end and a box in front of it. The effect or problem should be written in the box.

STEP 2: Write the major causes (man, material, machine, and method) in boxes placed parallel to and some distance from the main arrow. Connect the boxes by arrows slanting toward the main arrow.

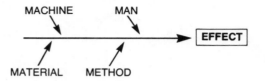

Sometimes it is possible, or may be necessary, to add more than four major causes.

STEP 3: List the minor causes on the chart around the major causes which they affect. They are connected by arrows pointing to the major causes.

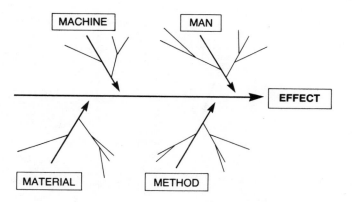

Some of the key features to remember are as follows:

1. Participation is necessary and all the members should be involved in analyzing causes.
2. A number of ideas (causes) should be generated.
3. Freewheeling should be encouraged.
4. Criticism should not be allowed.
5. The causes should be in before anyone takes any action. Sometimes all of this information is written on a large board and presented to the shop area personnel for consideration for one week to allow them to add more causes to the diagram as they think of them.
6. Members are asked to mark or vote on the causes they feel are the most important.

USES OF CAUSE AND EFFECT ANALYSIS

1. To recognize important causes
2. To understand all effects and causes
3. To compare operational procedures
4. To find major solutions
5. To figure out what to do
6. To improve the process

Figure 11–2 shows the actual applications.

Presentation Skills

When the Quality Circle members get ready to show their solution(s) to management it is important that they present their story effectively and appropriately so that management will accept their proposals without delay.[3] To do this Circle members need many different skills. Some of these skills are represented in:

FIGURE 11–2

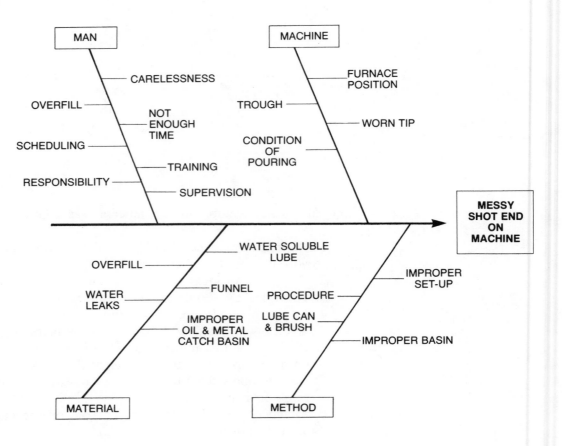

1. Oral preparations by the members
2. Preparation of the project report
3. Use of video and audio equipment
4. Visual aids
5. Group assignments in project presentations

REASONS FOR MANAGEMENT PRESENTATIONS

As has been previously stated, presentations to management help to improve the communications between management and workers; demonstrate management's involvement and interest to Quality Circle members; and foster a good working relationship among all the people. They also offer an opportunity to recognize the Quality Circle members' efforts.

ORGANIZATION OF THE PROJECT PRESENTATION

1. A presentation should not be more than 20-30 minutes long including opening and closing comments of the leader.
2. All members are introduced by the leader, and the leader closes the session by answering any questions asked.

FIGURE 11–3

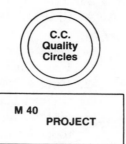

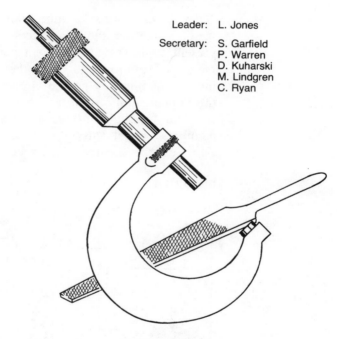

3. All members participate in the presentation.
4. All information gathered is used during the presentation, such as histograms, Pareto diagrams, and cause and effect diagrams.
5. Cost savings and other supporting information should also be discussed.
6. The outline should be prepared for presentation.
7. Good organization is essential.
8. All guests, steering committee members, and other related parties should be invited at least one week before the presentation.

TEN STEPS TO A SUCCESSFUL
MANAGEMENT PRESENTATION

1. Have a schedule and try to start and end on time.
2. Use a large enough room with plenty of seating.
3. Have a chairperson or coordinator present so that the meeting is under control.
4. Use an agenda with subjects and speakers outlined; leave room for taking notes.
5. Use visual aids such as slides, charts, graphs, and so forth.
6. Do not discredit other departments or people.
7. Use positive points as accomplishments.
8. Invite all interested parties.
9. Do not ask for additional funding or people.
10. Do not ask for on-the-spot decisions.

GENERAL COMMENTS ON PRESENTATIONS

There is no set time or time limit for the presentations to the management. Whenever the Circle feels they are ready, they may make the presentation. The management personnel who would be able to implement the solution and any others who would be affected should be invited. In this way people already know what is going to happen and the implementation phase is carried out smoothly.

All benefit from the management presentations. Quality Circle members benefit through personal development and job satisfaction. Also, all the members are recognized by the management for their

FIGURE 11–4

CYLINDER BLOCK REJECTS

contributions and achievements. Management benefits from improvement in quality, reduction in waste, and cost areas, which help to improve profitability of the company.

Finally, everyone in the Quality Circle program must remember that the management presentation—formal, or informal—is a must. Whether or not the project is completed or rejected, the management presentation must be arranged to recognize the Quality Circle members and to show appreciation for their efforts. Remember that this is the only final RECOGNITION the Circle program offers to the Quality Circle Member.

Notes

1. Donald L. Dewar, *The Quality Circle Handbook* (Red Bluff, Calif.: Quality Circle Institute, 1980).

2. This information was prepared by R. Oakland, Quality Control Engineer, Mercury Marine, Fond du Lac, Wisconsin.

3. This information was prepared by J. Dietrich, Die Casting Supervisor, Mercury Marine.

12

ADVANCED TECHNIQUES

We have discussed the basic techniques that can be used daily by Quality Circle members. These are mainly applicable to the solution of many repetitive manufacturing problems. However, the Quality Circle movement is now growing rapidly and people from management areas like engineering, manufacturing engineering, data processing, and many other similar areas are getting involved in solving problems through Quality Circle concepts. These people are already very knowledgeable in their fields, and in order to use their knowledge effectively, one must use more advanced statistical techniques. It is proved that these methods have saved thousands of dollars in many companies who took their time to use these methods effectively.

Some of the key advanced techniques that can be used effectively are listed below.

1. Cost avoidance team strategy
2. Red "X" theory
3. Realistic tolerancing
4. Process capability studies
5. Pre-control
6. The Run-sum control plan
7. Multi-vari chart
8. Component search patterns
9. Regression and correlation analysis
10. E.V.O.P. and R.E.V.O.P.

11. Experimental designs
12. Failure analysis
13. Extension of quality and reliability education

Cost Avoidance Teams

Cost avoidance teams are similar to Quality Circle groups.[1] Some of the objectives of the teams are:

1. To minimize internal scrap and rework.
2. To improve the communications between manufacturing, engineering, and quality control.
3. To cut down the costs.
4. To use statistical techniques as an aid to solve costly problems.

These teams generally consist of responsible, usually highly placed people from engineering, manufacturing, and quality control. Members are directed to the basic goals and asked to avoid using preconceived ideas (see Figure 12–1). Fresh data is collected and new parts are checked for proper analysis. For every event there is a cause, and C.A.T.'s (Cost Avoidance Teams) use this planned generation of new data to help find the root causes to eliminate the problems. Formation of cost

FIGURE 12–1

NO PRECONCEIVED IDEAS

FACTS

CONCEPTS

LET THE FIGURES TO THE TALKING

COST AVOIDANCE TEAM
Quality, Mfg., Eng.

For every event there is a cause. Find the root cause to eliminate the problem.

avoidance teams serves the same purpose as Quality Circles. When people work in the group, many more ideas are generated, and valuable experience is collected. Regular meetings are scheduled weekly to review the progress and assign the work to team members and their departmental assistants. Periodical meetings are then held with department heads.

The cost avoidance team can start by forming one or two teams, and expanding the scope later as required. Vice presidents of manufacturing and vice presidents of engineering generally initiate the corrective actions. The following agenda can be used as a guideline.

Formation of Cost Avoidance Team

Agenda

1. Objective
2. Team Formation:
   —Engineering
   —Manufacturing (Foreman or higher)
   —Manufacturing Engineering
   —Quality Control
3. Specific problems(s) to be attacked
4. Meeting schedule
5. Progress Report

It is extremely important to the success of the cost avoidance team that management review their progress every three months and lend help to the teams if the progress is not satisfactory. This is similar to what is done in management presentations in Quality Circle programs.

"Red X" Theory

The statistical technique called "Red X" theory has been widely publicized by Dorian Shainin.[1] Through his hard work and many successful applications, the technique has been sold to many companies in the United States. It is used effectively to solve complicated problems. The basic theory is now briefly described.

Every effect of importance, a "Y" (a product characteristic), varies as a result of a large number of causes—the variables in materials, ingredients, parts, machinery, operators, environment, and so forth. These causes always include some that are easily recognized, some that are suspected, and some that are completely unsuspected. The causes vary in three different ways during the operations (a) independently, (b) sometimes influencing others (auto-correlated), and (c) often operating to produce results influenced by combinations of causes (two or more at a time) which at certain levels cause synergistic results (interactions). Many companies which face chronic difficulties do not take the time to understand all these differences and generally content themselves with ready explanations. Some believe that the variation is due to inherent

FIGURE 12–2

variables in raw material that would be too costly to control. The cure is considered more expensive than the disease. The human element is also very often blamed. However, if you could take time to analyze problems properly, let the parts do the talking to reveal the leading cause, you will find that a "Red X" caused the largest variation in the process. Proper control of this variable can get rid of a major portion of the process variation and save thousands of wasted dollars.

The variables in the process generally do not contribute equally to the output variation. That would be too much of a coincidence. Most of the time one variable makes the largest contribution while another makes the smallest, with all others ranging somewhere in between. "X" usually designates the unknown in an equation. Because we need to find the largest single cause of variation, we should let it continue to function and thereby draw our attention, and we will symbolize it as an unknown in a very noticeable color—hence, the "Red X."

If you know the relative effect of each variable, you can rank the causes in sequence by the amount of their influence. You can then draw a Pareto curve to show how much of an effect each cause had on the final result. But the final result is *not* the direct sum of all the X influences, as shown in Figure 12–3.

The various causes that affect the process never seem to vary in such a way that at any moment they all tend to make "Y" go in one direction—like 100 throws of dice which never come up by chance to show 100 ones or 100 sixes. In other words, instead of the extreme values adding, they both compensate and accumulate in accordance

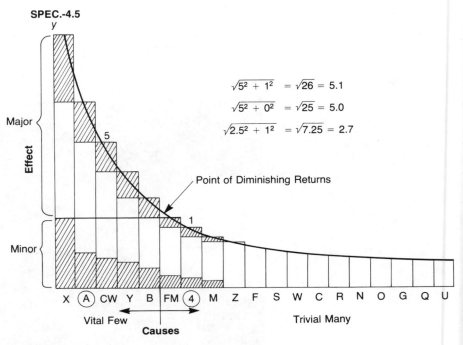

FIGURE 12–3

with the laws of chance. There is a well-known relationship which properly predicts how the laws operate: the total variation of Y is equal to the square root of the sum of the squares of the contributed variations of the independent single causes or independent groups of correlated and of interacting causes. The "Red X," being the largest contributor, will have its influence magnified in relation to the others, because each contribution is squared.

The magnification effect of a "Red X" can be very easily explained with a simple illustration.

In a particular process, suppose the performance of a part depends upon the diameter and the length at which it is manufactured, but nothing else. Let us say that the diameter has five units of influence on performance and that the length has only one unit of influence. The total influence of both factors combined will be 5.1.

$$\sqrt{5^2 + 1^2} = \sqrt{26} = 5.1$$

If the process shows 5.1 units variation, but the tolerance for performance allows only 4.5 units, you might expect that if you were able to cut the effect of length completely, you might cut the total variation to 4.1 units, and be able to hold the specified tolerance of 4.5. However, even if you do cut the effect of length completely, the effect of the two factors together will not be able to reduce to 4.1. This is because:

$$\sqrt{5^2 + 0^2} = \sqrt{25} = 5$$

The improvement was only 0.1. But, if you could reduce the effect of diameter by one half, the net effect of the two together will be reduced by much more. This is because:

120

$$\sqrt{2.5^2 + 1^2} = \sqrt{7.25} = 2.7$$

This shows a difference from the original reading of 47% improvement in the total variation.

Because these effects add as the square roots of the sum of the squares, the largest cause always has a disproportionately large effect on any outcome (product) in which it exists as a factor. All other causes have relatively smaller effects.

There are a number of areas where "Red X" theory can be applied and can be used effectively.

CASE STUDY

A paper mill in Minnesota was facing severe problems with the bursting strength of their manufactured paper. That quality was measured on completed paper, and it was difficult to find the source of the problem. Of course, the problem existed only at a certain time and would appear briefly and then disappear. For a long time, the quality of the wood used to make paper pulp (its natural fibre strength) was blamed.

After getting new data on the variation of strength with time, digester loads, reels, and within the reel, the "Red X" theory was applied to the problem cause. It resulted from an interaction between two variables in the digester (cooking) operation, and not the wood!

Realistic Tolerancing

It is necessary that a product be designed with realistic tolerances. Tolerances should have a practical functional role instead of being conservative. Many of the reasons given for declining productivity in the United States deal with problems of a scope beyond the control of one company. These include factors such as lack of capital investment, inflation, less research and development, and so forth. However, there is one key product improvement area that can be profitably addressed by individual manufacturing companies, and that is unrealistic product design.

Many tolerances found today are either unnecessary or too severe. Lack of formal statistical training has caused many engineers to tighten tolerances to make sure a product will work. As a result, many unjustified tolerances exist, and an unreliable product is often built at high costs.

There are many easy ways to cut down the costs, open the tolerances, and make more reliable products. Engineers should be required to justify any tolerances that are tighter than $\pm$ .015. Tolerance studies should be made through design layouts. Another easy way for functional output control is to ask the parts.

The following method of analyzing tolerances and then establishing realistic limits in any design is recommended.

Collect thirty random samples from the machine or from the process. Measure them carefully for the questionable product characteristic (x) that may be having an effect on the performance of the assembly (y). The results can be plotted on the graph, as shown in Figure 12–4.

Generally, one of these conditions will exist. When the readings show a horizontal plot, it indicates the tolerance for that x can be opened without causing deterioration in the quality of the final product. However, whenever there exist conditions as shown in Figure 12–4(a), the close relationship prevails between the tolerance under study and the final product characteristic (y). In this case, apply pre-control and control manufacturing process properly so that minimum scrap and/or rework will be produced in the process.

However, there are many problems in establishing realistic tolerances. Some of them are:

1. Many times engineers tighten the tolerances when problems are reported from the field. They often think that the problems can be fixed by tightening the tolerances.
2. Many times old drawing tolerances are copied without any evidence of their influence upon a (y). Use of handbook standards also does not help to establish realistic tolerances.
3. Many times parts do not confirm the print tolerance. These rejected parts are held for a Material Review Board. Many of them then get used by signature aceptance, and they generally function well. However, the drawings are not changed since many engineers object to losing control. Accordingly, the tolerances are no longer respected by manufacturing, vendors, and quality assurance.

CASE STUDY

A suitcase manufacturing company had to perform rework on its assembly lines to lower the gap between two metal strips at the edge of the top and bottom sections of all its attaché cases.

FIGURE 12–4

30 Random examples of units made
to the current tolerance

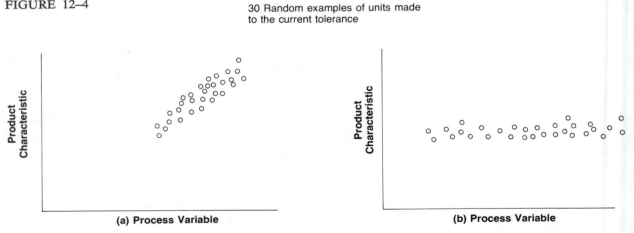

(a) Process Variable

(b) Process Variable

A Quality Control engineer who had recently attended a realistic tolerance course decided to study the various tolerances that seemed to affect the cases. Thirty random samples were picked from the assembly line. The key dimensions were measured, and graphs were plotted as previously described. Only one dimension showed a critical relationship between the dimension and the final product quality, the gap between the strips. Once that particular dimension and tolerance was adjusted, the cases built with new parts closed without any problem.

That costly rework on the assembly line was eliminated forever.

Process Capabilities

This is a very widely discussed subject in Quality Control. Many articles on this subject have been published, and any Quality Control book will have at least one chapter on it. Hence, we will cover only some key points here.

MEANING OF PROCESS

A process is a set of conditions or set of causes which work together to produce a given result. It may be:

1. A single machine or element of machine.
2. Single human being.
3. A piece of test equipment.
4. Method of measurement or gauging.
5. Method of assembly.
6. Method of process (chemical treatment plant).

The term "process capability" refers to the normal behavior of a process when it is operating in a state of statistical control, the predictable series of effects produced by a process when it is allowed to operate without interference from outside causes. The term can also be defined as the quality-performance capability of the process with given factors and under normal in-control conditions: i.e., process factors and process conditions.

Process capability is also the inherent ability of process to turn out similar parts.

PROCESS CAPABILITY STUDY

It is a scientific systematic procedure for determining the capability of a process by means of control charts and, if necessary, changing the process to obtain a better capability.

CONDUCTING THE STUDY

1. Form a team.
2. Obtain data from process and plot it on control charts and check the results.
3. See the pattern: (a) cyclic, (b) freaks, (c) gradual change in level.
4. Split the data into details—by machines, by product.
5. Use design of experiment technique.
6. Detect unnatural disturbances or eliminate or reduce.
7. Continue this until (a) process reaches the capability as shown by long continued natural pattern, or (b) process reaches a point beyond which large gains are not possible.

PRECAUTIONS

1. Take data, if possible in the same time sequence.
2. Take data on product as made.
3. Decide in advance on technique of measurement.
4. Decide where and how many measurements.
5. Make proper identification (day-date).
6. Note all changes in process.
7. Decide the scope—number of machines or number of stations.
8. Decide about conditions—one or more.

ESTIMATE OF THE PROCESS CAPABILITY

The capability of a process may be expressed numerically in two different ways: (a) as a distribution having a certain shape and spread, *or* (b) as a percentage outside of some specified unit. Mathematically the process capability is defined as a six-standard deviation unit (6σ)

$$\text{Process capability} = 6\ \sigma = 6\sqrt{\frac{\Sigma(x - \bar{x})^2}{n-1}}$$

σ = standard deviation of sample

Any book on Quality Control will show all the details on process capability calculations.

USES OF PROCESS CAPABILITY STUDIES

1. Acceptance of new pieces of equipment
2. Scheduling work of machines
3. Setting up the machines for production
4. Establishing control limits
5. Controlling process treatments: temperature, yield, pressure, and so on (steel industry or beer industry)
6. Evaluating and controlling any process
7. Machine repeatability and accuracy (NMTBA definition)

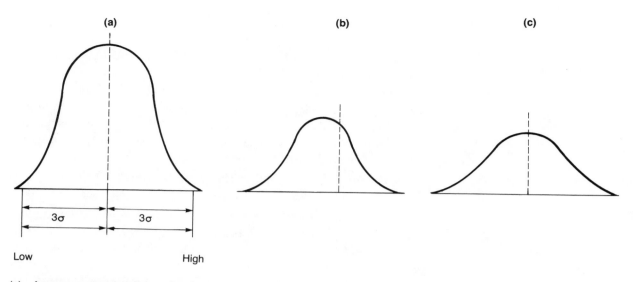

(a) Average centered and spread well within limit
(b) Average too low
(c) Average too high and spread too big

FIGURE 12–5

Pre-Control Technique

A good control technique should provide the manufacturing process operator with a set of decision rules for answering these questions reliably: Do I call for help? Do I adjust the process setting? Do I leave well enough alone?

Many quality control plans have been difficult to implement on the shop floor because of the complexity and mystery associated with the techniques. A simple, easily understood method is most desirable, since it can be implemented in the shop without too much difficulty.

Pre-control is such a technique. It helps an operator to produce good quality parts without having to graph data or record data on worksheets and make calculations.

Developed by Rath and Strong, Inc., a management consulting firm based in Lexington, Mass., the research for pre-control was sponsored by and conducted at Jones and Lamson Machine Company in Springfield, Vt.

Generally there are four requirements for quality pre-control. First, the operator must know the correct tolerances, must have ways of determining where in the tolerances the parts measure, must be able to adjust the process, and must accept the responsibility for preventing the violation of a tolerance limit.

The following case study shows how to set up and use a simple pre-control plan.

ZERO DEFECTS THE EASY WAY
WITH TARGET AREA CONTROL

When faced with a "Zero Defect" production requirement for the first time, the average shop is likely to hit the panic button and take refuge in aspirin tablets. If reluctantly the shop does agree to Zero Defect production, such agreement will usually be accom-

panied with the warning that engineering and inspection expenses will drive costs right through the ceiling. ZD is not a machination of the devil. ZD is a powerful tool for building quality into a product. The average shop can, provided it has the inherent machine capability, produce to a ZD specification without heavy additional expenses. Here is the story of how one job shop has produced over 30,000,000 parts to date on a ZD contract with no rejected shipments and without complicated statistics, inspection, or engineering services.

Every machinist worthy of the name keeps a good tool box filled with a complete set of the tools needed to do his job. Today there is a tool that should be in everybody's tool box—it's as basic and useful as a box wrench, a screwdriver, or a chuck key, but it's not made out of metal. It's a statistical tool—A Quality Control concept called Target Area Control. We'd like to show how we have been using this simple but effective concept at H&H Screw Products Manufacturing Company, to produce over 30 million tight tolerance screw machine workpieces to a zero defect level with no rejected shipments. Target Area Control is simple, effective and inexpensive.

H&H is an aggressive, fast-growing shop located in a new 26,000 square foot building ten miles outside Providence, R.I. It operates 42 Brown & Sharpe automatics, and 20 Davenports along with second operation equipment. In 1962, we were asked to bid on a large volume job in brass. The most difficult requirements were: (1) A plus or minus 0.00025 inch diameter tolerance on a half inch long body. (2) Competitive pricing—the parts had to sell for less than 2¢ each, including material. (3) Meet requirements for the Ford Motor Company's Zero AQL Program.

This looked like a job for a screw machine blanking with second operation finishing to the critical 0.0005 inch diameter tolerance on a centerless grinder. This approach had to be discarded in favor of sizing or shaving because the grinding was too expensive. To a Zero AQL the overall 0.0005 inch tolerance was considered too close to hold on the automatics. At this point our company President, Elwood E. Leonard, Jr., stepped in, and, with more confidence than was felt in engineering or on the shop floor, said we "could and would do it." We promptly took a trial order for 100,000 pieces, and all the brain-power we could muster in Engineering Production Control and Quality Control set to work on it.

From the Quality Control standpoint, after a discussion with the customer, we began using M-R type control charts at the machine, and applied Military Standard 414 ("Inspection by Variables") for final control. This meant calculating the Standard Deviation for every lot, a sophisticated statistical procedure that took a trained person 40 minutes with a slide rule. This procedure gave our production people effective control and gave sufficient protection to our customer, but it was also costly and complicated.

In February, 1963, I attended the National Technical Conference of the N.S.M.P.A., and heard Dorian Shainin, Vice President & Director of Statistical Engineering, Rath & Strong, Inc., Management Consultants, nationally known Quality Control expert, speak on "Pre-Control," or as we like to call it at H&H "Target Area Control." We applied this technique at H&H with the following results: (1) Our machine operators understand the control and do all the necessary measuring and recording themselves. There is no "roving" or "in-process" inspection. This has helped to develop a strong pride of workmanship in the operators who run this job. (2) Final inspection has been greatly simplified with the estimated savings so far at $5,000 in inspection labor. (3) Over 30,000,000 work-pieces have been made with no customer rejections on his Zero AQL sampling.

Here, clearly, we are using a very effective, powerful tool—a quality control tool. This tool is directly in the hands of the man who can make best use of it—the man who is operating the machine. This is the statistical background for this tool: (1) The Target Area is defined as the middle half of the tolerance. On a one half inch dimension with a plus or minus 0.002 inch tolerance, the target area is 0.499 to 0.501 since half the tolerance is plus or minus 0.001 inch (Figure 12–6). (2) If a job is just holding the tolerance, and the machine's average is right at the middle of the tolerance, 86 percent of the pieces made will be in the Target Area. If the machine is capable of doing anything better than just holding the tolerance, then more than 86 percent will fall in the target zone. As a useful rule of thumb, when you're just capable of holding the tolerance, 9 out of 10 must be in the target. Thus,

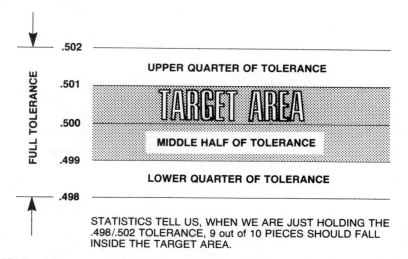

STATISTICS TELL US, WHEN WE ARE JUST HOLDING THE .498/.502 TOLERANCE, 9 out of 10 PIECES SHOULD FALL INSIDE THE TARGET AREA.

FIGURE 12–6 One of the fundamental statistical laws states that in a normal distribution of occurrences between two limits, 86 percent will fall within the middle half of the limits. For quality control purposes the figure is rounded to nine out of ten. Consequently, if nine out of ten production workpieces can be kept within the middle half or the Target Area, the entire production run will then be readily within the allowable tolerance.

we have taken a basic statistical law and reduced it to a very simple statement easily comprehended by anyone in the shop.

This is applied with two simple rules: (1) Set up: Sample five pieces in a row, and OK the job to run when 5 in a row are inside the target. (2) Running: Sample two pieces in a row. (a) If the first piece measured is within the target, put both pieces in the good bucket and let the job run. (b) If the first piece is in the tolerance, but outside the target, measure the second piece. (c) If two pieces in a row are inside the tolerance, but outside the Target there is a problem. Go back to set-up (Rule 1).

Remember we can allow some pieces outside the target—there's no talk here of cutting the tolerance. The ground rules allow about one piece in ten to be outside the target. Statistically, though, the chances of picking two in a row in a given "corner" outside the target are only one in 196. These are odds that any gambler would like to work with. This is the strength of Target Area Control—if the operator finds one piece outside the target he doesn't immediately jump to the machine and make an unneeded adjustment. He knows an occasional piece outside the target is permissible. When he finds two pieces in a row outside the target, however, he knows the odds are heavily against him that the job is OK, even though he has found no pieces outside the tolerance. He takes a good common sense approach when he has an indication of trouble—he inspects some more pieces, or as we say he "goes back to Rule 1—Set up."

We get valuable information by noting where the questioned pieces fall. If both questioned pieces are above the target then the process average has crept up and needs adjustment downward. If both pieces are smaller than the target the process probably needs an adjustment upward. If one piece is larger, and one piece smaller than the target there is probably too much variation or "spread" in the process.

The tool of Target Area Control, like any tool, doesn't help to get a job done if it sits unused in a tool box. There are several things that can be done to encourage operators to make use of this tool. One idea is to print the Target Area Rules on a piece of cardboard about the size of a playing card to be carried in a pocket or a tool box (Figure 12–7). Another idea is to provide gauging which has been designed for Target Area Control. Dial indicators can be marked, using bits of tape or a felt marker with half tolerance and full tolerance lines. One dial indicator manufacturer markets indicators with four specially colored tolerance hands just for this purpose. At H&H we use control charts at the machine with the Target Area marked off.

It's not necessary to upset an existing gauging system, or to change over to all direct reading dial type gauges. Let's take an example of a 0.500 inch plus or minus 0.002 inch hole which has been particularly troublesome on a second operation drill press. When this job is sent out to the floor, we send Target Area plugs (0.499

Target area rules

1.

SETUP—JOB IS OK TO RUN WHEN 5 PIECES
IN A ROW ARE INSIDE TARGET

2.

RUNNING—SAMPLE TWO PIECES
—IF THE FIRST PIECE IS WITHIN
TARGET, RUN
—IF THE FIRST PIECE IS NOT IN
TARGET, CHECK THE SECOND PIECE
—IF BOTH PIECES ARE OUT OF
TARGET, GO BACK TO SETUP, RULE 1.

MODERN MACHINE SHOP

CUT OUT AND PASTE IN TOOL BOX OR AT MACHINE

FIGURE 12–7 These simple rules are followed by the machine operator when producing to a Zero Defect requirement. They are either posted at the machine or in the tool box and are very simple and easy to follow. No complex statistical procedures are necessary.

and 0.501 inch) along with the full tolerance plugs (0.498 and 0.502 inch). The operator takes samples of two pieces every ten minutes and tries the Target Area plugs. If an occasional workpiece doesn't fit the 0.499/0.501 inch plugs, the operator tries the 0.498/0.502 inch set to make sure the workpiece is not out of tolerance. The operator knows it is OK to have about one in ten outside the Target Area. If he finds two in a row outside the target, he samples five in a row. If any of these do not fit the Target Area plugs, the operator knows he has an indication of trouble before any pieces have been made outside the tolerance.

(This article by N. Raymond Brown, Jr. is reprinted from MODERN MACHINE SHOP—July 1966—600 Main Street, Cincinnati, Ohio 45202.)

The "Run-Sum" Control Plan

This technique is similar to pre-control technique. The basic "run-sum" technique was developed in Japan to control process performance. Many variations have been developed and are being used in the United States. Some of the most recent variations have been worked by the manufacturing development section of General Motors Corporation.

129

The September 1978 issue of *Production* magazine shows how to set up the basic run-sum control plan. More details can be found in quality control handbooks.

Multi-Vari Charts

The multi-vari chart is a systematic method of collecting and recording data in a special way designed to isolate one of three different sources of the controlling cause: "within-the-piece," "piece-to-piece," and "time-to-time." A typical multi-vari study would plot, as a minimum, the measurements of three groups of three consecutive pieces. If the characteristic being measured is dimensional, say the diameter of the shaft, variation within the piece may be measured by taking several measurements on each piece: for the shaft, one might measure the diameter at each end. The difference between the two measurements of the shaft diameter indicates the amount of taper, a form of variation within the piece. This variation can be represented on the graph by a vertical line.

An entirely different set of variables would be associated with the type of variation which shows up from piece-to-piece. In order to pick up the effect of this source of potential causes, groups of three consecutive pieces from the same machine are measured. The value of piece-to-piece variation is based on the measure of the variation between the average values of consecutive pieces within the groups.

Time-to-time variation can be determined by measuring the first group of three pieces, then allowing a suitable period of time to pass before measuring the second group and then the third group. Calculate the overall average value for all the pieces in each group, and obtain the differences among the averages.

Every manufacturing process has different kinds of variables, and one of the three multi-vari charts will be most appropriate to the type of variable that most influences the output variation. The beauty of this technique is that the process or parts themselves reveal the answer to the problem. People are often surprised when they see a completely unexpected solution.

CASE STUDY

N.C.L. Company had a chronic problem with motor shafts which did not fit properly. Quality Control had made a process capability study that proved the present equipment could not hold the tolerance. Because the part was critical to the product, management approved the purchase of a new machine.

One of the quality control experts happened to visit the company around that time. He suggested exploring the problem with a multi-vari chart. To get a complete picture of the troublesome variation, the first trial included five groups of three consecutive shafts, measured at one-hour intervals. In order to pick up variation within the piece, the diameter of each shaft was measured twice at each end. Rotating the micrometer measured the maximum difference between diamether AA and minimum BB, indicating out-of-roundness, while the difference between the diameter at AA and CC indicated the taper (see Figure 12–8). The four readings were plotted on the multi-vari chart as shown in Figure 12–9. Variation at different times was the strongest, and tool wear was immediately suspected. The tool was changed between 11 a.m.

FIGURE 12–8

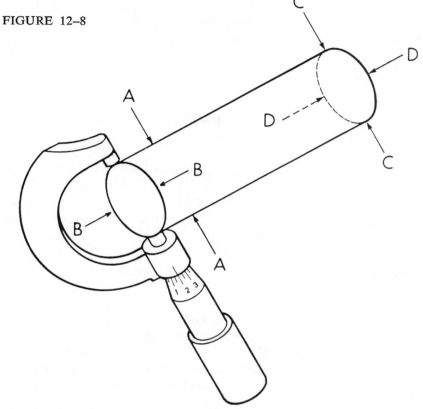

FIGURE 12–9

MULTI-VARI CHART

Part Name: ROTOR SHAFT	Part No.: 1031-1133-P	Dept: TURRET LATHE
Operator: S. JOSEPH	Machine No.: LT-76	Tool No.: TR-741
Operation No.: 100-249/251 Dia.	S.O. No.: L 10493-G	By

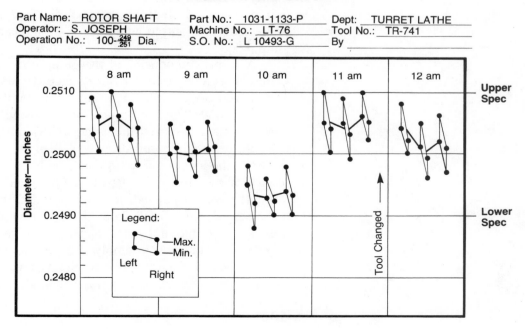

and noon and not between 10 and 11, when variation was greatest. The expert noted that the machine was shut down between 10 and 11 during the coffee break, and it might have cooled down at that time. A check also showed the level of coolant was low, so more fluid was added. Half of the variation disappeared. The next check made after the correction indicated all measurements within plus and minus .005".

Further analysis of the pattern showed a considerable out-of-round condition combined with a very consistent taper. These problems were also corrected later on, and all the parts were manufactured within a small fraction of the specification limit. The multi-vari chart thus separated variables into families and helped immensely to solve the problem.[2]

Component Search Pattern

Component search pattern is another valuable statistical tool developed by Dorian Shainin. This method is very useful in assembly areas where numbers of parts are assembled, and when one needs a short but sure way to solve a problem. The use of this technique can be explained briefly by the following case study.

CASE STUDY

N. G. Company in Chicago builds hydraulic pumps. One of the key requirements for the pump was a minimum output of 5 gallons/minute. Many pumps were rejected and rebuilt because their outputs did not meet the spec. Disassembly and repair costs were high, and the company did not know how to solve this problem. Many changes were tried, but without success.

Then one of the manufacturing engineers decided to apply a newly learned technique called "component search patterns." Two pumps were selected for the analysis (see Figure 12–10). "Hi = 6" indicated high output and "Lo = 4" indicated the unacceptable low output.

Various components of the pump were alphabetically divided into different sections, in order of expected decreasing importance. R stands for the rest of the component not disassembled. For example, the gears were called A. The two pumps were disassembled, rebuilt, and checked again to make sure that there was no assembly influence upon output.

A systematic procedure was then planned to interchange parts between the low output pump and the high output pump. The sequence used is shown in Figure 12-11. Component A was swapped; since the outputs were unchanged, it was concluded that A was not causing the problem. Component B from the low pump was put in the high assembly, and output then dropped to 3 gallons/minute. Placing the high B into the low assembly did not raise the output to 6 gallons/minute. A lower output than originally received in the low assembly is not discouraging, since this was a definite indication of an *interaction*

COMPONENT SEARCH PATTERN

H_I = 6
(Gals/Min)

Lo = 4
(Gals/Min)

		Result (Gals/Min.)	Analysis
1.	A̶_L R_H	6	A̶
2.	A_H B̶_L R_H	3	B+
3.	A_H B_H C̶_L R_H	2	C+
4.	A_H B_H C_H D̶_L R_H	6	D̶
5.	A_H B_H C_H D_H R̶_L	6	R̶

FIGURE 12–10

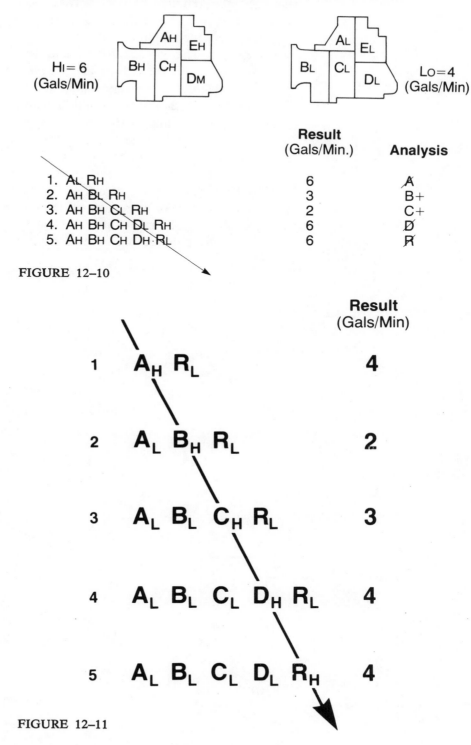

		Result (Gals/Min)
1	A_H R_L	4
2	A_L B_H R_L	2
3	A_L B_L C_H R_L	3
4	A_L B_L C_L D_H R_L	4
5	A_L B_L C_L D_L R_H	4

FIGURE 12–11

among two or more parts. Further testing was necessary to isolate the variable(s) causing it. *C* from the low assembly was then put into the high assembly, and the output was reduced to 2 gallons/minute. So far evidence indicated that both *B* and *C* were responsible. One additional variable *D* was suspected and checked; but the change made no effect.

To make sure the major variables were isolated, a "capping run" interchanged the remaining, non-disassembled parts of the assembly as though they were a single part. In that step, the output of the high assembly with the remaining untested components from the low assembly was analyzed. The test results of 6 and 4 gallons/minute indicated that the two key causes, namely B and C, were isolated.

After gathering the data and filling in the matrix and graph as shown in Figure 12–12, one would arrive at the proper conclusions that a $B \times C$ interaction existed along with smaller main effects of C and of B. The numbers also indicated that it was necessary to examine the parts of the B and C components.

When they were examined carefully, the improper drawing "call-out" and poor machining were found to be the root cause of the problem. Once these were corrected, all the pumps that were produced put out more than 8 gallons/minute. The rejects were completely eliminated. This procedure required only five pairs of tests out of the many possible combinations.

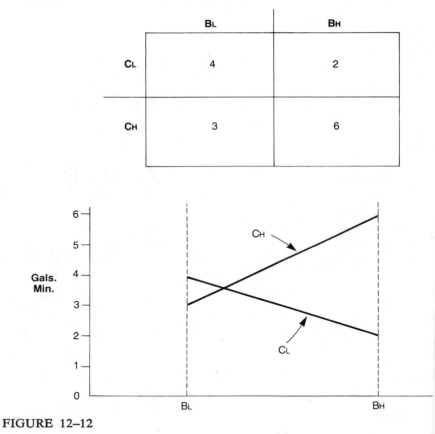

FIGURE 12–12

Regression and Correlation Analysis

This technique is also known as a scatter diagram. This method helps to check the relationship between two quantities. When we speak of the regression of one quantity or the other, we mean the relationship

134

of the average values of one quantity to the given value of the other quantity. The relationship of two quantities is expressed in the mathematical form:

$$y = mx + b$$

where y = extension = one quantity (dependent)
  x = weight   = second quantity (independent)
  m, b = constants

Multiple regression is another extension that is frequently used where there are a number of quantities in question. The mathematical representation is shown below.

$$y = Ax + Bz + Cm$$

where A,B,C = constants
  x,m,z = independent quantities

There is also another constant that helps to check the relationship between two or more quantities. It is known as coefficient of correlation (r). This is expressed as follows:

$$v = \frac{\frac{1}{n} \Sigma \, xy - \overline{xy}}{\sigma x \quad \sigma y}$$

where n = number of observations
  $\overline{x}$ = mean of independent quantities
  $\overline{y}$ = mean of dependent quantities
  σ = standard deviation

If *r* is between 0.8 and 1, the two quantities are related very closely to each other, as *r* gets smaller, the relationship between the two quantities becomes more remote.[2]

Process Improvement Through Evolutionary Operations

Evolutionary operation was introduced about twenty-five years ago by Professor George Box. In this view a manufacturing process, in addition to providing a product, should yield information to improve that product. The basic philosophy is that the process engineer needs to understand the effect on performance of changes in the process variables. This understanding helps to improve performance immediately, especially if he has a controlling variable (Red X) in his plan. In the basic procedure, you start with the point where you know the yield of the process and then run the tests above and below that level to find the yield at other locations. Then run further tests successively in the manner shown until you find a point at which the center value yield is optimum and each of the surrounding points shows a lower yield. The process of evolutionary operations is intended to find the optimum point of yield, like reaching the summit while climbing the mountain.

Evolutionary operations, while efficient and thorough, are time-consuming and costly when the number of variables exceeds four. This realization led to the development of random evolutionary operations (REVOP), which can be employed for optimization when the number of variables exceeds four. The theory, similar to that of evolutionary operations, introduces random directions to locate the direction of improvement. Experience indicates that near optimum conditions can be attained in sixteen to twenty tests.

Statistical Design of Experiments

This is another vast and fertile area that many companies should use. The proper use of this technique can save thousands of dollars and unnecessary waste of time to solve problems in companies.

A multifactor balanced experiment is far more efficient than varying one factor (variable) at a time—the old traditional way. The advantages of this technique are:

1. It works with more than one factor
2. Remaining factors do not have to be held constant
3. It helps to detect the effects of interactions
4. It is less costly and less time consuming

Fractional factorial designs and *random balance design* are two other useful techniques when dealing with up to thirty or forty different variables to be tested.

The University of Connecticut, Storrs, offers a special annual course in experimental designs in December. Details can be obtained by contacting the Division of Continuing Education at the University.

Failure Analysis

No product is perfect. Components fail at various stages because of "infant mortality," accidents, or wearout problems. It is extremely important at all times that failed parts be analyzed properly. The analysis should be a key function in any company and should be done on all the parts that fail the internal testing, as well as on external failures from the field. Two techniques that are useful in this area are as follows:

1. FMEA: *Failure mode effects analysis* attempts to predict all possible effects caused by the failure of a component. This technique can bring to light unexpected product design weaknesses.
2. FTA: *Fault tree analysis* is the opposite of the FMEA. It starts with the undesired event and works down to the possible causes of failure. This method becomes a shopping list of probable causes for each symptom of system failure. Details on this technique can be found in a few reliability engineering books.

136

Fault Tree Analysis

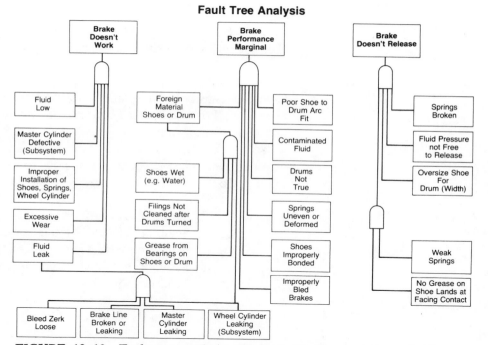

FIGURE 12–13 Fault tree analysis. (Kenneth E. Case and Lynn L. Jones, "Profit Through Quality: Quality Assurance Program for Manufacturers," reprinted with permission from QC&RE Monograph Series No. 2 AIIE—QC&RE —78-2. Copyright © American Institute of Industrial Engineers, Inc., 25 Technology Park/Atlanta, Norcross, GA 30092).

FMEA On Common Household Lamp
Failure Mode and Effects Analysis

Product 2C Lamp   Analyst J. A. White   Date 10 Jan. 1977

Component Name	Failure Mode	Cause of Failure	Effect of Failure on System	Correction of Problem	Comments
Plug Part No. P-3	Loose wiring	Use, vibration, handling	Will not conduct current. May generate heat.	Molded plug and wire	Uncorrected, could cause fire
	Not a failure of plug per se	User contacts prongs when plugging or unplugging	May cause severe shock or death	Enlarged safety tip on molded plug	Children
Metal base and stem	Bent or nicked	Dropping, bumping, shipping	Degrades looks	Distress finish, improve packaging	Cosmetic
Lamp socket	Cracked	Excessive heat, bumping, forcing	May cause shock if contacts metal base and stem. May cause shock upon bulb replacement.	Improve material used for socket	Dangerous
Wiring	Broken, frayed, from lamp to plug	Fatigue, heat, carelessness, childbite	Will not conduct current. May generate heat, blow breakers, or cause shock.	Use wire suitable for long life in extreme environment anticipated	Dangerous Warning on instructions
	Internal short circuit	Heat, brittle insulation	May cause electrical shock or render lamp useless.	Use wire suitable for long life in extreme environment anticipated	
	Internal wire broken	Socket slipping and twisting wires	May cause electrical shock or render lamp useless.	Use indent or notch to prevent socket from turning.	

FIGURE 12–14 Failure mode and effects analysis. (Kenneth E. Case and Lynn L. Jones, "Profit Through Quality: Quality Assurance Program for Manufacturers," reprinted with permission from QC&RE Monograph Series No. 2, AIIE—QC&RE—78-2. Copyright © American Institute of Industrial Engineers, Inc., 25 Technology Park/Atlanta, Norcross, GA 30092.)

137

Quality and Reliability Training

Commitment to build quality products started in Japan thirty years ago. The whole nation was involved in this movement, and today there are a number of quality programs being offered to the management as well as to workers by JUSE (Union of Japanese Scientists and Engineers). Over 38 courses to learn how to build a quality product are offered. Some of these courses are listed here:

1. Q. C. Seminar Top Management—45 hours
2. Q. C. Seminar Middle Management—72 hours
3. Q. C. Seminar Basic Course—180 hours
4. Q. C. Seminar for Sales Department—24 hours
5. Q. C. Seminar for Manufacturing—72 hours

"Company Wide Quality Control" (CWQC) is another key to success of the building of a quality product. This philosophy was taught to the Japanese people by Dr. Juran and Dr. Deming. We need to review our quality operations in the United States, and we need to implement effective quality systems in U.S. companies.

One should not forget the reliability in service of the product. Products may work well in the test laboratory, but the real test comes when they are in the customer's hands. It is important to concentrate on failure testing and to get away from the old success (no failure) testing philosophy.

Much has been published on the areas of quality control and reliability. We need to teach and train many people in these areas, to talk about quality, and to reinforce the concept that "Quality Is Everyone's Job."

Notes

1. Dorian Shainin, "How to Build Quality Products," talk given at Mercury Marine, Fond du Lac, Wisconsin, February 1979.

2. Sud Ingle, "Regression Analysis Made Easy," *Modern Machine Shop,* August 1971, pp. 68-70.

13

GROUP DYNAMICS

Many books and articles have been written and published on the subject of group dynamics. In this chapter we will discuss the basics of group dynamics and its use in Quality Circle training. Those who need additional details can review the references given in the bibliography.

Formal or informal groups are used widely in all types of undertakings and organizations, social, religious, political, and business. Religious and social institutions prefer groups, or committees, as they are sometimes called, to achieve a wider participation in their affairs. Most of the affairs of educational institutions are also run through formal groups called committees. Similarly, use of a committee is common in government and in business. One of the outstanding examples in business is provided by the "board of directors," the highest body in company management. Groups can accomplish many impossible tasks through widened participation and commitment of the people involved. Quality Circles also represent group participation in the company. Their notable achievements are only possible through the effective cooperation and larger participation of the people in the program. Quality Circles are used many times to accomplish a number of organizational goals. Group dynamics lend Quality Circles a number of advantages, which one realizes only through the formation of groups.

Advantages of Groups

An important reason for using groups is to gain pooled knowledge and judgment. Quality Circles are a very useful device for bringing collective

139

knowledge and judgment to problem solving. Some problems require the coordinated efforts of people from different areas. Through the use of Quality Circles it is easier to attain this cooperation. Similarly, when complex problems are resolved through integrated group discussions, the quality of decisions is generally better because of the group's interest, and implementation is a little easier.

Quality Circles can be formed in a number of different areas representing a variety of interests. Sometimes the members may seek advisors from outside their own organization to help them review problems from a different point of view. As Quality Circles expand, more departments and parties get involved in solving the company's problems. In the long run, Quality Circles enable the company to involve all types of departments and obtain a high degree of cooperation from them.

Quality Circles recognize the importance of cooperation and teamwork. Instead of individual competition, Quality Circles encourage team accomplishments. Those who work in Circles realize that all of the people in the group have to work together to solve problems. They criticize ideas but not the person who suggests them. Most of the members help each other and put aside their differences. In this way, group activities promote team work.

Groups formed in Quality Circles permit wider participation from a number of people. Members are also allowed to participate in the decision making process. This gives them a sense of belonging and a sense of security and self-fulfillment. Since each member participates in the decision, the implementation and execution not only becomes easier, but most of the members become enthusiastic in follow-up activities. If any difficulty or problem arises later on, members find a way to solve them. Some of the solutions may look impossible but can be made to work by Circle members dedicated to seeing their ideas succeed. This is called a commitment.

Group activities also help in transmitting and acquiring information. People get an opportunity to talk face to face—the best form of communication—which helps to clear up misunderstandings and eliminate the confusion that sometimes exists between people. It also gives people a chance to express themselves and exchange ideas. Improved communication through group activities is another advantage of Quality Circles.

Formal or informal groups also serve to train new leaders. As mentioned before, Quality Circle leaders in some companies are foremen, in other companies they are elected by the members. Some of those elected do not have formal leadership training, but groups provide leadership training grounds for these elected leaders. This also helps the company to find new foremen or managerial candidates.

Disadvantages of the Groups

Group activities are subject to certain limitations. It is necessary to recognize these limitations and proceed cautiously in implementing group work.

If the problems are simple and the solutions are straight-forward, groups work fine without any disagreement. However, if the problem is complex, all of the members may not agree with the proposals or actions. It then becomes necessary to discuss the various solutions and try to arrive at the best one. If members cannot compromise, and if the disagreement still exists, it may be necessary to vote on the proposals. A majority rule does not always lead to good decisions, and the team-work activities may fail if outsiders, like facilitators, do not watch them carefully, or if proper help is not forthcoming on time. In short, group activities are beneficial, but they need careful monitoring and proper care to operate successfully.

Training Techniques

Newly formed groups need training for teamwork. Members need to know the importance of teamwork and how to work in the groups. Most of them know their own work; however, it is necessary for them to understand that working together has greater advantages for the company as a whole. There are many ways to train the people for teamwork. One of the most effective and interesting ways is to get them involved in practical case studies.

Some case studies are discussed below:

1. *Telephone Exercise.* This is just a simple exercise. People in the training program are given a sheet of paper showing telephone numbers on the dial, and are asked to fill in the letters that go with each number. Even though one uses a telephone daily, it is interesting to watch the people figure out the correct answer.[1]

   The above exercise helps to get people free and makes them talk with each other in the class. It also helps to change the classroom atmosphere.

2. *Lost on the Moon:* This exercise deals with a situation on the moon, which is first reviewed independently by each member and then reviewed in small groups. Detailed analysis can be found in *Design News.*[3]

   ### Problem
   You are a member of a space team on a trip to the moon. You and your team have just crash landed on the moon's surface. Your spacecraft was ruined and everything on board was destroyed except the 15 items below. You are scheduled to rendezvous with the mother ship, which is 200 miles away on the lighted surface of the moon. Your survival depends upon reaching the mother ship.

   Rank the 15 items in order of importance to your successful and safe trip to the rendezvous location. Place number one (1) beside the item you consider most important, number two (2) beside the second most important, and so on through number 15, the least important item. This set of numbers is your individual priority ranking (second column, below).

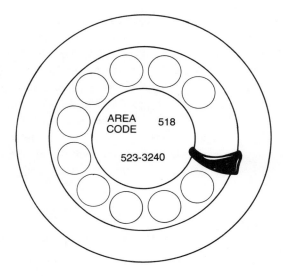

OBSERVATION PROBLEM
TELEPHONE DIAL

INSTRUCTIONS: Add the letters and numbers as they
appear on the dial.

FIGURE 13–1

When all have finished their individual priority ranking, teams of four to seven people will be formed. Team members will repeat the exercise, working together to arrive at a consensus, their group priority ranking (fourth column, below).

Next the instructor will provide the optimum priority ranking (first column). Individual error points (third column) are computed as the difference between optimum priority ranking and individual priority ranking. Similarly, group error points (fifth column) are computed as the difference between optimum priority ranking and group priority ranking. In both cases use absolute values only, that is, change any negative numbers to positive. Finally, total both columns of error points to obtain the individual and group scores.

3. *Lost in the Forest:* This exercise is similar to the exercise "Lost on the Moon." However, here the person is lost in a forest, and he has to analyze the situation similarly.[3]

Wilderness Survival Work Sheet

Here are twelve questions dealing with personal survival in a wilderness situation. Your first task is individually to select the best of the three alternatives given under each item. Try to imagine yourself in the situation depicted. Assume that you are alone and have a minimum of equipment except where specified. The season is fall. The days are warm and dry, but the nights are cold.

After you have completed this task individually, you will again consider each question as a member of a small group. Your group will have the task of deciding, by consensus, the best alternative

142

Item	Optimum Priority Ranking	INDIVIDUAL		GROUP	
		Priority Ranking	Error Points	Priority Ranking	Error Points
a. Box of matches					
b. Food concentrate					
c. Fifty feet of nylon rope					
d. Parachute silk					
e. Solar-powered portable heater					
f. Two .45-caliber pistols					
g. One case, dehydrated milk					
h. Two 100-pound tanks of oxygen					
i. Stellar map (of Moon's Constellation)					
j. Self-inflating life raft					
k. Magnetic compass					
l. Five gallons of water					
m. Signal flares					
n. First-aid kit with injection needles					
o. Solar-powered FM receiver/transmitter					

FIGURE 13–2

for each question. Do not change your individual answers, even if you change your mind in the group discussion. Both the individual and group solutions will later be compared with the "correct" answers provided by a group of naturalists who conduct classes in woodland survival.

1. You have strayed from your party in trackless timber. You have no special signaling equipment. The best way to attempt to contact your friends is to
   a. call "help" loudly but in a low register
   b. yell or scream as loud as you can
   c. whistle loudly and shrilly
2. You are in snake country. Your best action to avoid snakes is to
   a. make a lot of noise with your feet
   b. walk softly and quietly
   c. travel at night
3. You are hungry and lost in wild country. The best rule for determining which plants are safe to eat (those you do not recognize) is to
   a. try anything you see the birds eat
   b. eat anything except plants with bright red berries
   c. put a lot of the plant on your lower lip for five minutes, if it seems all right, try a little
4. The day becomes dry and hot. You have a full canteen of water (about one liter) with you. You should
   a. ration it—about a cupful per day
   b. not drink until you stop for the night, then drink what you think you need

c. drink as much as you think you need when you need it

5. Your water is gone, you become very thirsty. You finally come to a dried-up watercourse. Your best chance of finding water is to
   a. dig anywhere in the stream bed
   b. dig up plant and tree roots near the bank
   c. dig in the stream bed at the outside of a bend

6. You decide to walk out of the wild country by following a series of ravines where a water supply is available. Night is coming on. The best place to make camp is
   a. next to the water supply in the ravine
   b. high on a ridge
   c. midway up the slope

7. Your flashlight glows dimly as you are about to make your way back to your campsite after a brief foraging trip. Darkness comes quickly in the woods and the surroundings seem unfamiliar. You should
   a. head back at once, keeping the light on, hoping the light will glow enough for you to make out landmarks
   b. put the batteries under your armpits to warm them, and then replace them in the flashlight
   c. shine your light for a few seconds, try to get the scene in mind, move out in the darkness, and repeat the process.

8. An early snow confines you to your small tent. You doze with your small stove going. There is danger if the flame is:
   a. yellow
   b. blue
   c. red

9. You must ford a river that has a strong current, large rocks, and some white water. After carefully selecting your crossing spot, you should:
   a. leave your boots and pack on.
   b. take your boots and pack off.
   c. take off your pack, but leave your boots on.

10. In waist-deep water with a strong current, when crossing the stream, you should face
    a. upstream
    b. across the stream
    c. downstream

11. You find yourself rimrocked; your only route is up. The way is mossy, slippery rock. You should try it
    a. barefoot
    b. with boots on
    c. in stocking feet

12. Unarmed and unsuspecting, you surprise a large bear prowling around your campsite. As the bear rears up about ten meters from you, you should
    a. run
    b. climb the nearest tree
    c. freeze, but be ready to back away slowly

144

4. *Super Savers at Mini Company:* Mini Company was founded in 1970 in Fond du Lac, Wisconsin. The company manufactured energy-saving devices. Business was growing rapidly right from the beginning because of the high cost of energy. The company employed about 500 people and had recently expanded the business by hiring another 100 people.

Jack Schmidt was recently promoted to General Supervisor of the newly expanded area to build "super saver" energy devices. He had been for the last two years a hard working, skilled, honest employee from an old assembly area. The management thought he would be a good candidate for the job of general supervisor.

There were 50 assembly people working in Jack's area. After six months on the new job, Jack was confronted with a number of different problems. He considered quitting, and going back to the old assembly line area. Some of the problems Jack encountered were the following:

1. New employees, those who were hired recently, seemed interested in the jobs. However, after he gave verbal instructions in the assembly operations, many of them were still missing parts in the "super saver" assemblies.
2. In fact, 100 of the "super savers" built last month were returned to his department from the sales department. Because of his pride in his workmanship he felt ashamed, and decided to hide the returns so that no one would comment on his poor performance.
3. He recently saw that one of the employees was missing a small spring that was supposed to be assembled along with another large one. When questioned, the employee replied that he thought the small spring was unnecessary and decided to stop using it, thus saving money for the company.
4. Some labels were missing on "super saver" assemblies, and when he questioned another employee, the assembler told him that he tried to stick the labels on, but they would not stick. He did not inform anyone about the problem.
5. Jack also noticed many of his employees spending more time at coffee machines. When asked why, most of them told him that many castings and other purchased parts were of poor quality and would not fit together properly. Since they did not like to assemble poor quality work, they decided to wait until he came back from meetings to tell them what to do with the poor quality material.
6. Bob Hanson, Jack's new boss, was also becoming less friendly to Jack. When Jack was offered the new job, Bob praised him for his skills and abilities, and was very nice for the first three months. However, it seemed as though "the honeymoon was over."

What should Jack do- Quit and go back to the old job or try to solve the problems with the help of the people in his department. How can he accomplish this seemingly impossible task?

FIGURE 13–3

Group Formation

When Quality Circle training begins, the facilitator should first discuss the importance and objectives of Quality Circles. This helps to explain the program to all those who are interested in participating in Quality Circles. However, most potential participants are shy and reserved. They understand the need for the program, but really don't know how to participate in and enjoy the training. The previous exercises help to get people involved, and most of the members enjoy them. They participate in the discussion, they present their views, argue with each other, and start enjoying the training. Their reservations and shyness slowly disappear, and they look forward to the next training session. They get to know each other and slowly informal groups are formed in the training class. If the class is small, good communication and cohesiveness develops in the group. It is interesting to watch this change during a training program. Persons who are generally quiet in the beginning become very open and contribute much by the end of the training.

Likes and Dislikes

The following statements about Quality Circle groups are generally true:

1. Members like the discussion and the exchange of ideas.
2. Members enjoy working together.

146

3. Members feel happy when they accomplish a projected goal.
4. Members like to solve problems.

Members dislike some of the following routine work:

1. Members dislike routine work that does not offer challenges.
2. Members do not like to keep records.
3. Members do not like statistical work.
4. Members become impatient as they get closer to the solutions.
5. Members get shy when the formal presentation is arranged at the end.

In general, once the people are trained and the groups are formed, they enjoy working together. The exchange of ideas leads to more participation in subsequent meetings.

Effective Use of the Groups

Under certain circumstances a group can work effectively and serve very useful purposes in an organization. Active Quality Circles are prime examples of group activities.

In order to avoid confusion and to improve a group's effectiveness, the functions, scope, and purpose of the group activities should be clearly defined. A good Quality Circle policy serves this purpose. Such a policy also helps to explain to new members and new groups the purpose and objectives of the group activities.

Group work can become inefficient if there are too many or too few members participating. Too many members in the group sometimes create problems of management and leads to confusion and ineffective working conditions. Large groups cannot solve problems or work together if the members do not get to know each other. Too many members also make the group's work difficult because there is less interaction. In small groups there is too little knowledge and experience and too few members to do the job. It is essential that one find the proper size for a group. There is no magic number, no optimum size. Any group size between five and eight members works effectively. The actual size should depend on the abilities of the members to carry on different tasks and their willingness to cooperate.

Another important thing to remember for effective use of the group is to conduct the meetings properly. Quality Circle leaders should talk with the group members to arrive at the selection of a problem collectively, then solicit discussion and invite solutions.

Each member should be given a fair chance to express his or her views. The entire group should be made to think. The group leader should also divide the work and see that all the members are participating in solving the problems. The group leader should also keep notes and review them periodically so that there is proper follow-up in the work.

Group activities should be constantly evaluated so that judgment can be made on their effectiveness and use, and at the same time, guidance can be provided to those groups that are not functioning satisfactorily. Avoid forcing an issue or disturbing members; that will have an adverse effect on the group's work. Groups should be allowed to work freely, but at the same time should be watched for their performance to prevent an unnecessary waste of time and energy.

It is easy to see that groups can serve a useful purpose. Because of group interactions and the human behavioral problems that occur in group work, it is extremely important to monitor the group's work carefully.

Get People Involved

There are a number of different ways people get involved through Quality Circle activities.

Quality Circle meetings play an important role in getting people to work with each other. People get to know each other and get an opportunity to present their ideas. Well-managed meetings stimulate enthusiastic participation in the project. They also encourage the quiet and shy to express their ideas to the group through Circle leaders or through other Circle members.

People also get a chance to get involved in group activities during the management presentations. Most of these presentations involve every one, and it helps to develop "togetherness" in the group. Circle members work on the charts, graphs or slides, and speeches, and that helps to get them closer to each other. Members also get to know each other's likes and dislikes. Once a good feeling is developed in the group it generally lasts.

As the Quality Circle program grows, the impact of Quality Circle activities can be felt throughout the company. Many people who may not be involved directly get involved during the investigation and implementation phase. Quality Circles invite outside people whose help is required and who might be involved in the projects. The writer's experience has proven so far that these outside people not only help the Circles immediately, but also help the Circle program to expand. The good word about the success of the Quality Circle projects spreads, and people see the effect of group pressure on getting things done. Others, impressed by this success, gradually join the Circle program.

The influence of Quality Circles can be felt in community activities. Banks, department stores, and hospitals can use similar methods to save thousands of dollars that are spent unnecessarily. As group activities spread in the community, more and more people get involved for the betterment of the society.

Experiences of the Groups in Quality Circle Activities

Finally, let us share a few experiences that have taken place in the Quality Circle program.

1. *Spreading the Good Word:* Many Circle members or leaders might be quiet at the beginning. However, there is a tremendous difference in actions and behavior after six to eight months of Quality Circle operation. People are generally open and will talk well about the program. Most of them are convinced of the bright side and become good-will ambassadors for the program.

2. *Atmosphere Changes:* Some foremen will notice a change in the atmosphere. As they say, "an empty mind is a devil's mind." If people don't have anything to think about, they will talk about something that may not be interesting to others. Circle programs offer the group food for thought, and even during break or lunch time people keep thinking about the project.

3. *Overcome the "NO":* Many times ideas from the shop get crushed because someone in the top echelon says "no." However, group activities, like Quality Circles, do not take "no" from one person. Quality Circles demonstrate their success to many management personnel during the final presentation. This helps to alter the attitudes of those with short vision to the change proposed by the Circles. This group action is effective and works in many cases.

4. *We've Got to Make It:* Quality Circles also help to form groups—formal and informal. Many people get to know many of the problems that we are faced with today. Inflation, high costs, and foreign competition do not make our jobs easier. This message needs to be carried all over the company. The groups help to spread good will and to create a spirit of "we've got to make it."

5. *More "Informal" Groups:* Basic group formation is nothing new. However, Quality Circles expose management to the advantages of group actions. One informal group recently finished a plant layout job while others worked on the new engine model that was supposed to be in operation in less than one year.

6. *"There Is No Limit":* How would you like to cook for 100 people for $60, and serve them lunch in less than 30 minutes? Well, you can do it if you can get cooperation and help from the people involved. One of the plants did this successfully. That's what one calls "people power."

Notes

1. This information was prepared by R. Oakland, Quality Control Engineer at Mercury Marine, Fond du Lac, Wisconsin.

2. "Management Forum," *Design News,* July 21, 1975, p. 75.

3. Reprinted from J. W. Pfeiffer and J. E. Jones (eds.), *The 1976 Annual Handbook for Group Facilitators* (San Diego; Calif.: University Associates, 1976). Used with permission.

14

GUIDELINES FOR TRAINING PROGRAMS

An effective and successful training program for Quality Circle members, leaders, and management is the heart of a good Circle program. In the United States the work force is ingenious, but this brainpower needs training in statistical techniques. In the last decade, very little attention has been given to training the work force properly. I feel the most important task for the management is to make sure that this training phase of the program is carried out smoothly. Facilitators and coordinators play a critical role in training the Circle leaders and members.

Let us review the types of training that will be needed in a company.

1. Quality Circle member's training (eight hours)
2. Leader's training (eight hours plus additional training as required)
3. Facilitator's training (three and one-half days)
4. Middle management training (eight hours)
5. Top management training (four hours)

(Note: Hours and days suggested in brackets are a guideline. In reality, they are subject to change based on the type of company and conditions which exist in accepting this program.)

Quality Circle Member's Training

Figure 14-1 shows a sample of a training program. After members sign up voluntarily for training, they should be congratulated and should be notified of the time, place, and date for the training. Here is a brief review of the meetings to follow week by week.

First Week:	Welcome Introduce everyone Review objectives History Describe material Show slides Introduce code of conduct
Second Week:	Review Discuss brainstorming
Third Week:	Review Discuss group dynamics Do "Lost on the Moon" exercise
Fourth Week:	Review Discuss Pareto diagram Do exercise Ask members to think about a name for Circle and Leader
Fifth Week:	Welcome Discuss cause and effect analysis Review the techniques again
Sixth Week:	Welcome Review of last week Discuss check sheets and graphs Do exercise Select the Circle name Elect the leader and secretary
Seventh Week:	Welcome Review Discuss problem selection procedure Discuss histograms and control charts Select problem Review techniques
Eighth Week:	Review Describe management presentations Show successful projects Show how to work on a problem using all techniques Describe "KISS" principle
Ninth Week:	Graduation Talk by top management personnel Distribute starting material kits

```
          ┌─────────┐
          │  C.C.   │
          │ QUALITY │
          │ CIRCLES │
          └─────────┘

         Quality Circle Member's Training

Place: _____    Plant: _____

Time:  _____    Date:  _____


  Week    Date            Topic               Trainer

   1.           Introduction to Quality Circles   Mr. D.A.A.

   2.           Brainstorming                     Mr. R.L.O.

   3.           Group Dynamics                    Mr. D.A.A.

   4.            Pareto Analysis                  Mr. R.L.O.

   5.           Cause and Effect Diagrams         Mr. R.L.M.

   6.           Check Sheets and Graphs —         Mr. J.S.D.

                Circle Formation

   7.           How to select problems

   8.           Management Presentation

                Successful Case Studies           Mr. R.L.M.

   9.           Graduation                        Management
                                                  Speaker


Objectives:      1.   Improve Quality

                 2.   Improve Communication

                 3.   Reduce Waste



                                            Facilitator
```

FIGURE 14–1

Tenth Week:	Start Circle working on a project
Following Weeks:	On-going weekly meetings until the Circle is ready for a management presentation on project.

Leader's Training

To be effective, Circle leaders need additional training in leadership, communication, and management. They are the key persons in maintaining and keeping the Circle together. At Mercury Marine, we give additional training in these areas on a quarterly basis. Figure 14-2 shows one of the training programs conducted there.

Once a month leaders are invited to a luncheon meeting and outside speakers talk with them on a variety of subjects. Some of the topics covered are field failures, engineering functions, recognition, Quality Circles in other companies, and how to conduct meetings.

Figure 14-3 shows a suggested training program for leaders. This type of training helps the leader, but is not mandatory for the success of the program.

Facilitator's Training

A facilitator is another key person in a Quality Circle program. In Japan, most of his functions are carried out by the training department and management personnel in the company. In other countries, this concept is new and needs more attention in the training areas. The training of a facilitator is very important.

The basic training can start with consulting books or published articles (see Bibliography). There are, in addition, seminars and courses conducted by the International Association of Quality Circles (IAQC). These can be used as stepping stones. It should be realized that the needs of each company are different, and departments such as industrial relations or human resources are in a better position to construct proper courses for the facilitator.

The training for a facilitator should involve instruction in teaching techniques, learning techniques, human relations, statistics, group dynamics, and workings of the company.

1. Teaching Techniques: A facilitator needs to know how to teach. More than half of his time involves teaching in one way or another. He has to act like a teacher and make sure that students are properly trained to use the appropriate materials while solving problems. He oversees the brainstorming techniques. And he makes sure that management presentations are prepared and acted upon properly. He

153

```
                         ┌─────────┐
                        ( ┌───────┐ )
                        ( │ C.C.  │ )
                        ( │QUALITY│ )
                        ( │CIRCLES│ )
                        ( └───────┘ )
                         └─────────┘

              Quarterly Leader's Training


Place: _____    Plant: _____

Time: _____    Date: _____



                        AGENDA

MORNING SESSION:

              1.   Quality Circle Progress

              2.   Quality Control in Japan

              3.   Time of Your Life

              4.   How to Conduct Meetings

AFTERNOON SESSION:

              "How to solve problems and make good decisions"

              (Three Hours)


- - - - - - - - - - - - - - - - - - - - - - - - - - - - - - -

NAME: _____   Plant: _____

YES, I would like to attend the Leader's Training Seminar

                                            ┌──────┐
                                            │      │
                                            │      │
                                            └──────┘

Please return this form to the Plant Co-ordinator

- - - - - - - - - - - - - - - - - - - - - - - - - - - - - - -
```

FIGURE 14–2

154

LEADER'S TRAINING PROGRAM

TOPICS THAT SHOULD BE DISCUSSED

1. Introduction

2. Brainstorming

3. Group Dynamics

4. Leadership

5. Training Adults

6. Total Quality Control

7. Basic Quality Control Tools (data gathering)

8. Basic Quality Control Tools (data analysis)

9. Brief review of advanced Quality Circle tools

10. How to start and expand circles

11. Presentation techniques

12. Case Studies

13. Quality Circle stimulation

14. Communication

15. Review

Duration: Eight hours plus as required on a monthly basis.

FIGURE 14-3

even teaches the use of an overhead projector, slide projector, and other visual aids used to instruct group members or to illustrate presentations.

2. *Learning Techniques:* The facilitator also needs training in the learning process. There are many ways to learn how to do a good job. The basic principles of the learning process should be communicated by the facilitator. This helps the members to implement Quality Circle programs quickly and effectively.

3. *Human Relations:* Quality Circles involve people. There are a number of different personalities existing in a company. It is of the utmost importance to obtain cooperation from all people of differing personality in the company, from management as well as from the shop areas. Problems in human relations do arise from time to time and the facilitator should be prepared to handle them successfully. (See case studies in chapter 15.)

4. *Statistics:* The key areas in statistics are probability, histograms, control charts, sampling theory, experimental designs, regression and correlation analysis, and pre-control.

    There are many specialized books on industrial statistics that will give details on these subjects.

5. *Group Dynamics:* Specific books on group dynamics are listed in the bibliography. One has to deal with many facets of human relations, and only time and experience will make one expert and successful in this field.

6. *Workings of the Company:* Various aspects of the company business dictate the training program for the facilitator. Michigan Technological University, Houghton, Michigan, offers a three-day seminar called "Training the Trainer" which is very helpful as additional training for facilitators. The following is a brief outline of the course work.

    1. How to approach training systematically
    2. Understanding adult learning styles
    3. Developing a successful training style
    4. Principles and techniques for effective learning
    5. Training methods and strategies
        a. Demonstration
        b. Role Play
        c. Stimulation
        d. Case Study
        e. Discussion
        f. Group Dynamics
    6. How to get the most out of training aids: When to use them and why
    7. Appraising your program.

Training of Management

Quality Circles in Japan started at shop level under a foreman's direction. Top management and middle management personnel were already geared for "Total Quality Control." They welcomed the concept and

```
                          ┌─────────┐
                        ╱   C.C.     ╲
                       │   QUALITY    │
                        ╲  CIRCLES   ╱
                          └─────────┘
```

Training Program for Facilitator

<u>TOPICS</u>:

1st Day   1.   Introduction

             2.   History of Quality Circles

             3.   "If Japan can, why can't we?"

             4.   Circle presentation

             5.   Circle formation and operation

             6.   Circle program implementation plan

2nd Day   7.   Circle Models: Japan versus United States

             8.   Functions of facilitator, leader, members

                  and Steering Committee

             9.   Quality Circle Techniques

            10.   Brainstorming

3rd Day   11.   Pareto Diagram

            12.   Cause and Effect Analysis

            13.   Control Charts

            14.   Pre-Control and Histograms

            15.   Check Sheets, Graphs

            16.   Management Presentations

4th Day   17.   Leadership and Communication

            18.   Group Dynamics and human relationship

            19.   How to operate and help Quality Circles

            20.   Project Presentation

            21.   Implementation Plan: Review

            22.   Open Discussion

Note: One should also add material that was discussed on page ___.

Duration: Four days plus as required.

FIGURE 14–4

157

immediately offered help without any hesitation. However, the same is not true in the United States or in other countries where this concept has been experimental for the past four to five years. Top management in these countries recognizes the need for good quality; however, they still need training in the basic principles and workings of Quality Circles to build solid support from the top on down. Depending on the company size and location, a one-half day training course serves as a good foundation.

Problems with middle management are different. Personnel in such areas as industrial engineering, manufacturing engineering, and some other areas feel that they might lose some of their authority. Traditional systems of management in the United States do not allow the use of this participative management system in the company. To implement a successful program, it is necessary to have middle management's full cooperation. Four to six hours of training in principles and in operating a Circle should be conducted. As the program grows it is possible that Circles can be formed in middle management areas also. Experience also shows that Circles do not take away anyone's authority. On the contrary, they help to create more cooperation and better communication throughout the company and reduce the need to exercise authority.

Who Does the Training

A facilitator plays an important role in coordinating the training. He has to make sure that proper attention has been given to all necessary details such as training rooms, training aids, books, and other materials. He also arranges the courses for top management, middle management, and other people whose support is essential to the program. Departments like industrial relations and human resource development also aid in training. As the program grows, additional help may be sought from outside. Outside specialists in the field of Quality Control statistics and human relations help to educate the Circle members and enhance the training program.

It is always beneficial to use the experience of Circle members and leaders. Members can tell successful stories of their completed projects, which helps to give new members more confidence. Short speeches from top management help to demonstrate management's support of the program and create more harmony.

Training Material

Figure 14-1 shows a training format that can be used for training Circle members. The need for training material is unique, and proper arrangements for the material must be made before planning the train-

QUALITY CIRCLE TRAINING FOR TOP MANAGEMENT

Duration: Four hours plus as required

Topics:

1. Introduction

2. History

3. Brief review of "If Japan Can, Why Can't We?"

4. Total Quality Control concept

5. Quality Circle Operation

6. Functions of Members, Leaders and Facilitators

7. Statistical Techniques Used in Quality Circles

8. Project Presentations

9. Proposed Implementation Plan Along With

   Objectives.

10. Review and Discussion

FIGURE 14–5

ing course. At present, there is no prepared material which is available and suitable for all companies. Many articles have been published on this subject, and material from the Japan Productivity Center and the IAQC will serve as guides in the preparation of training materials. It is necessary that separate training material be provided for leaders, members, facilitators, and management. Each group has different needs. The member's material or handbook should be short and precise. It should include objectives, advantages, and operation of Quality Circles as well as various statistical techniques commonly used in solving quality problems. The leader's manual should include information not only from the member's manual but also should include additional details about training techniques, information about learning processes,

Quality Circles Training for Middle Management

Duration: Eight hours for four weeks or more

Topics:

    1. Introduction

    2. Why Quality Circles? Along With Objectives
        of the Program

    3. History

    4. Total Quality Control

    5. Operation of Quality Circles

    6. Functions of Members, Leaders, Coordinators
        and Steering Committee

    7. Successful case studies

    8. Statistical Techniques (details provided)

    9. Group Dynamics, Communication, Participation

  10. Review and Discussion

FIGURE 14–6

promotional techniques, and other information which will help leaders to manage Quality Circles more effectively. The facilitator's manual should be much more detailed and should cover the six areas in which the facilitator needs instruction. Figure 14-7 lists reference books that can be used to prepare training materials.

Lastly, remember that training is a never-ending process. People must be informed and constantly trained in modern techniques. Education helps to create new ideas and new solutions. That is how progress is made. No one should underestimate the people's brainpower, and in order to stimulate this power, remember a familiar saying, "Each one, teach one."

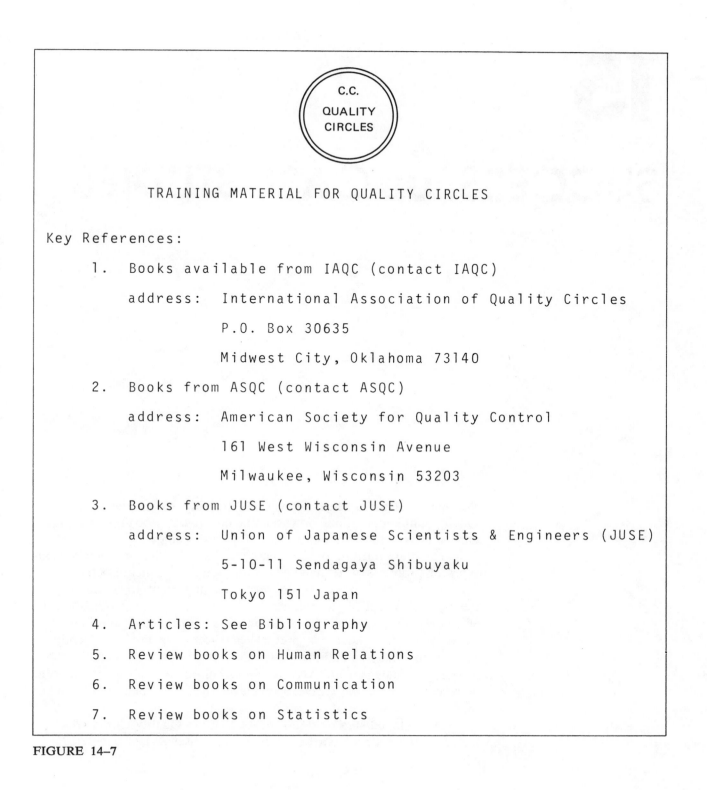

C.C.
QUALITY
CIRCLES

TRAINING MATERIAL FOR QUALITY CIRCLES

Key References:

1. Books available from IAQC (contact IAQC)

    address: International Association of Quality Circles

              P.O. Box 30635

              Midwest City, Oklahoma 73140

2. Books from ASQC (contact ASQC)

    address: American Society for Quality Control

              161 West Wisconsin Avenue

              Milwaukee, Wisconsin 53203

3. Books from JUSE (contact JUSE)

    address: Union of Japanese Scientists & Engineers (JUSE)

              5-10-11 Sendagaya Shibuyaku

              Tokyo 151 Japan

4. Articles: See Bibliography

5. Review books on Human Relations

6. Review books on Communication

7. Review books on Statistics

FIGURE 14-7

161

15

SUCCESSFUL CASE STUDIES

We have discussed thus far various training techniques as well as Quality Circle operation. However, the effectiveness of these techniques can be shown through some successful case studies.

The main purpose of these case studies is to illustrate how various types of problems were handled by the Circles. Generally, the Circle decides voluntarily to work on problems important to a majority of the people. Statistical techniques that were discussed before are used effectively to arrive at the solution. Brainstorming, Pareto analysis, cause and effect diagrams, and check sheets are used frequently to achieve the final goal. Finally, Circles always present their solutions to the top management. As was stated before, this is the main form of recognition for the Circle. Don't ever omit this final step, whether the project is successful or not.

The detailed step-by-step operation of the Quality Circle and how members solve a problem has already been discussed in chapter 7.

**Typical Procedures Used
in Quality Circle Projects**

Generally the following steps are followed in the Quality Circle operation:

STEP 1: Members get together and decide to list all the problems they would like to tackle. The statistical technique called brainstorming is used to collect and record ideas.

STEP 2: The leader then asks the group to vote for 2 or 3 key problems, or to choose another way to decide which key problems to work on.

STEP 3: The Circle then decides to concentrate on one major problem. The data is collected for analysis through the use of cause and effect analysis and Pareto diagrams.

STEP 4: Pareto diagram and group dynamic techniques are then used to analyze the problem further.

STEP 5: When a solution is reached that is acceptable to most of the group, a report is prepared for a management presentation, and finally a management presentation is arranged for final acceptance.

STEP 6: Solutions are then reviewed by management within the next two weeks. A follow-up report is prepared and actions are then reported to the Circle for their information.

Case Studies
from Japan and the United States

As discussed before, Quality Circles in Japan emerged in 1962 because of a real need to improve the quality image of the products built in Japan. Hence, most of the projects were related to quality. The concept of total quality control also has more thrust on quality. However, as the quality of the products improved, most of the companies turned their attention to other things such as cost reduction, waste reduction, absenteeism, efficiency improvement, and many other related matters in the companies. Today Quality Circles play an important role in management of the Japanese companies.

Even though the origin of Quality Circles and the basic principles were generated in the United States in the 1940s, and 1950s, the real applications and this new management style came into the picture here around 1970. A very few companies, such as Honeywell and Lockheed, showed keen interest in the idea and took the first bold step to use this approach in their companies. Most of the applications that we see are related to quality, cost reduction and communication improvement. However, I believe as time goes on, many more aspects of quality work will be grasped by the U.S. industries.

The following case studies will give an idea of the problems that can be tackled by the Quality Circle member.

CASE STUDY NO. 1

Subject: Written policy manual.
Problem: To prepare a written policy manual describing various policies and procedures of a firm covering health insurance,

163

welfare benefits information, an internal bargain sales, and so forth.

Solution: Each Circle member took responsibility for preparing a rough draft for a separate item. This took a long time to finish because it was in addition to routine work. Later, each item was discussed in the group meetings and a fair draft was prepared stating a written policy about every item tackled. This helped the employees to understand the firm's procedures better.

FIGURE 15–1

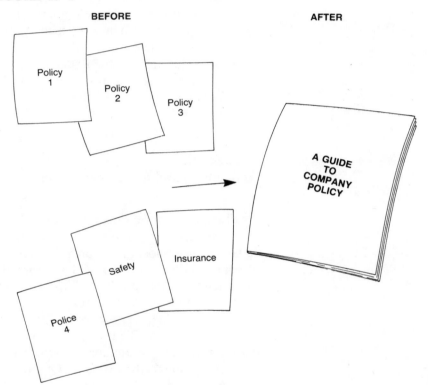

CASE STUDY NO. 2

Subject: Improvement of foot-board in the assembly area.

Problem: A foot-board that was too high made the workers tired, frustrated, and fatigued because it required constant climbing up and down the board for final finishing work. By the end of the day, the workers went home with tired feet, and this affected their work the following day.

Solution: Through group discussions, the Circle members solved the problem of making the last board a convenient height by constructing a step to go up and down. This avoided tired feet, and lessened the complaints about tiredness. It also contributed to efficient and speedy work.

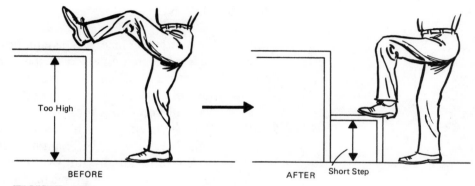

BEFORE   AFTER   Short Step

Too High

FIGURE 15–2

CASE STUDY NO. 3

Subject: Shortening the sludge treatment time on water tank of the grinder.

Problem: It took about one hour every morning to dispose of the sludge in the tank of the grinder and to fill it with water. This problem was demonstrated by all Quality Circle members. The Circle members studied the problem carefully and later demonstrated that maximum efficiency of the sludge treatment could be obtained by lowering the water level in the tank.

Solution: One day the Circle member who was cleaning the machines forgot to replenish the water in the tank. The next day the sludge treatment took less time. The Circle then studied the different water levels statistically to find the maximum efficiency of the sludge treatment.

After the detailed analysis it was demonstrated that most satisfactory results could be obtained without any trouble by reducing the water to 3/5 level. (See Figure 15-3.)

FIGURE 15–3

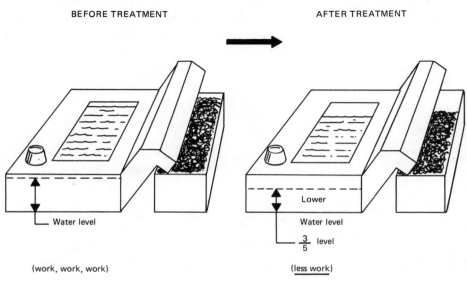

BEFORE TREATMENT

AFTER TREATMENT

Water level

Lower

Water level

$\frac{3}{5}$ level

(work, work, work)

(less work)

165

CASE STUDY NO. 4

Subject: Prevention of incorrect assembling of parts because changes were not communicated to the workers involved.

Problem: The workers often used the wrong parts because they were not informed of the changed specifications. Hence, better ways of communication were needed.

Solution: The Circle members hashed over the problem and came up with better ways of communicating the changes such as putting up signs by the worktable that indicated changes of specification or by preparing a checklist of such changes. Each worker was supposed to read the changes before going on duty each day.

FIGURE 15-4

BEFORE IMPROVEMENT

The specifications were changed, but what parts have been changed?

AFTER IMPROVEMENT

There will be no mistake since we can quickly verify what parts are changed simply by glancing at this.

CASE STUDY NO. 5

Subject: Safety through manufacture of conveyor stopper.

Problem: The parts falling from the conveyor could prove to be dangerous to a worker's life. Hence, improving the conveyor system was necessary.

Solution: The Quality Circle members, after discussion, found the cause of falling parts—wires wound up on the conveyor roller and other parts put on the conveyor would come loose. This resulted in parts falling off causing injuries to the workers. The members came to the conclusion that a stopper attached at the end of the conveyor chute would prevent the parts from falling off.

This not only improved the working of the conveyor system, but most of all, the workers were able to work with peace of mind.

CASE STUDY NO. 6

Problem: Damaged gaskets caused leaking components which necessitated rework and resulted in assembly problems.

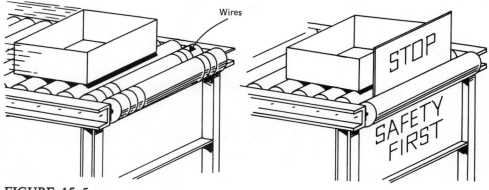

FIGURE 15–5

Solution: The primary problem is with handling gaskets from stock to the line, and then from line to stock. Guidelines established and directive memos to be issued relative to handling procedures as presented to management.

Results: Continual monitoring of the condition of gaskets throughout the assembly area has shown a considerable reduction in incidences of damaged gaskets and the cartons they are packaged in. (See Figure 15-6.)

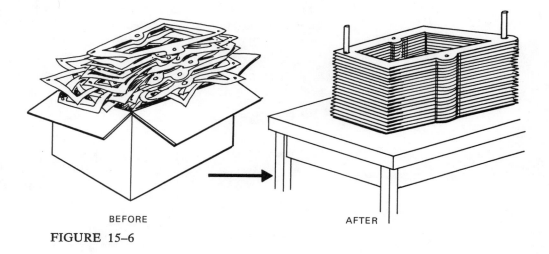

BEFORE   AFTER

FIGURE 15–6

CASE STUDY NO. 7

Problem: Rejects of painted V6 cowls because of dirt in the paint. The daily reject rate rose to as much as 25%.

Solution: The Circle members suggested the following improvements: Change the filters in the paint system; add plastic sheets on the conveyers, and avoid use of gasoline tow motors whose exhaust gases created turbulence in the air.

Results: Continued monitoring of the V6 painted cowl rejects showed the rate to have leveled off at an average of about 10%. (See Figure 15-7.)

CASE STUDY NO. 8

Problem: Engines on floor dollies are being damaged and some dangerous conditions exist as a result of poorly designed holding pins and a lack of maintenance.
Solution: Modify all dollies to conform to the proposed design.
Results: Management has accepted the proposed design change and maintenance program. The design change was even improved upon by management and is in the process of being implemented.

CASE STUDY NO. 9

The Fenton Art Glass Company, which employs some 500 unionized workers at Williamstown, West Virginia, began a participative problem-solving program after one of the owners received training in the technique in late 1973. Since its start, the program has been carried on by six groups of employees (including foremen) from single departments performing similar or closely related functions.[1]

One of the most successful groups has been a group of pressers, skilled glassworkers who operate by hand a press that shapes the glass and who function as leaders of a group of men who finish processing the item. They have responsibility for setting the pace of production and for solving quality problems.

The pressers have analyzed, developed, and tested solutions for

FIGURE 15–7

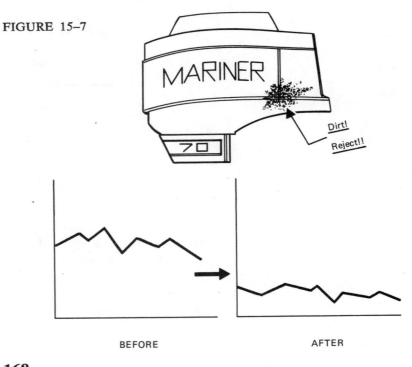

BEFORE   AFTER

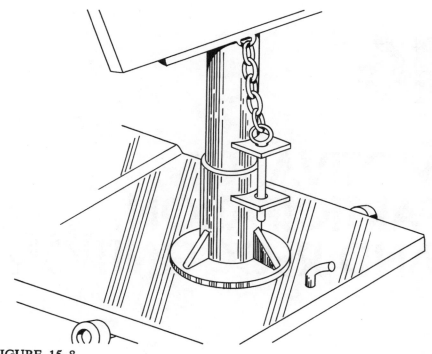

FIGURE 15–8

problems ranging from improvement in design and repair of equipment to review of new items for production feasibility, development of systems to improve communication, quality control, and problems involving materials, defects, and special production difficulties. They have handled approximately 30 projects on which progress was shown.

Perhaps the most successful project was the improvement in performance in the production of a new type of bowl. The yield on the item was improved from 17% good (of pieces pressed) to 51% good over the two months the problem-solving group worked on the problem. The solution involved changing the design of the mold and the piece, improving the tools, and revising the production method. The improvement in yield represented a labor savings of nearly $10,000 a year.

Members of the groups also mention the following improvements gained through group relationships:

—Development of communication between workers that allows them to learn from each other and to share the skills they have.
—Better communication between the company and the workers
—The ability to get suggestions implemented and to improve their pay by solving problems in their work.

Notes

1. Sidney P. Rubenstein "Participative Problem Solving: How to Increase Organizational Effectiveness." PERSONNEL, January-February 1977 (New York: AMACOM, a division of American Management Associations, 1977), pp. 30-39.

16

MOTIVATION, PARTICIPATION, AND RECOGNITION

People differ not only in their ability to do work but also in their will to do it. The motivation of people depends on the strength of their motives. Motives can be needs, wants, drives, or impulses within individuals. Most people work to satisfy individual and family needs and also to meet group and social pressures. However, keen competition and pressure makes people work harder. The degree of zeal varies from person to person. Some may work hard without any motivation while others need a push to do a good job. The Firestone Company recently released a film called *23-28* which explains these various types of personalities in a tactful way. Performance is often described as a function of an individual's ability, knowledge, and motivation. It is only when a person is properly motivated that he or she will use his or her ability, knowledge, and skill to produce optimum performance. Hence motivation is a key factor in business as well as in society.

Managers and foremen have to motivate employees constantly. America could put a man on the moon only because of President John F. Kennedy's commitment in 1960. His famous words, "This nation will commit itself to put man on the moon before the end of the century" cannot be forgotten easily.

Motivational needs vary from person to person, and a company needs to understand the types of people that are employed and then try to implement motivational programs that will fulfill the company's needs as well as society's.

There are currently a number of motivational theories. We will briefly discuss only the major theories that have a profound influence on the Quality Circle activities.

Motivation Theories

1. *General Model:* Mr. Paul Hersey and Mr. Kenneth Blanchard in their book called *Management of Organizational Behavior*[1] have discussed thoroughly various types of motivational theories. The relationship between motives, goals and activity can be shown in Figure 16-1.

   The strongest motive produces behavior that is either goal-directed or goal activity. With a broad goal such as food, it should be recognized that the type of food that satisfies the hunger varies from situation to situation.

   A similar illustration could be given for an intangible goal. If individuals have a need for recognition—a need to be viewed as contributing, productive people—praise is one incentive that will help satisfy this need. In a work situation, if the employee's need for recognition is strong enough, being praised by a superior may be an effective incentive to influence them to continue to do good work.

2. *Maslow's Theory of Hierarchy:* Abraham Maslow, a psychologist, developed a theory of motivation based on human needs arranged in a particular order from the lower to the higher needs. Maslow worked out a scale of human motivation based on the premise that higher order needs appear as other needs are satisfied. Also, no need can be treated as if it were isolated or discrete. Every need is related to the state of satisfaction or dissatisfaction of other needs. The five levels of need satisfaction he described are the following:

   A. Physiological Needs: Man lives for bread alone when there is no bread. Unless the circumstances are unusual, his needs for love, for status, for recognition are inoperative when his stomach

FIGURE 16-1   (From Paul Hersey and Kenneth Blanchard, *Management of Organizational Behavior,* © 1977, Prentice-Hall, Inc., Englewood Cliffs, New Jersey. Reprinted by permission.)

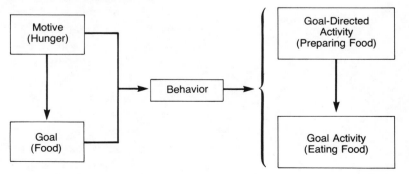

has been empty for awhile. But when he eats regularly and adequately, hunger ceases to be an important motivation. The same is true of the other physiological needs of man, for rest, exercise, shelter, protection from the elements.

B. Safety Needs: Safety needs are needs for protection against danger, threat, deprivation. Some people mistakenly refer to these as needs for security. However, unless man is in a dependent relationship where he fears arbitrary deprivation, he does not demand security. Since every industrial employee is in a dependent relationship, safety needs may assume considerable importance. Arbitrary management actions, behavior which arouses uncertainty with respect to continued employment or which reflects favoritism or discrimination—these can be powerful motivators of the safety needs in the employment relationship at every level, from worker to vice-president.

C. Social Needs: Man's social needs become important motivators of his behavior—needs for belonging, for association, for acceptance by his fellows. Management today is aware of these needs but often mistakes them as threats to the organization. Many studies have shown that highly knit, cohesive work groups may be more effective in achieving organizational goals than an equal number of separate individuals.

D. Ego Needs: The two kinds of ego needs are (1) those that relate to one's self-esteem, self-confidence, independence, achievements, competence, and knowledge; and (2) those that relate to one's reputation—needs for status, for recognition, for appreciation, and so forth.

Unlike the lower needs, these ego needs are rarely satisfied; man seeks indefinitely for more satisfaction of ego needs as they become important to him. The typical industrial organization offers few opportunities for the satisfaction of the ego needs of people at lower levels in the hierarchy.

E. Autonomy—Porter Modification: The Porter modification seems to have particular relevance to management, for while physiological needs have tended to decrease in importance, managers and supervisors have demanded control over their work environment and indeed, over their destiny. The need for autonomy which many participants express is based on the principle of self-government, self-control, and self-determination.

F. Self-Fulfillment: There are needs for realizing one's own potentials for continued self-development, self-fulfillment, and self-actualization, for being creative in the broadest sense of that term. It is clear that the conditions of modern life give only limited opportunity for expressing these relatively weak needs.[2]

3. *Elton Mayo:* Mayo of the Harvard Graduate School of Business Administration pointed out the existence of "informal" organizational groups and the impact of these groups on organizational objectives. Mayo reached a conclusion that people have a natural hunger for close associations with each other at work and that when the organization of work discouraged this, management's own goals would inevitably be thwarted. Instead of ignoring the instinct for

forming groups, management should encourage it; what's more, management should develop these groups by showing an active, first-hand interest in each individual member and by giving the group a reasonable share of control over its own work.

4. *Douglas McGregor:* There is a traditional theory of what people are like and what must be done to manage them. McGregor calls it "Theory X." The assumptions of "Theory X" are threefold. One is that most people just don't like to work. The second is that due to this dislike for work, most people must be coerced, controlled, directed, and threatened with punishment to make them work. The third assumption is that an average human being works a bare minimum, lacks ambition, refuses to take responsibility, and would rather be told what to do than to think for himself or herself. These assumptions guide management behavior and thinking. McGregor stresses that this set of assumptions, obsolete as it is, continues to have a very broad influence in American industry.

McGregor submits an alternative theory called "Theory Y," since he perceives the inadequacy of assumptions made in "Theory X" about human nature and motivation. The six important assumptions of "Theory Y" described by McGregor are as follows: (1) People do not like or dislike work inherently, but rather develop an attitude toward it based on their experiences with it. (2) While authoritarian methods can get things done, they are not the only method of motivating people to work for the organization. (3) People are not by nature resistant to the goals of the organization, or against assuming responsibility. It is the obligation of management to make it possible for people to recognize and develop these human characteristics. (4) Under the right circumstances people do not shun responsibility but seek it. (5) People possess enough imagination, ingenuity, and creativity to solve organizational problems, and (6) Under proper organizational circumstances and management, human beings will exercise self-motivation in achieving his or her own goals and those of the organization.

There is no royal road to the self-propelled, self-disciplining organization that McGregor describes. The evolution must start at the top and reach down to the lowest level. The superior staff member should act as a consultant and advocate rather than oversee. The focus of the organization becomes expediting business rather than struggling for power internally.

5. *Chris Argyris:* Behaviorists have been pointing out for ages that human nature is at least partially a function of maturation. According to Argyris, immature people are passive, dependent, have erratic shallow interests, have short time perspective, are in a subordinate position, and lack awareness of self. The characteristics of mature people are increased activity, independence, deeper and stronger interests, long-time perspective, equal or superordinate positions, and awareness and control of self.

Argyris concludes that the restrictions imposed on individuals by organizations for the sake of order and efficiency seem to create resistances which eventually hamstring the organization. Argyris finds three main mechanisms through which the organization

173

frustrates the mature employee and encourages the immature to stay that way. These are the formal organization structure, directive leadership, and managerial controls.

"Organization structure" typically concentrates power in the hands of a few at the top, and leaves almost none to those lower down the chain of command. He is convinced that concentrated power is unhealthy for the organization itself because it leads to apathy and inflexibility.

"Directive leadership" is the traditional style of supervision in which the superior makes all the decisions and his subordinates simply carry out those decisions. In effect, people are taught to trust their superior's judgment rather than their own.

"Managerial controls" consist of various restrictions on local initiative which require that certain decisions be made regardless of whether or not they seem appropriate to the man on the scene, for example, budgets, manpower restrictions, and standard operating procedures. Managerial controls therefore could be very harmful since they can put a damper on ingenuity and even on common sense adjustments to reality.

6. *Rensis Linkert:* Rensis Linkert of the Institute for Social Research at the University of Michigan emphasized the need to consider both human resources and capital resources as assets required for good management.

He developed four different systems of management that are found in various organizations. In system one, the management has no confidence and trust in the subordinates, hence, subordinates are not involved in any decision making. In system two, the management has some confidence and trust in subordinates, but still most of the decisions are made at the top and few by the subordinates. In system three, the management has substantial but not total confidence and trust in subordinates. Broad and general decisions are made by the top but specific decisions are permitted to be taken at lower levels. In system four, the management has complete confidence and trust in subordinates. Decision making is widely dispersed but well integrated. Workers' participation is encouraged. So everyone is engaged in efforts to achieve stated organizational goals.

In short, system one is a task-oriented, authoritarian management style, system four is a participative type of management style emphasizing teamwork based on mutual trust and understanding. Systems two and three are intermediate steps between the two extremes. In short, Linkert tells us that if the organization's management style fits in system four then one can expect a high productivity. Whereas the closer it is to system one, the more the likelihood of a sustained record of low productivity.

Since the root of productivity is the motivation of the individual, Linkert proposes an organization in which the individual can enjoy a sense of importance and influence. A consistent record of excellence would then become a matter of personal pride rather than a meaningless exertion for someone else's gain.

8. *Frederick Herzberg:* Frederick Herzberg and his colleagues at the Psychological Service of Pittsburgh interviewed about two hundred engineers and accountants who worked for eleven different firms in the Pittsburgh area. In the interviews they asked what factors made the respondents unhappy or dissatisfied and what factors made them happy or satisfied. Herzberg called the first category of needs hygiene factors or maintenance factors and the second category motivators. The best examples of hygiene factors were company policies and administration, supervision, working conditions, interpersonal relations, wages, status, and security. These factors produce no improvements but rather serve to *prevent losses* of morale or efficiency. They wouldn't really motivate the workers at all. But on the other hand, to have been deprived of them, would have caused motivation to deteriorate very rapidly. This would result in careless attitudes in doing their jobs. These factors contribute to the healthy or unhealthy environment of the worker.

A motivator, on the other hand, is an influence that usually has an uplifting effect on improvement, attitudes, or performance. Examples of motivators could be the sense of achievement, recognition for accomplishments, challenging work, and increased responsibility. These factors have definitely positive effects on job satisfaction, often resulting in an increase in total output.

In summary, the first (maintenance of hygiene factors) form an essential base for the second (motivators) and required fair treatment in such background factors as salary, supervision, and working conditions. If the background factors are in balance, the individual would not necessarily respond with any spurts of enthusiasm. He would do his job for the sake of doing it, and get

FIGURE 16–2

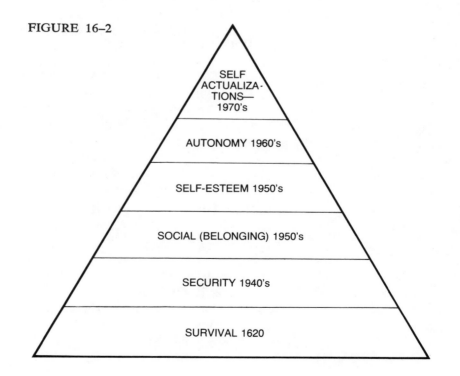

SELF ACTUALIZA- TIONS— 1970's

AUTONOMY 1960's

SELF-ESTEEM 1950's

SOCIAL (BELONGING) 1950's

SECURITY 1940's

SURVIVAL 1620

deeper into an uninspired rut. He would perform above the minimum expectations only when the second needs (motivators) were satisfied. A feeling of personal growth would exist when his work was not merely interesting but challenging, not merely prestigeful but significant, not merely fun but adventuresome.

What Do Workers Want?

An important question for managers to answer is, what do workers really want from their jobs? In one study done to attempt to answer this question, supervisors were asked to answer questions from the point of view of a worker and rank the answers by order of importance. In addition to the supervisors, the workers themselves also answered the same questions and ranked them by order of importance.[1] Following are the results (1 = highest, 10 = lowest in importance).

Table 16–1   What Do Workers Want from Their Jobs?

	Supervisors	Workers
Good working conditions	4	9
Feeling "in" on things	10	2
Tactful discipline	7	10
Full appreciation for work done	8	1
Management loyalty to workers	6	8
Good wages	1	5
Promotion and growth in the company	3	7
Sympathetic understanding of personal problems	9	3
Job security	2	4
Interesting work	5	6

Adapted from Lawrence G. Lindahl, "What Makes a Good Job," PERSONNEL, January 1949 (New York: American Management Association, Inc., 1949), p. 265.

Supervisors ranked good wages, job security, promotion, and good working conditions as the things workers want most from their jobs. On the other hand, workers felt that full appreciation for work done, feeling "in" on things, and sympathetic understanding of personal problems were the most important things.

Workers Group in the 1980s

Management can no longer assume that people come to the job with a built-in desire to work hard and to do the best job possible. At the same time, it does not mean that people do not work at all. Nor does it mean that American workers have all changed their motivations equally. One can divide the national working population into two overall groupings (Figure 16-4).

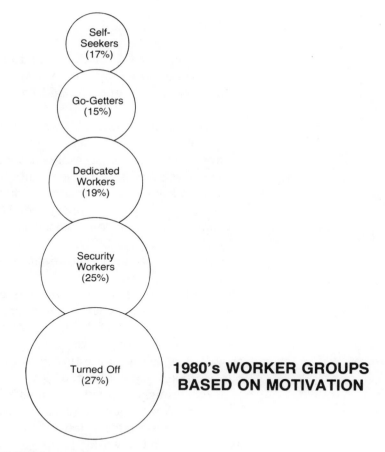

1980's WORKER GROUPS BASED ON MOTIVATION

Self-Seekers (17%)

Go-Getters (15%)

Dedicated Workers (19%)

Security Workers (25%)

Turned Off (27%)

FIGURE 16–3

THE OLD GUARD

This group is comprised of those for whom the old incentives still work fairly well. Although, it does show the effects of new social values and life styles. This group represents approximately 56% of all people who work and it consists of three subgroups.

1. Security Workers: About one-third of this 22% of workers, are white-collar clerical and service workers. For them, work is just a habit. They want job security and are not looking for meaning in their work.

2. Dedicated Workers: This subgroup, about 19% of workers, is more positively work oriented. Money is important to them but not as important as the work itself. These workers are older in age— mostly above 35 years.

3. Go-Getters: This subgroup represents 15% of workers and is younger, most of them under 35. People in this subgroup are the real "go-getters." They are motivated primarily by money and getting ahead. They are ambitious, and management has no problem understanding them or providing the incentives to motivate them.

The remaining 44% of the work force can be divided into two sub-groups. Both subgroups are young, that is, under 35, but they are socio-economically opposite and have opposite attitudes.

1. *Turned Off:* About 27% of all working people fall within this category. Of all the subgroups, this one is the least motivated to work hard, the least well-educated, and has the lowest earnings. There workers have the least internal motivation to do a good job.
2. *Self-Seekers:* About 17% of workers fall in this subgroup. It is the youngest subgroup, college educated, white collar, and middle-management professional men and women. This group is the hungriest for responsibility, challenge, autonomy, informality, and less rigid authority in organizational structure.

One of the drawbacks of all theories of motivation is that workers are treated as homogeneous. People are different—with different value structures. The idea of having a work force stretched out on a wide spectrum—with people who still are turned toward the 19th century as well as people who are turned toward the 21st, is a difficult concept, but one that must be grasped.

Increasingly, we will need a cafeteria concept of motives, tailoring the motivational package to each individual. Throughout our history, and certainly during the last century, American individualism stopped at the door of the work place. Now it's knocking the door down demanding entrance. In order to satisfy the need for individualism at work, we need new kinds of human technology.[2]

Motivational Aspect of Quality Circles

Men and women are social animals and like to work with each other in the society. Most of their activities take place in groups, and it is essential that these groups be motivated properly to reach high achievements. A number of the needs discussed in motivation theories are combined in Quality Circle philosophy. (Figure 16-4.) Job satisfaction and teamwork should be the two driving forces behind all motivational activities.

Participation in Quality Circles

Participation is the key to successful Quality Circle programs. Without effective participation from various levels this program cannot achieve a high degree of success. Motivation and participation go hand in hand. Motivational workers and managers can accomplish wonders.

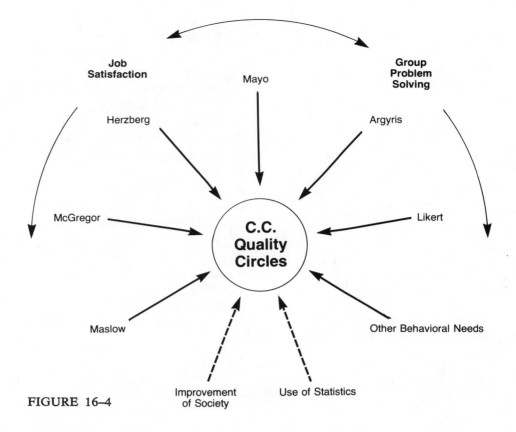

Job Satisfaction

Mayo

Group Problem Solving

Herzberg

Argyris

McGregor

C.C. Quality Circles

Likert

Maslow

Other Behavioral Needs

Improvement of Society

Use of Statistics

FIGURE 16–4

The best example of this is in Japan. People are convinced when they see the benefits of the program and how it can grow in any society. However, in order to maintain the continuity it is essential to get effective participation from various groups.

The Quality Circle program needs participation from various areas. Some of the key areas are:

1. Top management
2. Middle management
3. Foremen
4. Circle leaders
5. Facilitators
6. Circle members

The type of participation that is expected from these groups has already been discussed in the chapters 5 and 6.

We will briefly review the key points here:

1. Top Management:
    A. Should attend presentations done by Circle members
    B. Give speeches and talks
    C. Promote Quality Circles in various areas in the company wherever they might apply
    D. Help to establish policies
2. Middle Management:
    A. Support the program
    B. Participate actively

C. Spread the good word
D. Form their own Circles
3. Foremen:
   A. Be a leader as a member of a Circle
   B. Participate actively
4. Facilitators:
   A. Talk of work with Circle members and leaders
   B. Promote and expand the program
5. Leader:
   A. Show consideration to all members
   B. Use brainstorming
   C. Try to calm down the "talker"
   D. Distribute work to all
   E. Call outside help, if required
   F. Listen to people and encourage all
6. Circle Members:
   A. Be active members
   B. Work with everybody to make projects successful

Recognition

The recognition aspect of a Quality Circle program also goes hand in hand with motivation. Motivated people do not care too much about recognition. The basic philosophy in Quality Circles is to promote recognition of the workers.

1. *Management Presentation:* This is the best method of recognizing people that is being used in the Quality Circle program. Often people are neglected, workers are treated like machines without brains or feelings. This creates feelings of worthlessness among the workers. These feelings can be vanquished slowly by instituting Quality Circles. Workers get a chance to participate, to express their ideas, to let everyone know that they know their jobs. They get the opportunity to discuss ideas with the management on a one-to-one basis. They feel proud to show their achievements and feel free to ask for solutions to their problems on the job. Through all these activities they start getting the recognition that they have never had before.

2. *Luncheon Meetings:* Many times top management is busy with long-range planning and other policy matters. They may not be available when the management presentations are held. One of the best ways to show Circle achievements to the top management is by planning quarterly luncheon meetings with the members present. Two or three of the best presentations can be put on during the luncheon meeting to demonstrate the work the Circles accomplished throughout the year.

3. *Free Trips or Paid Vacations:* Many companies award free trips or paid vacations to the best Circle leaders. Along with the recognition,

this creates healthy competition in an organization and also attracts more people to the Quality Circle program.

4. *Annual Convention:* An annual convention is another way to recognize the Circle activities. In Japan, this method is used all over the country. There are company conventions, there are regional conventions, and finally there are national conventions held annually in November in Tokyo.

There are a number of other possible activities to recognize Circle accomplishments and Circle members. It is up to the facilitators and the steering committee to think of new ways to show appreciation to the Circle members who are the backbone of the program.

Motivation, participation, and recognition are three major aspects of the Quality Circle program. They are like spices in food. Without their presence, the program will be bland and ineffective. One has first to motivate the people, then keep them interested at all times in the program, and finally, recognize their achievements to the full extent throughout the year. The program belongs to the people, and with their cooperation amazing things are possible.

Notes

1. Paul Hersey and Kenneth Blanchard, *Management of Organizational Behavior,* 3rd edition, © 1977, Prentice-Hall, Inc., Englewood Cliffs, New Jersey. Reprinted by permission.

2. Notes from Dr. E. Bogard, Assistant Director, Instructional Operations, Morain Park Technical Institute, Fond du Lac, Wisconsin.

17

IMPROVING COMMUNICATION

Importance of Communication

Communication is a vital process in the smooth functioning of any organization. Without proper communication it is difficult to exchange ideas, thoughts, or information. Effective communication may be defined as the exchange of information and thoughts between two or more persons to reach mutual understanding and to carry on the activities of the organization successfully. Communication cannot take place unless people are involved in exchanging information. People, therefore, are the most important element in the communication process.

Communication is a continuous process. Most managers spend more than 80 percent of their time in communicating information and thoughts verbally, by telephone, or in memos. Good communication is also important in the execution of the company's plans and new strategies, in the enhancement of the program, and in the taking of necessary corrective actions. It also helps to get rid of confusion and misunderstanding between parties. People can be brought together for a common cause through good communication. Thus, communication is vital in all areas and activities of the organization.

Ways of Communication

Communication within an organization takes place in a number of ways. Some of them are as follows:

1. Oral communication
2. Written communication
3. Telephone, Telex
4. Pictures
5. Posters
6. Video tapes
7. Audio tapes
8. Films
9. Blue prints
10. Samples—models
11. Personal behavior
12. Closed circuit television
13. Cameras
14. Meetings
15. Seminars
16. Annual gatherings, parties, and picnics

Whenever people talk with each other, oral communication takes place. Oral communication is short lived and quick and is influenced by personality, self-interest, and attitude. It helps elminate paper work but sometimes leads to confusion especially if words are carelessly used. Oral communication also takes place in meetings, during training, and in seminars. The group discussions that take place in Quality Circles are another form of oral communication.

Written communication is long lasting, more formal, and more effective. Memos, letters, and reports are also forms of written communication. Personalities and personal behavior do not significantly influence the outcome of written communication. However, words can be interpreted differently, and so confusion may arise between the parties. It takes time to write messages or thoughts, and this may result in delays.

The most popular means of communication in today's society is the telephone. People spend from 10 percent to 80 percent of their time on the telephone. At the higher levels of an organization employees may spend more and more time on the phone. Even though the phone media is oral and direct, the effect of personality is less dominant. The conversation can also be taped for future use. Telephone communciation is quick and also saves paper work and writing time. Conference calls are a popular way of enabling more individuals to talk together at the same time.

Pictures, blue prints, and posters are other forms of communication to a mass audience. Pictures are self-explanatory and can carry messages and information quickly and in small areas. Blueprints explain different kinds of technical information which cannot easily be explained in words. Posters are powerful tools to impress mass audiences with short messages which can be remembered easily. They can be posted in a number of places and be read quickly by all. Films, audio tapes, and video tapes are modern ways of presenting information quickly and effectively. Samples and models are also used.

Finally, personal behavior or body language during conversation or discussion also communicates good or bad information. If a meeting is a success and no major problems arise, people generally talk with each other in a friendly manner. On the other hand, if a meeting goes sour or gets a little hot, people leave the meeting abruptly, sometimes with grim faces.

Formal and informal communication is commonly used in the organization. Seminars, meetings, memos, and letters are some of the formal ways of communicating, and are the backbone of the exchange of information in a company. Formal communication is generally carried out between superiors and subordinates at each level. There is also formal communication between departments. Along with the formal communication, there always exist informal channels of communication, sometimes known as the "grapevine" or "rumors." People talk with each other informally or have understandings at various levels. They continue their contacts outside the company and come to know each other. This creates a different type of communication. Sometimes it is healthy, sometimes it is harmful. Rumors spread rapidly through this channel, sometimes with important details omitted. People try to interpret the signals and add their own irrelevant, additional information which can cause confusion, misunderstanding, and an inferior message.

If meetings become bull sessions, the leader bears the responsibility for reminding people of the "code of conduct" and getting them back to the business at hand. It is not an easy job. Some groups go great guns, others progress slowly.

Communication Methods Used in Quality Circles

There are a number of different ways in which Quality Circles can improve communication in a company. Quality Circle meetings, project presentations, training, steering committee meetings, and monthly leaders' meetings, all of which have already been discussed in other parts of this book, present opportunities to help improve communication. At these gatherings people talk with each other more freely, they exchange ideas, and develop a kind of unity. The following list shows some of the other methods that are popular in promoting effective communications in a company:

1. *Graduation Party:* Every training program should be concluded with a ceremony honoring those who went through the training. Top management personnel should be invited to show the company support and should be asked to congratulate the graduates. This impresses the newly-trained members and improves participation right from the start.
2. *Monthly Newsletter:* It is of the utmost importance that information related to the Circle program be disseminated throughout the company. A monthly Quality Circle newsletter provides this source. The letter can include names of new graduates, information on new Circles, new project presentations, or anything that is thought to be provocative and positive.

3. *Posters:* Posters help to communicate effectively many messages about the Quality Circle program.
4. *Information Boards:* Quality Circle information boards are another effective method that can be used in any type of organization. The facilitator can post the accomplishments of Circle members, as well as other informative material which will create more interest in Quality Circle programs.
5. *Annual Gatherings and Picnics:* These are some of the other methods that a company can adopt in any country. It is necessary that a company support the program in many different ways to keep people "involved."
6. *Annual Conventions:* This method is very common in Japan. Many companies hold bi-annual conventions with the employees and discuss the best Quality Circle projects from various departments. Similar conventions are held on a regional basis, and finally, the national convention is held in November in Tokyo. Many employees win free trips or paid vacations as rewards for the best project work accomplished. These types of conventions help to get people together and once again improve the communication in the company.
7. *Recreational Activities:* People need change during work to break the monotony. Showing work-related or recreational movies helps to create more interest in the work. In addition people become relaxed and refreshed from watching something different. It also encourages people to sit together and exchange information on a variety of subjects.

Many companies in Japan have provided workers with facilities for physical recreation also. Bodies as well as minds need to be in good condition to do a good job.

Difficulties in Communication

A number of problems exist in the field of communications. We will discuss some of them here.

In formal communication in an organization information is generally passed from the top down. If a problem exists between a superior and a subordinate, complete information might not be passed on to all the people concerned. A manager might try to hide some detail or try to treat some part as confidential, this might create an atmosphere of mistrust, which is unhealthy for the company. In some cases, the superior may feel that the subordinates do not need to know all the details, which also creates problems in some cases. Sometimes incomplete reports or information, or messages that are too cumbersome may also raise difficulties within the company.

In many companies, departments are created to serve specific functions like engineering, manufacturing quality control, and so forth. Even though all of these units are supposed to work together for the same purpose, because of the departmentalization people do tend to look out for their own departments. Sometimes the information flow is

C.C.

QUALITY

CIRCLES

QUALITY CIRCLE MONTHLY NEWSLETTER

T R A I N I N G:

On November 1, 1981, twenty-two people were graduated
in Plant #2 upon completion of the Quality Circle program.

On November 21, 1981, thirty people graduated in Plant #15
upon completion of the Quality Circle program.

P R E S E N T A T I O N S:

Plant #4: Rods Unlimited gave their presentation on mis-
alignment of bolt holes for 619 and 622 connecting rods.

Plant #17: The Pit Crew presented their project, Reorgani-
zation of pre-set and wash tanks on October 20th.

Plant #15: Presentations were given by the Quest Quenchers
on October 8, 1981, Bleed barb fitting. Also, on October 9th
the Added Touch gave their presentation of Publication change
notices.

CONGRATULATIONS TO ALL OF YOU AND THANKS!

- -

FLASH:

CBS news with Walter Cronkite on October 27, 1980 carried
a story about a North Carolina shoe company (Barry of Goldsboro)
whose productivity has increased tremendously with the implementation of an "Employee Participative Program". The company
is one of the most profitable shoe companies in the U.S. today.
Workers have helped by reducing waste and increasing quality.
There has been a notable reduction in absenteeism as well.
Regular meetings are held by the company to keep employees informed of business conditions.

- -

THERE'S NO LIMIT TO WHAT WE CAN DO TOGETHER!

FIGURE 17-1

186

Quality
Circles
Working
Together!

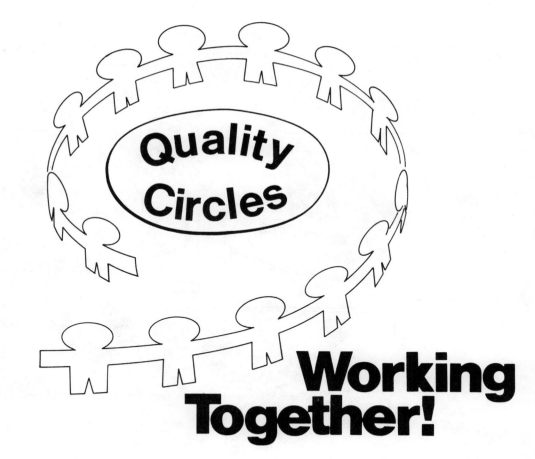

FIGURE 17–2

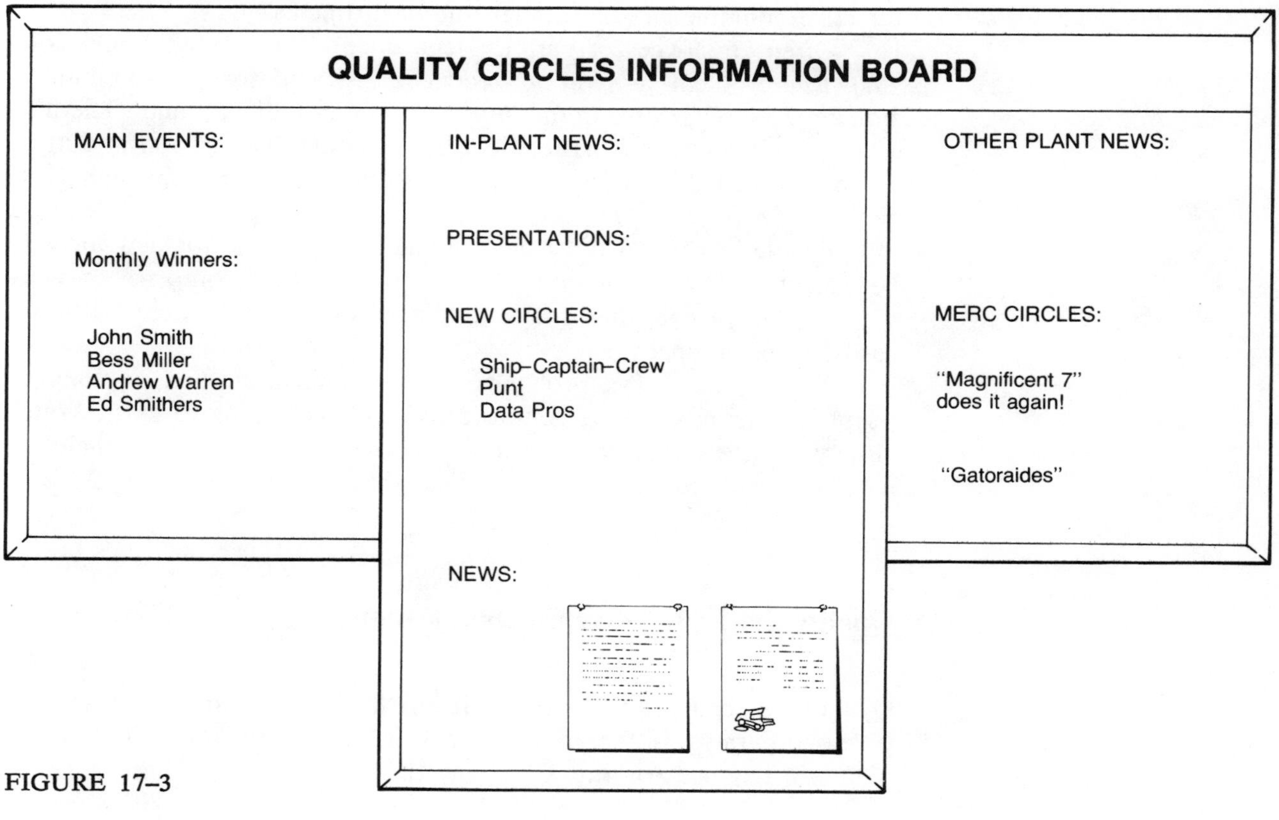

QUALITY CIRCLES INFORMATION BOARD
MAIN EVENTS:
Monthly Winners:
John Smith
Bess Miller
Andrew Warren
Ed Smithers
IN-PLANT NEWS:
PRESENTATIONS:
NEW CIRCLES:
Ship–Captain–Crew
Punt
Data Pros
NEWS:
OTHER PLANT NEWS:
MERC CIRCLES:
"Magnificent 7"
does it again!
"Gatoraides"

FIGURE 17–3

FIGURE 17–4

not completely smooth. It is necessary to eliminate the impediments to effective communication between the departments.

Often employees of various departments arrive at different solutions to a problem and will not reconcile their differences. Communication between the people in this situation becomes difficult and sometimes leads people to become irritated with each other. The person in authority must watch these situations closely to prevent permanent damage to the organization.

People in general resist change and it takes time for new ideas to be accepted. On the other hand, information that conforms to one's views or knowledge, that does not go contrary to one's thoughts moves easily in the company.

There are always problems in communication and as long as people are involved these complex problems are going to exist. Watch closely for them and try to get rid of them immediately to maintain harmony and cooperation in the company.

Quality Circles Improve Communication

One of the benefits that results from the implementation of Quality Circle programs is the improvement in communication. One of the plants in Hughes Aircraft Company on the West Coast has promoted improved communications as the objective of the program and has achieved great success. Some companies have seen a reduction in grievances through improved communication. The following cases show how this was accomplished with Quality Circles:

1. Quality Circle programs establish one of the best training programs for people in the shop as well as in the office area. The people who join the program voluntarily and attend the training enjoy that training very much because the training is unique and allows them to use their imagination. There is no force used to command attendance, and people enjoy discussing their views and exchanging the ideas in the meetings. Since the training is open for shop as well as for office staff, information flows freely between a number of different areas, and communication is improved.

   After one of the training sessions, participants not only expressed satisfaction with it, but asked to continue the training periodically. Many felt that the training brought the department together and made the group more cohesive. People also got to know each other, and healthy informal channels were established within the group and with others outside the group.

   A training class also helps to get rid of misconceptions about the Quality Circle program. One of the union stewards was opposed to the program for a long time. But after he went through the training, he was convinced that the program is really for the benefit of the people and he became one of its strongest supporters. He is still a very active Circle member and helps to promote the Circle program in the rest of his company.

2. Completed Quality Circle projects are published periodically and distributed within the company. This type of information flow also helps to improve communication. More people read about the projects, recognize that the ideas come from a variety of people, start talking with interest about the program, and decide they would like to present their ideas to the company. This is another way to see improvement in communication. One of the projects involved a safety survey with 300 people in the company. It created great curiosity about Quality Circles. When it became known that many of the suggestions had been implemented, people realized the scope of Quality Circles—they help not only to improve the quality of product but also aid in other vital areas. Information was passed around and new communication channels among people in the company were opened.

3. Quality Circle programs have another unique characteristic. The functions of the facilitators or mini-coordinators allow the Circles to float freely in the organization. Whenever there is a need for someone outside the immediate project area to attend the meetings, the facilitator can make the arrangements and request help which is usually immediately forthcoming. This unique characteristic of the program helps immeasurably to improve communications in the company—from top to bottom in the organization as well as horizontally between the departments. Quality Circle programs in this way help to eliminate barriers.

4. Quality Circle programs also offer individual or group counseling. The facilitator generally contacts people and seeks their advice to improve the program. At the same time he may try to explain the program to new people and point out its benefits. He acts as an ambassador to the program. Exchange of information takes place all the time, and a healthier relationship is created. These are a few examples of improved communications in the company. The actual benefits of the Quality Circle program in the communications area are unlimited and ever-expanding. Trust is created between people and most of them feel free to talk, express their views, and exchange their ideas with the management. This is what we need today to create harmony and progress in the society.

18
PROMOTIONAL ACTIVITIES

One of the essential and significant ingredients in the success of a Circle is publicity. People in the company need to know what is going on and what has been achieved through the program.

It has been observed that good programs die because of too little or too much publicity. Handling the publicity of the program is a delicate matter, and has to be carried out carefully to achieve the goal—to inform the people and build a positive attitude to the program. It is of the utmost importance that people be convinced that it is their program, and understand the need for acting in unity to achieve prosperity for the company. Hence, most of the promotional activities should aim at this objective.

Some, but by no means all, of the promotional activities that can be used to promote and expand the program are listed as follows:

1. Management attendance at the presentation
2. Appreciation letters
3. Certificates
4. Finished projects display
5. Posters, slogans, flyers
6. Pictures of the Circle members
7. Employee meetings
8. Monthly letter
9. Slides and video tapes
10. Movies and other recreational activities
11. Small gifts

12. Reports on business trips
13. Outside speakers and visitors
14. Trip to IAQC conferences
15. "Quality Circle" Day

1. *Management Attendance at Presentations:* Quality Circles generally pick out their own problems and then propose solutions. Later, a presentation is arranged to show their achievement. It is important that middle management and the concerned parties attend these meetings to indicate their open support. Presentations should also be used for exchanging ideas. Management should later use every opportunity to comment on the projects performed by the members. These actions help to promote the program and build the morale of the people. Thus the program gathers momentum and a warm reception in the shop.

2. *Appreciation Letters:* Once the project is complete and the presentation is made to management, the next step is to review the presentation and prepare follow-up lists and responses to the Circle. However, there is another important function that management should perform. It involves a "thank you" letter to all of the Circle members. Figure 18–1 shows a sample letter. It is recommended that this type of letter be sent to the home address of the Circle member. Some companies have found that when the letter is sent to the home, wives or husbands get curious about the program, and participation proceeds more rapidly.

3. *Certificates:* Once the project presentation is given to management, a certificate showing the completion of the project is presented to the leader and copies given to each member. (See Figure 18–2.) Copies of all the certificates are also proudly displayed on the notice board to show the Circle achievments to the rest of the employees of the company.

4. *Finished Project Display:* When the project has been presented to management many details and actual test samples from it can be displayed in a showcase. This helps to generate more interest and may encourage workers in other areas and in people who are still waiting to join the Circles.

5. *Posters, Slogans, Flyers:* Many simple posters can be prepared, with the help of the Circle members, aimed at promoting the Circle's people-building philosophy. (Figure 18–3.) Slogans like "there is no limit to what we can do together" help to show the power of unity. Sometimes flyers are sent to the employees with the paychecks. These flyers inform the people of business predictions, Quality Circle progress, or new developments in the company.

6. *Pictures of Circle Members:* Many companies have used this method to promote Circle activities. Honeywell Company has used it very successfully. Group pictures of the Circle members at work are taken and displayed in the work area.
   Circle members are proud to show their participation. This method also helps to identify Circle members.

7. *Employee Meetings:* Many companies hold monthly or quarterly employee meetings to explain to the employee the business condi-

```
                    L.B.C., INCORPORATED

                    Oshkosh, Wisconsin


                                           March 4, 1981


James J. Jones
605 E. Hickory Street
Oshkowh, Wisconsin 54935

Dear James:

     In regard to your voluntary membership in the Quality

Circle program at L.B.C., Inc., we wish to thank you for

participating in the "Miracle Workers'" project presentation

on January 18, 1981.

     You, as well as your circle's members, did an excellent

job in presenting the problem and solution for the presentation.

     Your cooperation and dedication to the improvement of

our product reflects on you as an outstanding employee of

our company as well as of our community.

     We offer you and your family our sincere thanks and

appreciation for your fine performance.


                              Sincerely,


                              S.G. Deer
                              Plant Manager
                              L.B.C., Incorporated
```

FIGURE 18–1

FIGURE 18–2

**C.C.
QUALITY
CIRCLES**

CERTIFICATE

N.R.B. Company proudly presents this Quality
Circle certificate for successfully completing the

project on: _____

Circle Name: _____

Project: _____

Circle Members: _____

_____

_____

_____

_____

_____

_____

_____
Plant Manager

193

THERE IS NO LIMIT TO WHAT WE CAN DO TOGETHER!

FIGURE 18–3

tions, any new events, or any new intentions the company has to promote a Quality Circle program. The president or vice-president of the company can show his or her full support of the program by talking positively about it to the employees. Such support from the top management helps to promote the program in the company.

8. *Monthly Newsletter:* A monthly newsletter can be published by the company to report Quality Circle activities. Training programs, management presentations, and other interesting topics can be reviewed in a newsletter.

9. *Slides and Video Tapes:* Slides describing Quality Circles and their achievements can be put together and shown to the employees at lunch times or during breaks. Today, video cassettes are easily available to record the programs at a reasonable price. Video cassettes can be used to record management presentations and other pertinent discussions. Later this recorded data can be used in the shops and in other areas to promote Quality Circle programs. This mehod also offers an opportunity to view the accomplishments of the Circles to those who have never attended a program.

10. *Movies and Other Recreational Activities:* During a recess or lunch break people need some kind of recreation. Card games are commonly played in cafeterias. However, there are other kinds of recreation available. Sometimes a movie related to the work or other topics can help to increase people's knowledge without taxing their minds too much. It is reported that the General Motors Corporation has even shown football games and has set up table tennis tables in various plants. This indirectly helps the employee to form groups, which also indirectly prepares their minds for them to join the Quality Circles at a later date.

11. *Small Gifts:* Some companies hold monthly leaders' meetings in which various general topics are discussed. Small door prizes are awarded to the active Circle members at those meetings. The prizes may consist of gift certificates, invitation cards for dinner for two, or T-shirts, and so forth. Pictures of the lucky winners are displayed on the Quality Circle display board. This is yet another way to get more people interested in the Quality Circle program.

12. *Reports on Business Trips:* Many times Quality Circle members while they are involved in Circle projects visit other companies. It is advantageous to publicize these visits to the rest of the Circle members. This generates interest and encourages growth of Circle membership.

13. *Outside Speakers and Visitors:* Quality Circle members are always in need of more training to improve their skills. Sometimes it is profitable to call on well-known speakers from outside, and to promote the event all over the company. This helps to attract more people and to interest them in the program.

FIGURE 18–4

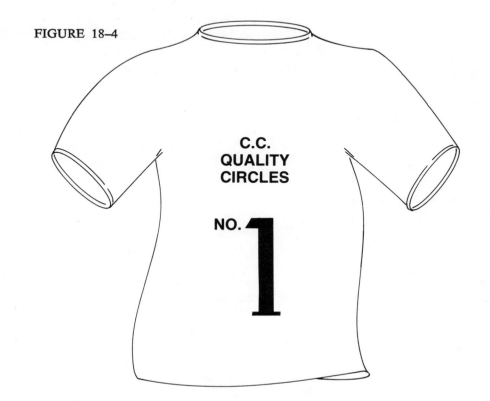

C.C.
QUALITY
CIRCLES

NO. 1

Visitors from outside companies should also be welcome since such visitors quite often become a topic of conversation with Circle members and their fellow workers, and this in turn helps to attract more people to the Circles. The outside guests also reinforce Circle members' pride in their own achievements.

14. *Trip to IAQC Conference:* The International Association of Quality Circles holds an annual conference in the United States. This is similar to the annual conference held in Japan and in Korea. Many papers and workshops on Quality Circles are presented in these conferences. It is recommended that those companies who wish to promote Quality Circles send a representative to these conferences. This gives the companies an opportunity to hear new ideas expressed by different experts, and it also gives them an opportunity to examine other people's Quality Circles. Some companies send the Circle members and, believe it or not, this generates interest among the employees.

15. *"Quality Circle" Day:* "Quality Circle" day is another exciting idea that a company can use to promote Quality Circles. Generally, one can arrange a picnic in the summer and provide free food and drinks. Or arrange a dinner meeting at Christmas time and invite all of the Circle members. This helps to bring people together and creates a cohesiveness and cooperation among them. It also attracts an increase in membership. It is reported that Dover Electric Company in Memphis, Tennessee, celebrated such a "Quality Circle" day with great success.

These are just a few suggestions that can be used to publicize Quality Circles. There are many other things that can be done to suit an individual company. In the long range, a company should try to achieve 100 percent participation in the program from the employees and think of ways to get there. Then, and then only, has one achieved the true *success* in a Quality Circle program!

19

PROBLEMS IN MANAGING QUALITY CIRCLES

A Quality Circle program can be very exciting, but if it is not administered properly it may run into a number of unforeseen difficulties. These problems can cause serious setbacks and if not properly resolved may destroy the program completely. One should anticipate some of these problems and be ready to deal with them efficiently when they occur.

This chapter is divided into three sections: general problems in Quality Circle programs, specific problems and suggested solutions, and human relations—case studies.

General Problems

As discussed before, a Quality Circle program involves participative management. Like any new program the success of this program will depend on overcoming the difficulties that may arise in the program.

Some of the general problems to watch for are

1. Poor training
2. History of previous programs
3. Existing suggestion system
4. Union relationships

5. Insufficient support from top management
6. Insufficient cooperation from middle management
7. Inadequate publicity
8. Difficult or unrelated problems
9. Unrealistic expectations
10. Poor or slow response from management

Precautions should be taken to prevent or resolve the following problems.

1. *Poor Training:* The Quality Circle program cannot start or survive without adequate training of the participating personnel. People must be trained properly and must be convinced that the program is a "people-building program" based on a sound training system. Some companies do not realize the importance of this training, and in those cases, the program is almost certain to face serious problems right from the beginning.

2. *History of Previous Programs:* Many companies start new programs without adequate planning. The programs begin in response to high level pressure, or just to keep up with others. Normally, such programs do not last long. If a company is known to follow the practices indicated, its Quality Circle program will also be a fatality.

3. *Existing Suggestion System:* Many companies have a suggestion system in which a person is awarded a part of the savings realized from an accepted suggestion. In recent years, this system has been growing rapidly in Japan. In companies where the suggestion system exists, it is important that the introduction of a Quality Circle program be planned very carefully. Quality Circles do not have monetary rewards, therefore companies which have a suggestion system should modify their rules and procedures so that these two programs will not conflict with each other and cause more problems.

4. *Union Relationship:* Timely help from labor unions can make Quality Circles a tremendous success. However, the history of Circles in Japan indicates that the union barely supports this program. It seems also that there is limited involvement from union leaders. In other countries where the relationship between union and management is different, it is highly recommended that union leaders be informed of the basic principles of Quality Circles, such as, that it is a people-building philosophy and that it aids in the development of a higher quality of workmanship. The cooperation between union and management will vary in different companies. However, experience shows that people like this program, they like the involvement and participation and get satisfaction from seeing the results of the program. It is essential to be patient with the union leaders and keep striving for more cooperation.

5. *Insufficient Support from Top Management:* This is the other side of the coin. Top management in support of Quality Circles is a must, but it has to be earned. Many companies really don't know what kind of support should be expected from top management. One of the key things for top management to do is to issue a

Quality Circle policy and attend management presentations to show their interest in the program.

6. *Insufficient Cooperation from Middle Management:* The operation of Circles and the implementation of projects that are completed by Quality Circles sometimes increases the feeling that middle management is losing its authority in various manufacturing areas. However, it should be realized that no one loses authority in a participative management style, even though it appears like that on the surface. On the contrary, this concept helps to improve cooperation in different departments and also betters communications. In countries like the United States, the success of Quality Circles will depend on convincing middle management that "there is no limit to what we can do together."

7. *Inadequate Publicity:* Recognizing the Circle's achievements is a must. Circle members and Circle leaders appreciate being publically recognized. It is essential to advertise recognition programs adequately. A monthly newsletter, posters, pictures, small seminars, and many other similar programs, such as dinners or picnics help to publicize the program throughout the company. However, one should be very careful not to give too much publicity to any or all programs at too early a stage because there may be many problems later on. Everyone is generally enthusiastic at the start of a program. But sometimes it is possible to create dissatisfaction in the groups by neglecting some key points in the publicity. Hence, great care should be taken with publicity, and the advice of the Circles should be asked.

8. *Difficult or Unrelated Problems:* Quality Circles are just like infants in the beginning; they don't know how to walk, talk, or laugh. They don't know where to go or what to do. It is necessary for them to be nourished, guided, and given proper direction. Problems selected for solution should be simple and work-related in the beginning. Circle members should be guided in the use statistical problem-solving techniques. At the same time, a facilitator should avoid getting Circles involved in solving problems like material planning or scheduling. Quality Circles cannot contribute much in this area since they have very little control and knowledge of its working.

9. *Un ealistic Expectations:* It must be realized that Circles are not a panacea for everything. The program is most useful for solving daily problems where members know more than anybody else about the work. However, the program will not solve the research problems or financial problems of the company. One should not expect quick results from the program either. It is a new management philosophy, and it will take time to build confidence in it. Remember, "Rome wasn't built in a day."

10. *Poor or Slow Response from Management:* It is essential that Circle members present a final report on their project to management. It could be an interim report, a final proposal, or a report on a discontinued project. No matter what the outcome the presentation is a must. If you recall, it is the only real recognition that Circle members get. It is their opportunity to share their pride

and happiness with management. At the same time, management must make sure that suggestions or proposals are analyzed properly and as soon as possible. A timely response should be offered to the Circle member so that they will understand that a follow-up is in process and their efforts have not been wasted. If management does not start a follow-up system, the Circle members will get discouraged, communications will break down, and members will soon lose interest in the program, putting it in jeopardy.

These are the general problems of Quality Circles. In the next section we will review some specific problems and some proven solutions that have been used in these cases.

Specific Problems and Suggestions[1]

PROBLEM 1: POOR IMPLEMENTATION

Suggestions: To eliminate poor implementation of the program, prepare a plan for your management organization.

1. Use the existing Quality Circle organization.
    a. Introduce the concept
    b. Conduct a complete training course
    c. Monitor and measure results
2. Report back to management the results of this trial run.
    a. Measure the success in dollars, time invested versus savings achieved
    b. Assess the improvement in product quality
    c. Analyze any improvement in the relationship between floor worker and management
3. Form an operating committee to consist of the plant manager as chairman, plant superintendent or general foreman, personnel manager, and quality control manager. Have them meet weekly to resolve any problem associated with the program.
4. Establish your Circle policy and submit it for upper management's approval. Include items such as:
    a. Meeting times and places.
        1. Should they be on company time?
        2. Will participants be paid?
        3. Rate of pay
        4. Recognition for projects
        5. Coffee and rolls for training
        6. Lunches for completed projects
    b. Movement from Circle to Circle
        1. By department
        2. Because of layoffs
        3. Because of dropouts

The key here is to develop a consistent policy and to avoid unnecessary changes.

5. Plan an introductory meeting with your union's top leaders.
   a. Stress the importance of quality in keeping the company going
   b. Show how the thoughts and ideas of the workers now have a vehicle in which to be heard and used
   c. Suggest that they support the program or at least not oppose it, since no one is opposed to the improvement of quality.
6. Have all foremen participate in the training program. The training should be mandatory, even though their involvement in the Circle program will be voluntary. However, this involvement should not interfere in any way with the functions of the Circles in their area.
7. Choose an area in your plant where you feel the program has its best chance for success.
8. Prepare a short summary of your program that could be made available to production workers and distribute it along with a sign up sheet for anyone interested. Indicate the place and time of the meeting.
9. Begin your training and upon completion form your Circles and choose a project.

PROBLEM 2: INHIBITING FOREMAN

Suggestions: One of the roles of the facilitator is to recognize the problem of the foreman who inhibits the activities of the Circle and to resolve the situation tactfully:
   a. Offer examples of how other Circles work
   b. Direct communication with the foreman
   c. Get assistance through the steering committee and down through the chain of command

PROBLEM 3: UNWANTED FOREMAN

Suggestions: Some Circles may not want the foreman as a member. To resolve this problem separate the desires of the group into the following categories:
   a. Personalities: If there are some conflicts in personality, these should be examined to see if the members are being too critical or if their concerns are valid. Consult with the general foreman to determine the best approach to resolving these matters. If the problem lies with the members try to let the program work to change their attitude.
   b. Some members feel more comfortable without the foreman. By advising him that this is perfectly natural the foreman should not be hurt or discouraged. Try to get him involved with another Circle.

PROBLEM 4: UNWILLING FOREMAN

Suggestions: Some foremen do not want to participate in Circle activities.

Be sure to examine the reason for non-participation. He may feel that if he becomes a member of one group other groups in this department may feel slighted. If he has a negative attitude to the program, it may be necessary to review this part of his performance through the plant manager or general foreman. This procedure has proven to be quite helpful.

PROBLEM 5: UNION OPPOSITION

A. Your program will eliminate jobs.

Suggestions: This can be a problem. It should be addressed immediately through the steering committee. Direct your approach to this problem by relating to waste. Waste is all around and adds to the cost of the product. The reduction of waste will reduce the cost of the product which will in turn make the product more competitive in the market place. This will increase sales and result in more jobs.

B. Why should I help the company?

Suggestions: The workers *are* the company. Their minds are a sleeping giant and represent a resource well worth tapping. Circle involvement helps reduce the monotony of their jobs, and there is satisfaction in helping to reduce problems.

C. This is work simplification which eliminates jobs.

Suggestions: Stressing the reduction of waste and the improvement of quality and not stressing the elimination of jobs or operations, will still result in the job improvements as a side benefit to the program. The program may also create more jobs because of an increase in sales.

PROBLEM 6: NONMEMBERS' INTERFERENCE

Suggestions: If catcalls and negative remarks made during meetings held on the floor or negative references to the meetings made at any time are a problem for the Circle, move the meetings, possibly to private meeting rooms. This may still generate nonmembers' interference. The union may also oppose such a meeting with its people because it is held behind closed doors. The best approach to this objection is to issue an open invitation to anyone who wishes to attend to sit in on meetings.

Nonmembers' interference may also be expressed in phrases such as "Why are they, the Circle, getting credit for that idea? I've been telling them, the company, the same thing for years." This situation provides an opportunity to show the difference between a suggestion and a solution. The most powerful attribute of a successful Circle project is the proven solution. Making a suggestion places the burden of proof on someone else. By following the format learned in training, these same suggestions are put to the test during the trial run. Suggestions that don't work when tested are eliminated. Proven suggestions with back-up data become solutions. It is far easier to implement a solution than to prove a suggestion.

There is also the effect of group dynamics upon the quality of a decision—an important factor with or without a Circle program.

PROBLEM 7: PRESSURE AGAINST PARTICIPATION

Suggestions: Counter pressure against participating or joining in the Circle program through the steering committee. Get back to upper management and if the problem stems from the union, arrange a meeting with the union leaders and the company president. The message should be: Help us by joining the program. If you do not want to join in, don't interfere with others who do wish to participate. *All* unions want to produce quality goods or will not openly suggest making products of poor quality. Therefore it is important to talk of good quality and waste reduction. Again, stress the difference between suggestions and solutions.

PROBLEM 8: OTHER PROGRAMS

Suggestions: Other programs, such as value analysis or work simplification, can work against a successful Circle program. The best approach is not to carry any of them over into or along with the Circle program. Quality Circles should be kept separate.

If work simplification is offensive to workers because of fears that it might eliminate some jobs, keep it at the foreman's level. Never put them together, even though some training may be similar.

PROBLEM 9: MEETING TIMES AND PLACES

Suggestions: If meetings are held during lunch hour, be sure to check if participants will be paid for the meeting time. If all items of pay are negotiable, it may not be possible to pay some without paying all. If the operation permits, it is best to meet on company time, or at the least 50-50—50 percent on company time and 50 percent on lunch time. Down time may be a practical time to consider for meetings.

PROBLEM 10: MEETING LENGTH

Suggestions: Thirty minutes is not usually long enough for a meeting, forty-five minutes to one hour is more productive. If this seems to be too much time to take away from the normal work schedule, consider meeting once every two weeks for the longer period.

PROBLEM 11: SPECIAL MEETINGS

Suggestions: Getting special groups together to work on improving the Circle program can be a problem. Some ideas that have been surprisingly successful are meeting after hours, utilizing inventory downtime, evenings, or vacation time.

PROBLEM 12: ALERTING TOP MANAGEMENT

Suggestions: To make top management aware of projects select typical finished projects and have the Circle make quarterly presentations to the company president.

PROBLEM 13: ASSESSING CIRCLE EFFECTIVENESS

Suggestions: To determine whether your program is as effective as you would like it to be prepare a questionnaire for Circle members and nonmembers. Questions should be prepared properly and may include the following: What more can the program do to help you as a worker? Why don't you belong to a Circle? What can we do to make involvement easier?

PROBLEM 14: HANDLING APPARENT INFRINGEMENT

Suggestions: Often a problem or project will lead you into a department or to a person responsible for a particular problem and will create an appearance of infringement on someone else's authority. Here the facilitator or mini-facilitator will have to prepare the way. This is done by focusing on the problem and forgetting about assigning blame. Usually the people affected will be happy to see someone trying to help them out of a jam. Invite them to the meetings to allow them to explain their view of the problem.

PROBLEM 15: ARRANGING EXTRA EVENTS

Suggestions: Pass the requests for extra meetings or trips to other plants through the steering committee. Usually giving advance notice will allow for planning on the floor. Trips to other plants should be allowed if they pertain to the project under consideration. Schedule trips in advance and be sure to work through the other plants.

PROBLEM 16: GETTING STARTED

Suggestions: Getting the first project started is probably one of the most difficult times for a Circle. From experience, it has been found, that if the first project is fairly easy the Circle gains confidence and keeps its momentum and interest going.

It has also been found that some groups can tackle for their first projects problems that initially appear to be insurmountable, and do extremely well.

PROBLEM 17: MINUTES OF MEETINGS

Suggestions: Have Circles submit minutes of each meeting to the facilitator so the progress of each Circle can be monitored.

PROBLEM 18: PROJECT PRESENTATION

Suggestions: Samples of the project showing the problem before Circle work and after project was completed are displayed in a display case at the entrance of the plant to show all employees the results of Circle work.

PROBLEM 19: MAINTAINING AN EFFECTIVE STEERING COMMITTEE

Suggestion: A Circle steering committee is generally comprised of a plant manager, a plant superintendent, a plant personnel manager, a facilitator, a manager of quality control, and one Circle leader representative. The group should meet for one hour to discuss problems that have been encountered by the Circles. Examples of problems that can be discussed:

    a. Need for additional time.
    b. Need for time to go to outside vendor.
    c. Meeting room taken over by somebody else.
    d. Picnic tables and chairs needed for meeting place.
    e. Interference by union, and so on.

With the steering committee meeting weekly and with the key plant personnel present, many problems can be resolved before a major problem is created.

The Circle leaders attend steering meetings on a rotating basis for one month so all leaders and Circles are represented. They are usually selected in alphabetical order. The steering committee is vital to a successful Circle program.

Communicate and learn from other people's mistakes.

The basic defense against negativity is a strong offense. A very effective part of this offense is a good publicity program. Posters provide a means of driving home your points. This program can be very inexpensive if you enlist Circle members in the preparation of posters, and use blue prints. Notice boards for Circle activities, pictures of new accomplishments, and monthly meetings are additional means of good publicity. Don't overlook the obvious. Be sure news of Circle activities is posted in all critical areas or pass out newsletters. Never assume that everyone knows all.

Case Studies in Human Relations

Problems in human relations are complex and no two of them are alike. The five case studies presented here will help you in analyzing similar situations in your company when they occur. It must be remembered that no two situations are alike nor are any two solutions. Each problem must be handled on its own and must be resolved according to the company's administrative policy.

CASE STUDY NO. 1: MEMBER SELECTION—INITIAL

The industrial engineering group consists of about fifty people in two groups. The steering committee decided to initiate two Circles, one in each group.

Volunteers were solicited and approximately 90 percent volunteered. The steering committee decided to limit Circle size to seven members. The department members were allowed to determine how the seven should be selected. One group used a random selection (names drawn out of a hat).

The other group voted for seven people each. What problems do you foresee?

CASE STUDY NO. 2: MEMBER SELECTION—LATER

Both Circles and the steering committee had agreed that the Circle members could approve visitors.

The steering committee had established a policy that in any department with Quality Circles every person in the department would be offered an opportunity to join a Circle.

When the Circles had been in operation four months, a member of the department tried to join the Circle. The Circle members refused to admit him.

The facilitator said the members had to admit him. The Circle members said they had the right to keep unwanted visitors out. When the facilitator insisted that the visitor must be admitted, the Circle stopped meeting.

Can you analyze the problem?

CASE STUDY NO. 3: LIP SERVICE

The Quality Circle program in one of your plants started off with three Circles.

All three leaders were junior supervisors. Two were on the second shift.

When the program had been in operation for six months, one leader left the company. His Circle was continued by the facilitator.

A second Circle stopped meeting because they weren't informed that equipment required for their solution had ben ordered and would be six weeks late in arriving.

The plant manager indicated he actively supported Circles, made space available, allowed them to meet, but couldn't spare his key supervisors.

Any comments?

CASE STUDY NO. 4: BOYCOTT

Approximately six Circles were meeting at one location. Three more were planned. The program was well received.

At the time, the use of hot plates had become common in the shop. The management decided to discontinue this. And when the use of hot plates was discontinued, the members began boycotting every Quality Circle.

The boycott has gone on for two weeks.

CASE STUDY NO. 5: SLICK PRESENTATION—
BAD CORRECTION

The "Wild Bunch" presented an excellent solution to a machining problem. There were four solutions.

An operator who worked on the parts led the presentation. He fielded all questions well. Management accepted all recommendations.

Later, the facilitator asked the quality supervisor if he could see improvement.

He answered, "No, and we won't until the man who made the presentation learns to run the part."

Do you agree?

Notes

1. This information was prepared by G. Hodkiewicz and G. Scott, Quality Control Managers at Mercury Marine, Fond du Lac, Wisconsin.

20

HOW TO MEASURE QUALITY CIRCLE PROGRESS

In 1973 the Lockheed company was responsible for publicizing Quality Circles in the western world. Many educators and business people had doubts about its survival at that time. However, in 1981 the survival of the idea is assured in the United States for about the next ten to twenty years, provided there is sufficient support and nourishment from middle and top managements.

The question is how to cope with the astonishing growth of the Circles so that the people involved will not get discouraged and will not lose their interest in the program. At the same time the significance of the cost and benefit relationship cannot be overlooked.

At present there is no one way to measure the progress of the program and it is hard to say whether one can ever develop one because of the complexity of the program. Because there are various aspects to the Quality Circle program, there needs to be more than one way of evaluating the program.

It is not only the pure numbers or the financial aspect that must be reviewed, but also the human element. Changes in human relations brought about by the Quality Circles have a far-reaching impact on any organization. After implementation of a Circle program, one company reported that during break times, instead of talking about politics or football games, more and more people started to talk about the projects they were involved in with the Circles. Supervisors noticed that discontentment and dissatisfaction at work was slowly disappearing in the areas where Circles had been in operation for about six to eight months. How can one easily evaluate and measure such an organizational change or progress brought on by these Circles?

Many organizations are using one or more of the following ways to keep track of progress and to evaluate the impact on the organization. This list can be expanded as time goes on, and as new needs arise to evaluate the progress.

1. Quality improvements
2. Participation
3. Cost reduction
4. Waste reduction
5. Machine utilization
6. Safety
7. Productivity
8. Machine maintenance
9. Communication
10. Attitude
11. Product improvement
12. Customer satisfaction
13. Absenteeism
14. Grievances
15. Work satisfaction

1. *Quality Improvements:* This is where it all started! Quality Circles were formed to eliminate poor quality work. Quality improvements can be measured in any of the following ways:
   a. Percentage reduction in rejects
   b. Reduction in defective products
   c. Reduction or elimination of rework
   Example: In one industry, plastic parts were painted with black color. At times, daily rejects were up to 50%. Quality Circles attacked this problem and suggested changes in the filtering and cleaning systems. After implementation of the above suggestion, the rejection rate dropped to 2% daily.
   Example: In another industry, black sleeves were used which sometimes were melted and torn. Quality Circle suggested the use of a different material for sleeves. Rework on the original sleeves was approximately 30%. Rework on the new sleeves was reduced to less than 1%.

2. *Participation:* One can keep track of the number of Circles and the number of people participating in the program. If the number of programs is growing as desired, there should also be an increase in the membership.

3. *Cost Reduction:* In Japan one of the biggest movements in the manufacturing area is to reduce the cost of manufacturing a product without lowering its quality. Quality Circles are vigorously and continuously working in this area and helping the nation to compete successfully in the world.
   Example: Assembly of electronic guidance system. A Quality Circle was formed in this area and came up with a cost-reducing solution—a 46% reduction in cost over a period of two years.

4. *Waste Reduction:* This measure goes hand in hand with cost reduction. However, we concentrate on eliminating the waste and in turn save money.

   Example: Cartons were used in the assembly area to pack material. Later they were delivered to another area where the material was to be used and the cartons thrown away. Following Quality Circle suggestions, the cartons were returned to the original department, and that waste was reduced by 100%.

5. *Machine Utilization:* This is another unique area that can be used to measure the effectiveness of the program. Proper machine utilization helps to improve efficiency and consequently reduces the cost of production.

   Example: The time required to set up the die with an old machine was approximately 6 to 7 hours. One of the Quality Circles worked on this and reduced the set-up time to only half an hour and thus increased the speed of production.

6. *Safety:* The importance of safety is known to everyone. Savings and improvements are measurable but the achievements gained in this area benefit mankind.

   Example: Quality Circles interviewed about 300 people in one plant and came up with a list of important safety items that should be taken care of immediately. Pareto analysis was used and key items were highlighted. Many critical situations were fixed within six months.

7. *Productivity:* For the last few years, the rate of productivity in the United States has declined tremendously. This is causing a lot of anxiety among the business people. Quality Circles are one vehicle that can be used to improve productivity. However, to eliminate jobs is not the objective of Quality Circles.

   Example: One of the famous electronic industries started assembly of printed circuit boards under two different conditions. Three pilot lines where Circles were in operation showed significant improvement in their productivity as compared to the six other lines where there were no Circles in operation.

8. *Machine Maintenance:* Many times companies talk about well-designed, systematic, maintenance programs. However, in reality these are myths. Many machines are overlooked because of a lack of manpower or time. Quality Circles can improve this situation by proposing short but necessary maintenance to keep the machines running.

   Example: A machine was purchased about 12 years ago. Because of customer demand for production there was no good maintenance plan. When the machine broke down it would be fixed over the weekend. Quality Circles showed how a preventive maintenance program could be carried on to fix the worn-out parts of the machine before the machine got completely out of order. The use of holiday and vacation repair periods was also proposed to avoid hampering production.

9. *Communication:* Good communication is one of the critical ingredients in running an efficient business. Without proper communication many important matters are delayed, orders get lost, and dissatisfaction arises in many areas. After the implementation of one Circle project, a phone call came from one of the Circle mem-

bers complimenting the company for starting the program. The caller said that things were changing in his area. People talked with each other openly and were starting to get to know each other, which had never happened before.

Example: Information regarding die work at the end of the run and die transfer in the shop was not clearly conveyed to all of the people working in that area. A written procedure was prepared by one of the Circle groups to communicate with various departments and to eliminate confusion and misunderstanding.

10. *Attitude:* This is another element that is difficult to measure. One can take an attitude survey before and after the Quality Circles are introduced in the organization. All the indicators that are measured will without doubt show dramatic improvements. Mike Donovan, Honeywell Corporation, Minneapolis, Minnesota, has developed a "Reaction Survey" to survey the reactions of the people. The following indicators were used in the survey:
    1. Cooperation
    2. Communication
    3. Management responsiveness
    4. Use of job knowledge
    5. Role clarity
    6. Participation
    7. Feedback
    8. Task significance
    9. Recognition

11. *Product Improvement:* Quality Circles are not involved so much in this area at present. However, as the program grows and experience is gained, one can see definite improvments in the product through Quality Circle work.

Example: One model was studied by the Circle to improve the performance. The Circle came up with the suggestion to eliminate four parts and add one that would improve the performance of the model.

12. *Customer Satisfaction:* Progress can be measured by reviewing customer satisfaction. The service department can also help to gather feedback on what is happening in the field so that quality can be improved in the shop.

Example: The Toyota Company was trying to improve customer satisfaction. Customer complaints were presented to the Quality Circles who were asked to eliminate the problems. The information created a lot of constructive action in the shop which resulted in good projects for Circles.

13. *Absenteeism:* This is another measure of the effectiveness of the Circles. It is reported in many companies that people enjoy the Circle work and participation in it. Jobs become more interesting, people look forward to work, and this consequently helps to cut down on absenteeism.

14. *Grievances:* This is also a powerful indicator of the success of the Circles. If the Circles can work on the problems that are job related, many causes of unhappiness can be eliminated before they become major problems. This consequently should result in less dissatisfaction and fewer grievances.

Example: General Motors has used this measure in the Tarrytown, New York, plant. The study showed grievances were reduced markedly in the last three years.

15. *Work Satisfaction:* This will be the ultimate measure of the Quality Circle success, but it will not be an easy measurement to take. It will be necessary to design a survey and test the results using statistical methods. Rank order statistics or non-parametric statistics can be used to measure the improvements.

Since a Quality Circle program is based on a people-building philosophy one has to keep in mind that Circle members should achieve happiness in the long range so that the program can have a lasting impact on the organization.

A company may start this kind of program because of the amount of publicity that the program has received. It is crucial, however, that the financial aspects of the progress are evaluated continuously so that a progress report can be provided on request to the top management.

Without such review, there is a great danger that when times are bad, a company may decide to stop these activities and go back to the old system. This kind of review of the Circle progress also helps the company to know where the program will go. In addition, it helps to plan the future needs of the program. Progress indicators can act as a compass that helps to sail the ship in the proper direction toward its destination.

21

QUALITY CIRCLES IN SERVICE INDUSTRIES AND MANAGEMENT

Quality Circles in Japan started in the manufacturing areas and resulted in tremendous growth in the manufacturing facilities. However, the basic ideas are spreading into other areas also. In the United States there are more service industries than manufacturing industries and it is necessary to see how the Quality Circle philosophy can work in those service industries.

Quality Circles in Service Industries

During the 1980s there will be an unbelievable explosion of Quality Circle concepts in all industries and at all organizational levels. A few of the organizations that may welcome the Quality Circle concept are banks, hospitals, schools, insurance companies, government agencies, department stores, restaurants, and motels.

Since there is historically no broad base for applying this concept in the service areas, the integrity and validity of the program in this area are still open to question. However, let us review the basic objectives of the program.

1. *Quality:* Improving quality is a never-ending job whether you manufacture a product or offer a service. People demand quality service and if they don't get it, they turn to another firm that offers better quality services.

2. *Cost Reduction:* Cost reduction is also of great concern in today's inflationary conditions. Operating costs of hospitals or other service industries are increasing at a rapid pace, so it is necessary to find ways to eliminate the waste so that the services remain competitive without loosing the quality image. If through small groups better attention is paid to these areas, it is possible to achieve cost reduction in service industries.

3. *Communication:* One cannot deny the importance of communication in service industries. As long as different people with different personalities are involved in giving services confusion and misunderstanding are bound to exist. Poor communication can cause dissatisfaction and create undue tension. The use of Quality Circles based on a people-building philosophy would help to improve communication in the service industry.

4. *Productivity:* Productivity in the United States is lagging behind other countries. In fact, the recent statistics show that growth is almost nil. In Japan, West Germany, and France productivity is growing at more than 5% annually. Reducing costs and eliminating unnecessary efforts should help to improve productivity.

5. *Job Satisfaction:* We have discussed this element at various places in this book. A person has to feel happy and enthusiastic at his work and should take pride in that work. Quality Circles help people feel important and help to bring harmony into an organization.

As has been shown, these major objectives are also applicable to the service industries. Consequently, there is no reason why this program won't work in any service industry. However, a major hurdle to overcome in implementing Quality Circles in the service industry is that in 1981 most of the material being written and published is based on conditions in the manufacturing industries. Similiarly, many of the case studies that are published also deal with industrial problems. There seems to be a great need at present for material applicable to service industries.

This writer is using the following 10-hour training program in one hospital and a department store, and it is being well received so far.

Proposed Training for Quality Circles in Service Industry
Week 1: (a) Orientation
         (b) Importance of good communication, good quality, waste reduction, and so on.
         (c) Quality Circles: What are they, and why?
Week 2: Group dynamics (See Chapter 13)
Week 3: Brainstorming (See Chapter 11)
Week 4: Pareto analysis
Week 5: Cause and effect analysis
Week 6: Check sheets, graphs

Week 7: Flow process and operation analysis
Week 8: Operator activity analysis
Week 9: Importance of quality, work sampling
Week 10: Circle formation
Graduation

Most of these techniques have already been discussed. The three techniques that need a little more explanation are flow process and operation process analysis, operator activity analysis, and work sampling.

1. *Flow Process and Operation Analysis:* Flow process and operation process analysis involve studying various operations and the flow of the material or product in the hospital or in a department store. Special forms are designed to study these operations. The principal aim is to eliminate unnecessary operations, reduce waste, and improve efficiency. For example, a lot of unnecessary paper work and paper handling can be eliminated by using this technique.

2. *Operator Activity Analysis:* This is another useful technique where you study one work area and try to redesign that work area to eliminate unnecessary operations. The technique is discussed in a number of other books, including *Motion and Time Study* by B. W. Niebel. To implement this technique it may be necessary to reshuffle the employee while balancing the workload and elminating unecessary functions in a service industry. This task should be pursued very diplomatically.

3. *Work Sampling:* This technique is also known as the "ratio-delay" technique. With the help of this technique one can analyze how the job is performed and how much time is spent in doing various activities. For example, a medical technician's functions can be observed and can be broken down as follows:

Write reports	10% of time
Take samples	10% of time
Answer phones	25% of time
Take messages	10% of time
Examine samples	25% of time
Other	10% of time
Rest period	10% of time

After studying the above analysis, one can evaluate each activity and improve efficiency by eliminating unnecessary activity or reducing the time spent doing such an activity.

It must be remembered that activities and work handling conditions in hospitals, banks, and other service industries are quite different from those in manufacturing industries. The types of people employed and their skills are different too. Hence, it is necessary to employ specific techniques to analyze the various activities and work handling methods in the service industries.

The following cast studies are designed to show the application of techniques and principles of Quality Circles. (The actual facts have been altered to provide anonymity to the cases.)

CASE STUDY NO. 1

JSK Hospital in Lakin, Oklahoma, was trying to reduce operating costs of the hospital. Many areas were studied to discover excessive expenses. Management put together the report which showed the following operating costs (excluding salaries).

- —Heat
- —Water
- —Telephone
- —Outside services
- —Garbage collection, disposals
- —Office and other supplies
- —Insurance
- —Car license fees
- —Rental cars
- —Emergency services
- —Postage and telex
- —Medical supplies
- —Accounting services

Many employees were anxious to help. However, Mr. White, president of the hospital, was puzzled about how to solve the problem. Can you propose any advice? How and why?

CASE STUDY NO. 2

ABC Savings and Loan Assocation recently hired Mr. Jones as assistant vice-president of the association. During the first two weeks of his tenure he noticed the following:

1. There was excessive paper handling between various departments and very little talk and communication among the groups of people.
2. Many employees arrived late and left promptly at closing time.
3. Rest rooms and surrounding areas were shabby and unclean.
4. Many suggestions given by Susan, Bill, Bob and Debbie, the tellers and loan officers, were ignored.
5. There was no discipline at windows and many customers were showing impatience at being kept waiting for a long time to get service.

Mr. Jones recently heard about the Quality Circle. What kind of advice can you offer him? Propose an implementation plan.

CASE STUDY NO. 3

Mr. Williams, President of Flanagan Insurance Company, recently noticed that the insurance business was showing a drastic decline. He decided to improve the situation by instituting a training program for insurance agents. The following plans were proposed to Mr. Williams.

1. Send an angry letter to each insurance agent along with new training program.
2. Call each agent individually and explain the problem and ask for mandatory improvements by offering training.
3. Call groups by area and explain the problem to them. Later, ask for suggestions and show them the training program that would contribute to increased sales.

Based on Quality Circle principles, analyze each proposal and discuss the consequences.

CASE STUDY NO. 4

The State of New Jersey's Department of Labor and Industry has had participative-problem-solving teams in operation for more than a year. The technique was initiated with 16 pilot teams whose members scored such high-quality results that last September department officials offered to train 18 additional department employees and supervisors as trainer/consultants to put the program on a permanent basis.[1]

Among the problem-solving achievements recorded by the pilot groups were suggestions by a payroll section on how to speed preparation of payrolls and thereby eliminate in-week and Saturday overtime for an annual savings of approximately $3,600. An accounting unit having problems with microfiche copies proposed remedies expected to save nearly $3,000 annually in materials and production time. Another section reduced the delay frequency of a major report from six days late to zero while increasing the accuracy of source information by 75 percent.

A clerical group reduced error frequency on rush jobs by establishing a workflow-quality checkpoint system. Their procedure, which saved a total of 30 hours a week, is now being used for other work and to reduce pressure on other rush jobs.

In addition there was a general increase in employee satisfaction, morale, and more effective teamwork within the work groups. For instance, one group identified their problem as being employee motivation and increasing productivity. During the pilot program, they identified the areas that were counterproductive and made efforts to improve them.

But the amount of dollar savings effected by these activities isn't the major point. Rather, what is germane, a department official said, "is the demonstration that employees at all levels within an organization can provide solutions to their daily work problems and thereby increase their own productivity." Another gain was a "significant increase in job satisfaction."

Quality Circles
in Management Areas

Quality Circles in management areas are growing rapidly in the United States. Companies like Westinghouse, Hewlett-Packard, Mercury Marine, and others reportedly are involved in training many management people in this type of activity.

The following areas have generally shown more interest in Quality Circles:

1. Engineering
2. Purchasing
3. Material control

4. Industrial engineering
5. Data processing
6. Finance or accounting

As discussed many times before the basic Quality Circle principles are applicable to any group, and one should not consider the above list complete.

Quality Circles in management areas are new in style. However, many departments hold project meetings which can be considered informal Quality Circles in action. Many times companies form "task forces" to solve complicated problems. These are also informal Quality Circles. However, the major difference between the informal and formal Quality Circle is the basic principle of "voluntary participation" and the training offered to the members. Similarly, even though the problems solved do help the company, the problems that are picked by the Circle members create more interest in the group in addition to satisfaction later.

TRAINING AND IMPLEMENTATION

The training proposed earlier, is also applicable in the management area. Most of the problems and the type of work is similar. Hence, the type of training can be similar. Any additional specific training based on the particular needs of the group will be highly useful. But it is not necessary at the beginning of the Circle program. As time passes more training can always be added to improve the efficiency of the group.

Implementation plans can also be similar as shown in chapter 8. Always go slow. Try pilot plans and then expand. To join a winning team, follow these rules to achieve the success. Always remember the voluntary aspect and the people-building philosophy of the program.

Let us review a few case studies that will show the success of the program in management areas.

CASE STUDY NO. 5

Data Processing: Many people in the data processing department of Lysing Company had heard about Quality Circles. A sign-up sheet was circulated in the department for volunteers. After the circulation was completed, the sheet was sent to the facilitator who later conducted eight hours of training for all members.

Members formed the circle called the "M.I.S." Circle. Brainstorming was used to select the project. The Circle aided in the analysis of excess paper consumption for computer reports. Approximately 25 reports were analyzed for the sample study. Discussions were held with various personnel. A sample study conducted showed the reduction of paper use to about 15 percent. The M.I.S. Circle later presented the solution to the management and asked permission to study more reports in a similar way.

CASE STUDY NO. 6

This case study was presented at the second annual IAQC Conference held in San Francisco in 1979.[2]

Westinghouse Electric Corporation of Baltimore is very active in Quality Circles. At present there are more than one hundred Circles in this company. Many of them also operate in management areas. The following project was presented by their purchasing department.

Like death and taxes, the problem of material overshipment is a sure thing among large procurement organizations. Some suppliers repeatedly deliver more material against a given purchase order than is ordered. Yet the magnitude of this problem is rarely perceived. The purchasing department Quality Circle group at the Westinghouse Defense Center in Baltimore, Maryland, undertook this type of analysis to address the problem of overshipments.

Recognizing the complexity of the problem, the V.O.S.R. began to apply Quality Circle techniques to find the causes of the problem. A cause and effect or "fishbone" diagram (Figure 21–1) was constructed and all potential causes were listed.

Each invoice was analyzed by the Quality Circle members and categorized according to this analysis. From the data, a Pareto diagram was constructed ranking the causes in order of occurrence from the highest number to the lowest.

The Pareto diagram indicated that the leading causes could be pinpointed as the vendor's attitude or rather as the vendor's apathy. Anything in excess of the 10 percent was considered as an overshipment.

Once this was established, the Quality Circle members began to find ways to implement the solutions they had agreed upon. One that is somewhat obvious is to print Westinghouse's standard terms and conditions regarding overshipments on each purchase order issued. Figure 21–2 shows the trend of over-shipments before and after issuance of the letter through May 1979. As is shown, a definite decrease resulted in a very large cost savings to Westinghouse. Needless to say, the solution recommended by the V.O.S.R.'s was effective and the value of Quality Circles proved itself.

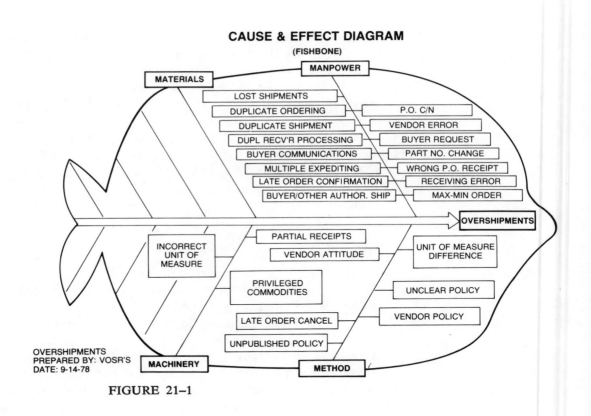

CAUSE & EFFECT DIAGRAM
(FISHBONE)

FIGURE 21–1

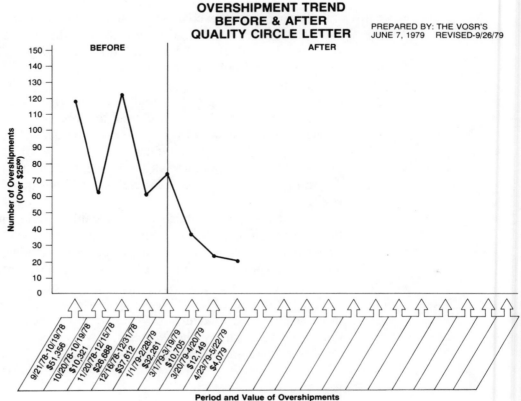

FIGURE 21–2   Overshipments trend before and after Quality Circle letter.

OVERSHIPMENT TREND
BEFORE & AFTER
QUALITY CIRCLE LETTER

Notes

1. Sidney P. Rubenstein, "Participative Problem Solving: How to Increase Organizational Effectiveness," PERSONNEL, January-February 1977 (New York: AMACOM, a division of American Management Associations, 1977), pp. 30-39.

2. D. F. Aiello, "Material Overshipments," presentation delivered to Second Annual IAQC Conference, San Francisco, February 1980.

22
QUALITY CIRCLE ACTIVITY SURVEY

Quality Circles have been in existence in Japan for the past 18 years, and the concept is just beginning to catch the eyes of U.S. industries. Few companies in the United States had this type of program in the 1970s. However, the real publicity was generated by the Lockheed program in 1973. Many articles were published on the program that was developed in the Lockheed company. Many visitors watched the program. Since then the Quality Circle activities are growing by leaps and bounds in the United States. A number of companies have installed pilot or full scale versions of the program. The formation of IAQC (International Association of Quality Circles) has also helped to promote these activities in the United States.

It may be helpful to review major surveys that were conducted recently in the United States. This information should be helpful to new companies in the formation of a Quality Circle program.

The following information was collected by IAQC during 1979 and 1980: [1]

1. Quality Circle growth in U.S.A. (See Figure 22–1.)
2. What areas do Quality Circles operate in? Manufacturing, engineering, office, stockroom, warehouse, accounting, data processing, purchasing, quality control, maintenance stores.
3. When do you hold the meetings? (See Figure 22–2.)
4. Do you pay for the meeting time? (See Figure 22–3.)

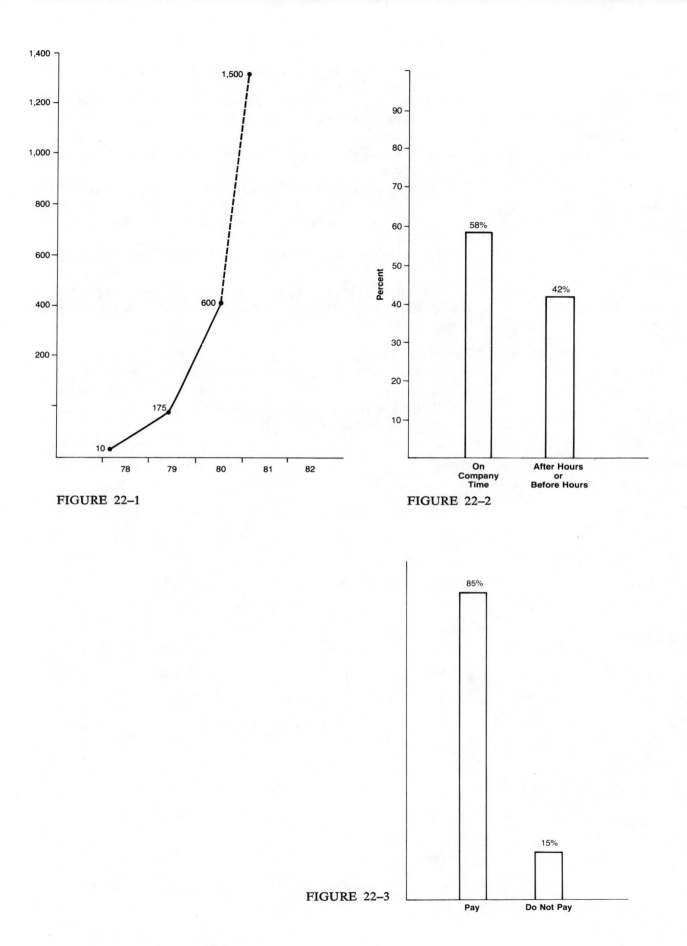

FIGURE 22–1

FIGURE 22–2

FIGURE 22–3

223

5. How long do you train the Quality Circle members? (See Figure 22–4.)
6. How long do you train the leaders? (See Figure 22–5.)
7. How do the Quality Circle leaders get elected? (See Figure 22–6.)
8. What kinds of problems are studied by Quality Circles? (See Figure 22–7.)
9. How many Circles did you use in your pilot program? (See Figure 22–8.)
10. What is the frequency of your Circle meetings? (See Figure 22–9.)
11. How long was your pilot program? (See Figure 22–10.)

During our visit to Japan we visited a few companies. The following points are based on the information that was discussed with these companies.

1. How many people are involved in the Circles in your company? Most of them answered between 80 percent to 90 percent. However, all Circles and Circle members are not effective.
2. Do you pay for the Circle activities? Some do and some do not.

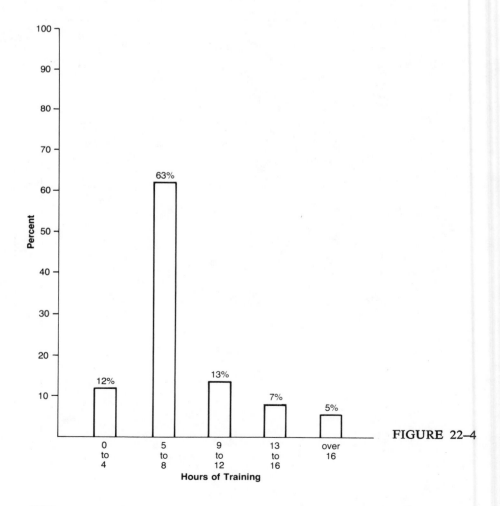

FIGURE 22–4

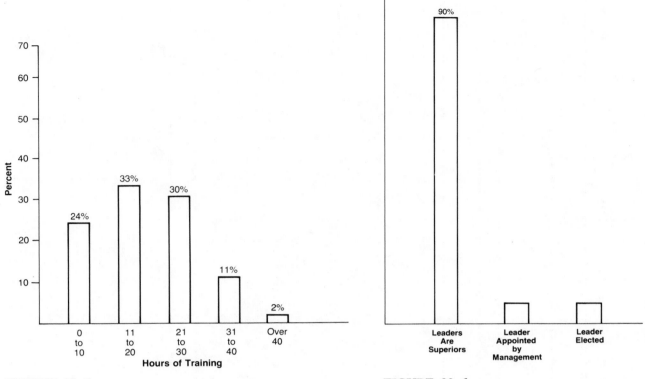

FIGURE 22–5

FIGURE 22–6

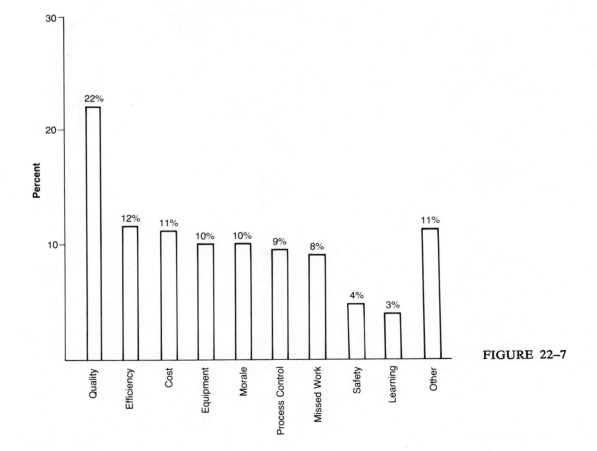

FIGURE 22–7

225

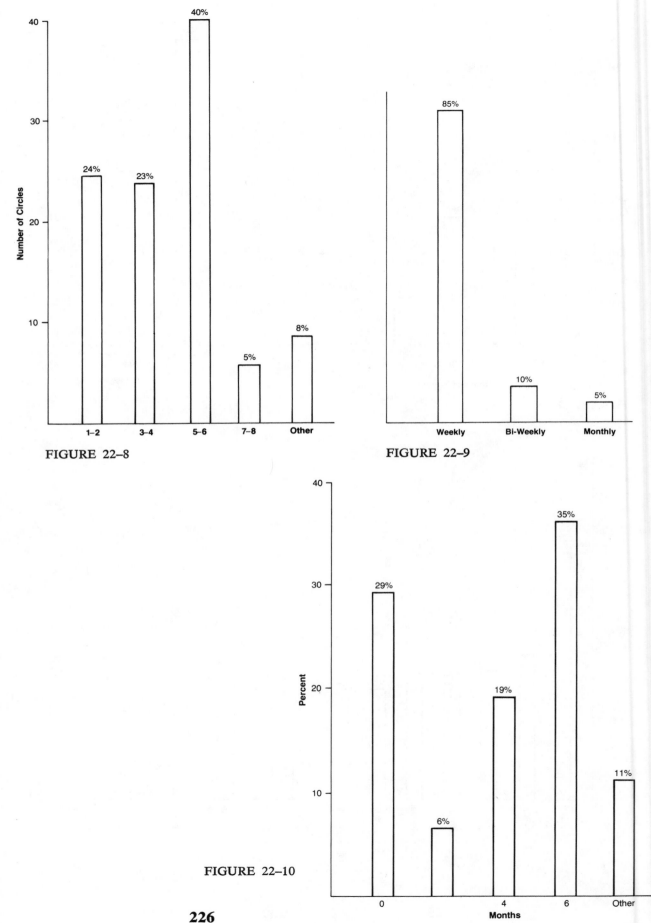

FIGURE 22–8

FIGURE 22–9

FIGURE 22–10

3. What is the feeling of union leaders toward Circle activities?
   Most of them are neutral.
4. When are the Circle meetings?
   Some of them work on company time and many of them meet after work.
5. What kind of problems are solved in Quality Circles?
   Cost reduction, quality, safety, maintenance, and many others.
6. What kind of statistical techniques are used in the Quality Circles?
   Pareto diagrams, cause and effect diagrams, histograms, control charts, graphs, plant-layout, sampling, check sheets.

JUSE (Union of Japanese Scientists and Engineers) does a similar survey in Japan and will supply more information.

As mentionted before one of the major reasons to include these surveys in the book is to guide new companies to a smooth start. Many of these industries need direction, and the information on this program should be valuable to the newcomers. It is not necessary to follow the majority but at least it helps to discover the many old avenues before deciding to create new ways. Surveys also help to exchange good information which finds its way directly and indirectly to many companies. As the Quality Circle program grows in the United States, no doubt many changes will occur in the procedures, however the basic foundation and the philosophy will remain the same for a long time.

Notes

1. "Survey of Quality Circle Activities," *IAQC Quality Circle Quarterly*, 2nd quarter 1980, and "Results of Recent IAQC Survey," *ibid.*, 3rd quarter 1979.

23
APPROACHES TO STARTING QUALITY CIRCLES

We have discussed the various elements that are involved in the Quality Circle program. We have analyzed why Quality Circles can and will work in any kind of environment.

Basic statistical techniques that are commonly used in analyzing problems have also reviewed in other chapters. In short, anyone interested in promoting and planning to implement the Quality Circle program should be able to digest this material and propose a plan to the management of his or her company.

There are many ways to start the program. The following are four major ways to proceed:

1. Design your own program
2. Use available material
3. Attend seminars
4. Seek outside help

1. *Design Your Own Program:* As mentioned before in chapter 2, many companies in the United States have had informal Quality Circles in operation. Even today these informal Circles exist in small companies.

It is reported that one company in Pennsylvania uses what is called the "team approach" strategy. Whenever there is a problem that needs to be tackled, people in the shop area are brought together with the office people. A team is formed to solve the specific problem. The team is then given an opportunity to do whatever is necessary to eliminate the trouble spot. When the problem is solved or minimized the team is given appropriate recognition by the management. That team is dissolved and another team or teams are formed when needed in some other area of the company. This process goes on continuously.

Another small company in Iowa has adopted a slightly different approach. The president of the company holds monthly meetings with all employees present and briefs them about the business and about problems the company faces in various areas. Then the employees are asked to help in solving daily problems. Those who come up with good ideas are recognized in the next meeting, and dinner certificates are awarded for the family.

Huron Machine products, a Fort Lauderdale, Florida, based company, has introduced productivity teams in that company. These groups are asked for their advice on managing the company. The employees helped to cut costs, improve work flows, improve communications, and reduce conflicts in the company. The details of this were discussed in June 1980 issue of *Modern Machine Shop*.

When Japanese firms purchase companies in the United States they follow similar informal Quality Circle patterns. Generally, at the end of the shift the foremen hold daily meetings with the employees. These last about 15 minutes. Problems and suggestions are discussed and analyzed. The top management also follows the same system by holding weekly meetings and tries to implement resulting suggestions as soon as possible. One of the companies reported that the reject rates were reduced from 140 defects per 100 units to less than 4 to 5 defects per 100 units. One can achieve this type of success only with enthusiastic partcipation from the entire work force.

There is nothing wrong with these informal circles. Improved efficiency and effectivness can be achieved by offering good training programs in statistical techniques so that many problems can be solved systematically and not reappear. The training and group interaction are important in improving the quality of workmanship. Small companies which do not want to form large elaborate formal Quality Circle programs can follow an informal system and still achieve cohesiveness and unity in the company.

2. *Use Available Material:* Today many articles are published on the Quality Circle subject. More and more material on Quality Circles is available through I.A.Q.C., A.S.Q.C., and J.U.S.E. A study of all the material and an understanding of the basic principles can aid in formalizing a program suitable for an individual company's needs. Consult the bibliography for more references.

A company which is interested in this type of informal approach should appoint a person to collect all the material. That person can be employed part-time at the beginning. As the program grows, a full-time job can be created for him or her as a coordinator or a program manager. Generally, a person in quality control or industrial relations departments can do a good job. Those companies who cannot commit substantial financial support can try this approach. However, it is important to select the candidate carefully and to make sure he or she is really interested in promoting this participative style in the company. This approach is slow and also requires a lot of time spent in convincing others. It also involves a lot of homework by the assigned person. The coordinator or program director has to be patient and persistent, since progress in this case is predictably slow, and sometimes the program can die if support from the management is not forthcoming on time.

3. *Attend Seminars:* Today seminars on Quality Circles are offered at many places. There are three main types of seminars that are offered to the public:

One-Day Introductory Seminar
1. Introducing the Quality Circle concept into your own organization
2. Behavioral aspects of Quality Circles
3. Implementation of a Quality Circle program
4. Functions of the Quality Circle groups
5. Quality Circle Techniques
6. Maintaining Quality Circle operations

Two- or Three-Day Leaders' Seminar
1. Introduction
2. Objectives and goals
3. History
4. Functions
5. Group dynamics
6. Leadership
7. Communication
8. Motivation
9. Participation
10. Management presentation
11. Quality Circle techniques
12. Successful leader
13. Open discussion

Four- or Five-Day Facilitators' Seminar
1. History of Quality Circles
2. Circle operation
3. Circle implementation plan
4. Functions
5. Quality Circle techniques
6. Training techniques
7. Group dynamics
8. Leadership
9. Participation
10. Coordinator's role
11. Functions of the coordinator
12. Circle maintenance

13. Project follow-up
14. Planning for training
15. Promotional activities

Companies who plan to use this approach should first send one or two people to an introductory seminar and later on preferably one person to a facilitator's seminar. The wealth of knowledge that can be gathered in these courses helps to give Quality Circles a little faster and better start in new companies. Some companies in the United States adopted this method in 1979 and 1980. It is also reported that those companies who used this approach achieved remarkable progress within a short period of time.

4. *Seek Outside Help:* This method helps to expedite the Quality Circle program effectively and smoothly. Many mistakes that might occur are avoided with experienced help. However, since sometimes this type of outside help is unwelcome, great care must be exercised in employing people from outside the company. Financial constraints also become critical factors in employing outside help. However, companies should evaluate the need, its objective, and benefits, and then arrive at a final decision as to whether to rely on internal sources in implementing this program or go abroad for it. In some cases a company might decide to drop this possibility completely because of old traditions and influences.

Planning for Quality Circles

Quality Circles deal with human management and it is this unique management style that is new to most U.S. companies. It is necessary to proceed slowly and cautiously in implementing this program. It should only be undertaken after many hours of careful planning. It is advisable to start a pilot program and if that succeeds, then expand. Figures 23–1 23–2 will show two different plans that were followed in two companies in the United States. The step-by-step planning that is outlined will demonstrate how to adopt the Quality Circle program in the new environment slowly but surely and still make it successful in the long run.

Consider the following examples to avoid making the mistakes that might occur when a new Quality Circle program is started.

Case Study No. 1: Management of NCB Company in Iowa recently sent two people to a Quality Circle seminar. When they returned from the seminar, they made an enthusiastic presentation to the management. Management decided to start the Circle program. Volunteers were called for from various departments and within two months approximately fifty Circles were started. However, no provision had been made for a facilitator or meeting areas. Similarly, management presentations were made but there was no systematic follow up. After six months, management noticed that many Circle members were dropping from the program.

231

PRODUCTION DIVISION PROJECT SCHEDULE

PROJECT: **QUALITY CIRCLES**

Task	8/2	8/9	8/16	8/23	8/30	9/6	9/13	9/20	9/27	10/4	10/11	10/18	10/25	11/1	11/8	11/15	11/22	11/29	12/6	12/13	12/20	12/27	1/3	1/10
Form Steering Committee			■																					
Appoint a Facilitator	■																							
Train the Facilitator								■																
Pick Team Leaders									■															
Train Team Leaders										■														
Inform Union Officials									■															
Inform all Employees											■													
Pick Trial Departments											■													
Indoctrinate Trial Depts.												■												
Pick Circle Members													■											
Train Circle Members															■	■	■							
Begin Official Operation of Circles																				■				
Determine Additional Circles																								■

FIGURE 23–1

Case Study No. 2: SKL Company in Chicago recently heard a lot about the Quality Circle program. The management decided to hire an outside consultant since there was no one in the company who knew enough about the program. A meeting was arranged with the consultant. After the first meeting the consultant sent a proposal. The management felt that installation would cost too much and decided to drop the program.

Case Study No. 3: CBN Company in Hillside, New York, recently decided to start the Quality Circle program. However, George Huck, the newly-hired president, was unaware of the other programs that were in operation in the company. A "suggestion" system had been in operation for six months. Work simplification training had been completed recently by the plant managers to improve productivity. An MRP system was under consideration. The parent company was considering introducing "B.A.D." (Buck-a-Day) program within the next three months.

Any comments?

Case Study No. 4: RCD Company realized that in order to stay in business and compete with foreign companies, it was necessary to involve their people. George Hamilton, plant manager, decided to talk with the union leaders and inform them of the newly

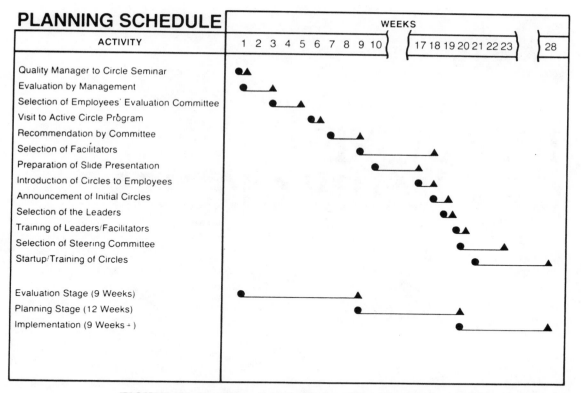

PLANNING SCHEDULE

ACTIVITY	WEEKS

Quality Manager to Circle Seminar

Evaluation by Management

Selection of Employees' Evaluation Committee

Visit to Active Circle Program

Recommendation by Committee

Selection of Facilitators

Preparation of Slide Presentation

Introduction of Circles to Employees

Announcement of Initial Circles

Selection of the Leaders

Training of Leaders/Facilitators

Selection of Steering Committee

Startup/Training of Circles

Evaluation Stage (9 Weeks)

Planning Stage (12 Weeks)

Implementation (9 Weeks +)

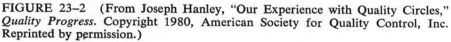

FIGURE 23–2 (From Joseph Hanley, "Our Experience with Quality Circles," *Quality Progress.* Copyright 1980, American Society for Quality Control, Inc. Reprinted by permission.)

promoted Quality Circle program. Union leaders showed no interest at all.

George wondered what to do next.

Case Study No. 5: Mr. Wright, President of "Do It" Company, read a lot of material about the Quality Circle program. He instructed the subordinates to arrange a meeting with all department heads and plan to start Quality Circles in "Do It" Company. Mr. Wright personally attended the meetings and wrote an enthusiastic article in the company paper. However, Mr. Wright later got involved with joint ventures in China and Europe. The program was forgotten for the next six months. When he returned to the main office he found that very little action had been taken on the program. He ordered that the Quality Circle program start right away; however, very few people showed any interest in the program.

Any comments?

24

THE FUTURE OF QUALITY CIRCLES

The story of Quality Circles is by no means complete. Quality Circles have no cultural or economic boundaries. The underlying philosophy can work in any society—all that is needed is a strong will and determination. The world is in constant turmoil and no one can stand still and hope to get rid of the many problems confronting business today.

We are moving in a jet age and tomorrow conditions may be even worse. As Alvin Toffler stated in his *Third Wave*, "things are going to happen much faster in the future and only those companies who will keep up with the fast pace will stay alive in the 21st century."

Human management in the 1980s is going to be a critical issue and careful attention must be paid to the participative management style if future management patterns are to be changed.

Review

So far we have discussed the various aspects of the Quality Circle program. As the new needs arise there will be more and more different problems needing increased attention. Historically, this program has proved to be of a universal nature. It is up to each society to modify it and use it to its fullest extent. No one can force this type of change in management nor a change in the attitude of the people. It has to be arrived at voluntarily and nurtured slowly.

This book began with a historical background of Quality Circles and revealed the superb work that has been accomplished by the Japanese people. "Informal organization" of the Quality Circle and the functions of each individual have been discussed, as well as statistical techniques and how to use them. Figure 24-1 briefly summarizes the various elements of Quality Circles.

Cautionary Notes

Honeywell, Inc., the Minneapolis-based control and information giant, recently held a quality conference to promote the use of the Quality Circle philosophy in all of its divisions, which involve approximately 90,000 people. Dr. R. Cole, professor of sociology and the director of the Center for Japanese studies at the University of Michigan, Ann Arbor, was the keynote speaker for the conference. Dr. Cole contends that Quality Circles are "about to boom" in the United States, but he warns that if Circles are implemented in an organization because "everyone else is doing it" the effort could "boomerang." Cole's expertise comes in part from spending five years in Japan studying the work,

QUALITY CIRCLE REVIEW

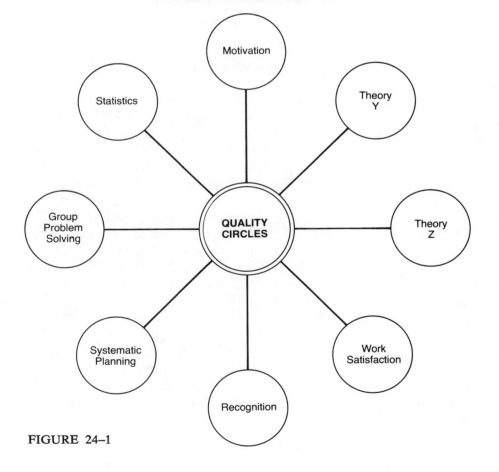

FIGURE 24–1

workers, and work systems. Much of Cole's message is that Quality Circles work, but American management needs to think through the potential problems and the ramifications of installing them. Among Cole's other points to ponder are these:

—Never underestimate management's ability to mismanage. Middle management can be very threatened by Circles and that can be a big obstacle to successful implementation. They have to see a positive payoff—Quality Circles are not a program but a way of managing. There is no free lunch to be had from Quality Circles, and it is hard work to bring them into being.

—The issue of measuring ROI (return on investment) from Circles can be a red herring. The Japanese don't try.

—Quality Circles do contribute to the improvement of the quality of working life, but their primary purpose is to improve quality of product and productivity. The further the focus moves from that objective, the further you get from the technological base, the quality control tools that make them work. People respond better to the technical problems. They know how to make things work. The QWL is a side effect, not a reason for being.

—You have to *keep* challenging the Circles to function properly. A few years ago at Toyota, they stimulated the Circles by challenging them to eliminate customer complaints. That kind of thinking is necessary to keep the effort alive. You cannot start Circles and then walk away from them.[1]

Copy Wisely

In NBC's *White Paper* program called "If Japan Can, Why Can't We?", commentator Lloyd Dobbins said, "copying won't work, we are two different societies." This remark may create doubts in many people's minds about the viability of Quality Circle programs in the United States or any other country. Simply copying the Japanese in Quality Circle techniques may not result in lasting benefits because of the difference in cultural backgrounds.

Therefore it is important to understand the basic concept accounting for the success of Quality Circles. Only then can other aspects, such as the use of statistics or group dynamics, be modified to suit the needs of U.S. society. Since Quality Circles are based on a "people-building philosophy," and since the basic motives of recognition and self-fulfilment exist in all people, the concept should work anywhere, if copied properly rather than superficially.

In the NBC program, Dobbins commented further that "All humans think, and nowhere is it chiseled in stone that those in management think best." It is this belief that will make some form of the Quality Circle work anywhere in the world.

Do We Need Quality Circles?

The Quality Circle program is growing rapidly in the United States and many companies have heard a number of stories of successes.

Many of these companies will wonder how those successes were achieved. They will ask themselves "Do we need Quality Circles?" There is no simple answer to this question. From the discussion so far it is apparent that it is not easy to implement this program overnight nor to see immediate results. Another fact about the program is that it does not cure all the problems, nor is it for everyone in the world.

But one can draw the conclusion that to keep up with the future world happenings, there is an urgent need to change management styles. More attention must be paid to the people. Their brainpower can be used to improve the business climate, as well as the society we live in. Participation doesn't mean giving up authority. Top management will still establish the goals and be responsible for the results. However, management can let *all* the people in the organization help them to achieve those goals by letting them participate in decision making during various phases of the business. Remember, "There is no limit to what we can do together." The world is in economic turmoil and it is up to all of us together to build the future. No one else is going to help us, and once the horse is out of the barn, there is no use in closing the door.

Many companies under Japanese management do not at present have "formal Quality Circles." However, many changes have occurred in these companies which have led them to use the full potential of the workers. The result was big profit. The United States has the same pool of people.

Some of the key changes are as follows:

1. *Use Proven Designs:* Before anyone starts manufacturing the product, the design must be reliable and quality oriented and must be able to be duplicated in the manufacturing processes.
2. *Maintain Close Relationship:* Maintaining a close relationship between manufacturing engineering and design engineering helps to eliminate problems in implementing any new process or product without too much difficulty.
3. *Stop the Assembly Lines:* The basic philosophy is "build the product right the first time." The idea being, it is cheaper to fix the product in assembly rather than later on in other areas. It is much more costly to fix it in the field.
4. *Worker Participation:* There are many different ways to get workers involved in many decision-making processes. The following are just a few:
   a. Daily 15-minute meetings with the foremen or supervisor at the end of the shift
   b. Monthly meetings with foreman and management

c. Use informal "Quality Circles" by getting workers' help in implementing or analyzing the problems

d. Group discussions

5. *Effective Communication:*

a. Monthly or weekly meetings on performance and business

b. Display of charts and graphs throughout the company

c. Training programs fit for different levels in the organization

6. *Quality Not Just Quantity:* The importance of quality is stressed at all times. Many areas in the shop have made their own signs. Some of the signs read as follows:

—"Working Together"

—"Be Proud of Your Product"

—"All Aboard——The Quality Train"

—"Cut Down on Scrap"

—"Quality Is Everybody's Job"

7. *Use of Theory "Z":* In America, and for that matter, almost all over the world, most corporations have been organized according to what is called "Type A" with the brass at the top. In a new book entitled *Theory Z,* William Ouchi, a management professor at the University of California, Los Angeles, projects a broader base of decision-making authority with more supervisors and employees brought into the process. A few of the results of implementation of this Theory "Z" would be more efficient running of plants, reduced absenteeism, a lower turnover of employees, and improved quality of product. One can generalize that the Quality Circle is only one way of managing people effectively. But "participative management" is really the key to success in the future and it is essential to plan business activities accordingly.[2]

Random thoughts on Quality Circles presented in the next section should help in determining whether or not to initiate the Quality Circle concept in an individual organization.

Random Thoughts on the Future of Quality Circles

1. *Future Variations:* As the use of Quality Circles increases throughout this country and the rest of the world different forms and types of Circles will emerge. Since different people work in different ways, the successful Circles will be those adapted to the particular society in which they are developed. In the United States, we will probably see a growth in the number of both formal and informal Circles and a use of "communication centers" to disseminate information and increase the effectiveness of interfunctional activities.

2. *Increased Participation:* As mentioned before, there are only 300 to 400 companies actively participating in this program. However, there is growing activity all over the country. Many unions and management people are taking a second look at what is happen-

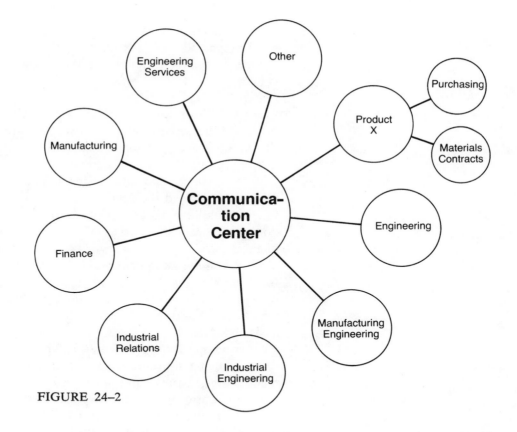

FIGURE 24-2

ing to our economy and to the business world overall. Quality Circles offer a good opportunity to alter the downhill trend of our business. I predict that overall participation is going to increase in the next 10 to 20 years. This is the only way to beat the competition. People will lean towards Theory "Z" when participative management is called for to manage the business.

3. *Union Cooperation:* Unions play an important role in American business. They negotiate the contracts, work on grievances, and function in other related areas in the business. However, there are some basic problems regarding Quality Circles and the participation needs of the company that need the attention of the union leaders. It is essential to eliminae the "we" and "they" spirit that exists between the union and the management and constantly keep in mind that we are all together in business and the only way we are going to survive is to work together in the company. Meeting the competition and putting out quality goods go hand in hand, and cooperation from the union is extremely important to meet this goal for survival in the future.

4. *Quality of Work Life:* The quality of work life program started in General Motors in 1973. For the first few years there were only 4 to 5 plants involved in the program. Today there are approximately 50 plants involved in this program, and the number is growing every year. The quality of work life program tries to use ideas similar to those used in the Quality Circle program but on a broader scale. Many other companies are planning to start similar programs. GM's plant in Tarrytown, New York, is a prime example

of the benefits that can be expected from this program. This plant has changed its image from one of poor quality and performance to one of the best quality and the most efficient plants in GM system.

5. *Labor Management Teams:* Labor management teams will be formed. This is another upcoming development in factories and other similar organizations. Once an agreement is reached with the union leaders, "labor-management teams" will be formed to attack quality problems, communication problems, and thus to help the company improve business. The famous historian, Edward Gibbon, explained the decline and fall of the ancient city of Athens in a few chilling words, "In the end, more than they wanted freedom, they wanted security. They wanted a comfortable life and in their quest for it all—security, comfort and freedom, they lost it all. When the Athenians wanted finally not to give to society, but for society to give to them, when the freedom they wished for most was the freedom from responsibility, then Athens ceased to be free." The question that comes to mind is "Can America escape a similar fate?"

6. *Expansion in Service Industries:* The idea of Quality Circles is recently being introduced to service industries. Hospitals, department stores, banks, and insurance companies also need to cut down on waste and to improve the quality of service they render. I predict that these service units will make use of the basic philosophy slowly and cautiously. As discussed before, benefits are there for all types of people, but judgment must be employed in using this technique.

7. *Growth in IAQC Activities:* The International Association of Quality Circles was formed in 1978. Two years later there were more than 1000 members in the society. By the end of 1990, the prediction is that membership will exceed 50,000 members, and chapters will be formed in many cities. Regional conventions and seminars will increase and participation in annual conventions will also grow astonishingly.

8. *Thrust on Quality:* Recently published reports indicate that Americans view the "quality of the product" as an important factor. The quality of the product built in America in 1981 does not carry the same strong image that it used to in the 1960s and 1970s. Products built in Japan are considered superior and more reliable. Many companies in the United States see this as a threat in 1981 and are trying to put together their efforts to change this picture. The philosophy of "total quality control" is emphasized more emphatically. "Quality from womb to tomb" is being considered vital for success.

Many companies have also elevated quality functions to a higher level of importance. In auto and electronic industries, the quality function is independent and generally the vice-president for quality control reports directly to the president of the company.

9. *Use of Higher Statistics:* Quality Circles today use mostly basic statistical techniques. However, as the Circle members gather experience in problem solving they will face tougher, more complex

manufacturing and engineering problems and will then need to use more complex statistical methods. Refer to chapter 12 to review some of these methods, and also consult books on statistics and quality control engineering.

10. *Quality Circles and Government:* Chapter 21 shows one of the simple uses of Quality Circles in the U.S. Government. The writer believes that in the coming years there will be more and more use of Circles to cut down waste and improve productivity. Many people from the Navy, Army, and other areas have contacted me to gain more insight. Tinker Air Force Base in Oklahoma has been very active in Quality Circles. I hope the effective use of Quality Circles in the U.S. government will eliminate many unnecessary OSHA standards and other waste that leads to inefficiency.

11. *International Role:* The Quality Circle phenomenon is going, sooner or later, to touch every country on the earth. There may not be the same contribution or growth in every country; but it is to be hoped that it will help all of us to build a better society. Dr. Juran has discussed this in detail in an article "International significance of the Quality Circle movement," published in *Quality Progress,* Nov. 1980.

12. *Think Human Development:* Quality Circles are organized based on a people-building philosophy. People like to get together, work together, and see something happen. They feel they can accomplish something by using their brainpower. We need to let everyone in the society contribute to the improvement of life. Alone no one can

FIGURE 24–3

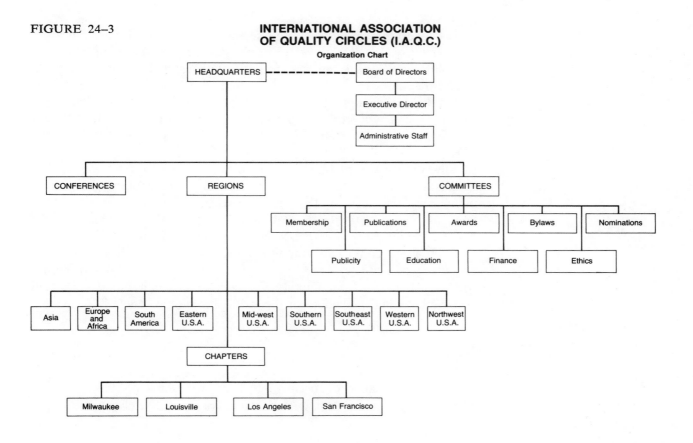

INTERNATIONAL ASSOCIATION
OF QUALITY CIRCLES (I.A.Q.C.)

TOTAL QUALITY SYSTEM

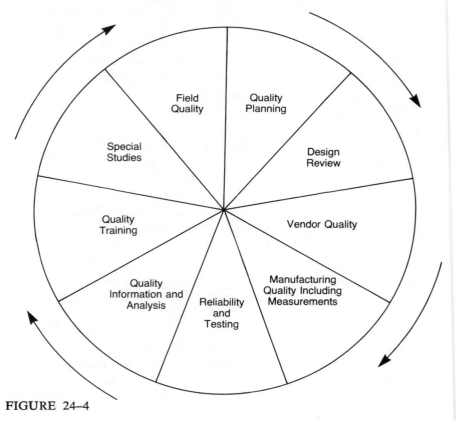

FIGURE 24–4

do everything, not even the scientist or the most gifted person; generally, it helps to seek cooperation and to share the responsibilities. We will see that many countries will follow this path. More and more programs will emerge to improve the work life of human beings and to better the society we live in. The only thing that will stop us from creating new programs and new ways to achieve high standards is the lack of imagination.

Finally, one of the well-known authorities on Quality from Japan, Dr. Ishikawa, has said "Quality Circle activities are rapidly growing in many countries such as Taiwan, United States, Mexico, Brazil, Thailand, Malaysia, Netherlands, Belgium, Denmark, and the United Kingdom. Judging from the common acceptance of the Quality Circle concept, I am convinced that Quality Circle activities have no socioeconomic or cultural limitations. Human beings are human beings wherever they live and Quality Circle activities can be disseminated and implemented anywhere in the world for human bnefit."

Notes

1. Reprinted with permission from the August 1980 issue of TRAINING, The Magazine of Human Resources Development. Copy-

right Lakewood Publications, Minneapolis, MN, (612) 333-0471, pp. 94-95. All rights reserved.

2. For more information, see "An Attractive Japanese Export," *Time,* March 2, 1981, or "The World of Z," *The New York Times,* December 13, 1980. See also William Ouchi, *Theory Z* (Reading, Mass.: Addison-Wesley, 1981).

BIBLIOGRAPHY

The subject of Quality Circles is exciting and popular and there is no end to the materials published daily.

The following is a list of major articles and books on the subject that are both stimulating and innovative.

Books

Amsden, D., and R. Amsden, eds., *Q. C. Circles: Applications, Tools, and Theory*. Milwaukee: ASQC, 1976.

Case, K., and L. Jones, *Profit through Quality; Quality Assurance Programs for Manufacturers*. Atlanta: American Institute of Industrial Engineering, 1978.

Cole R., *Work, Mobility and Participation; a Comparative Study of American and Japanese Industry*. Berkeley, Ca.: University of California, 1979.

Crosby, P.B., *Quality if Free*. New York: McGraw-Hill, 1979.

Dewar, D., *The Quality Circle Handbook*. Red Bluff, Ca.: Quality Circle Institute, 1980.

Drucker, Peter F., *Management*. New York: Harper & Row, 1954.

Hersey, P., and K. Blanchard, *Management of Organizational Behavior: Utilizing Human Resources* (3rd ed.). Englewood Cliffs, N.J.: Prentice-Hall, 1977.

Herzberg, Frederick, *Work and the Nature of Man*. New York: World Publishing, 1966.

International Association of Quality Circles, *Transactions: 2nd Annual Conference*. Feb. 20-22, 1980.

Ishikawa, Kaoru, *Japan Quality Control*. Tokyo: JUSE, 1972.

Likert, Rensis, *New Patterns of Management*. New York: McGraw-Hill, 1961.

Likert, Rensis, *The Human Organization: Its Management and Value*. New York: McGraw-Hill, 1967.

Maslow, A. H., *Motivation and Personality*. New York: Harper & Row, 1954.

McGregor, Douglas, *The Human Side of Enterprise*. New York: McGraw-Hill, 1960.

McGregor, Douglas, *Leadership and Motivation*. Boston: Massachusetts Institute of Technology Press, 1966.

Articles

Alexanderson, B. Orjan, "Quality Circles in Scandinavia," *Quality Progress*, 2, July 1978, 18-19.

Beardsley, J. F., "Training Is the Heart of the Lockheed Quality Control Circle Program," *ASQC 30th Annual Technical Conference Transactions*, June 1976.

Beardsley, J. F., "The Quality Circle Steering Committee," *IAQC Quality Circle Quarterly*, 4th quarter, 1978, 26-30.

Cole, R., "Made in Japan; a Spur to U.S. Productivity," *Asia Magazine*, May/June 1979.

Cole, R. E., "Will Quality Control Circles Work in the U.S.?," *Quality Progress*, July 1980, 30-33.

Deming, W. E., "Japan's Turnaround in Quality," *Quality*, Feb. 1980.

Fenney, E., "Quality Circles Using Pooled Effort to Promote Excellence," *Training HRD*, Jan. 1980.

Guest, R. H., "Quality of Worklife; Learning from Tarrytown," *Harvard Business Review*, July-Aug. 1979, 76-87.

Hanley, J., "Our Experience with Quality Circles," *Quality Progress*, Feb. 1980, 22-24.

Hill, C., and W. Courtwright, "Quality Circles Work," *IAQC Quality Circle Quarterly*, 3rd quarter, 1978, 27-36.

Irving, R. R., "Quality Control Circles Spur to U.S. Productivity, Improve Product Quality," *Iron Age*, June 5, 1978.

Johnson R., and W. Ouchi, "Made in America Under Japanese Management," *Harvard Business Review*, Sept. 1979.

Juran, J. M., "Japanese and Western Quality—A Contrast," *Quality Progress*, Dec. 1978, 10-17.

Konz, S., "Quality Circles: Japanese Success Story," *Industrial Engineering*, Oct. 1979, 24-37.

McClenahen, J. S., "Bringing Home Japan's Lessons," *Industry Week*, Feb. 23, 1981, 62-72.

Naumann, A., "The Importance of Productivity," *Quality Progress,* June 1980, 18-26.

Rieker, W. S., "What Is the Lockheed Quality Control Circle Programs?," *ASQC 30th Annual Tech. Conference Transaction,* June 1976.

Rieker, W. S., "Quality Control Circles," W. S. Rieker, Inc., 1978.

Rubinstein, S., "Participative Problem Solving: How to Increase Organizational Effectiveness," *Personnel,* Jan./Feb. 1977, 30-39.

Shearman, R., "How Can America Increase Productivity in the Next Decade?," *Quality Progress,* Jan. 1979, 22-26.

Swartz, G., and V. Comstock, "One Firm's Experience with Quality Circles," *Quality Progress,* Sept. 1979, 14-16.

Weimer, G., "Blue Collar Workers Are People Too," *Iron Age,* May 18, 1980.

Yager, Edward, "Examining the Quality Control Circle," *Personnel Journal,* Oct. 1979, 682-684.

——— *Wall Street Journal,* Thurs. Feb. 21, 1980, 44.

——— "Humanagement," *Industry Week,* Jan. 7, 1980, 84-90.

——— "More Companies Adopt Quality Circles," *Industry Week,* Aug. 1, 1977, 67-68.

——— "Productivity and Morale Sagging, Try the Quality Circle Approach," *Personnel,* May/June 1980, 43-44.

——— "Quality Circles Become Contagious," *Industry Week,* April 14, 1980, 99-103.

——— "Quality Control Circles Pay off Big," *Industry Week,* Oct. 29, 1979, 17-19.

——— "Quality Control Circles: A Productivity Tool," *Small Business Report,* May 1980.

——— "Quality Control Circles Save Lockheed 3 Million Dollars," *Quality,* May 1977.

——— "Honeywell Imports Quality Circles as Long-Term Management Strategy," *Training/HRD,* Aug. 1980, 91-95.

——— "Japanese Managers Tell How Their System Works," *Fortune,* Nov. 1977, 126-140.

Periodicals

The following periodicals are also a rich source of articles on the topic of Quality Circles.

Fortune	*National Productivity*
Harvard Business Review	*Newsweek*
IAQC Quality Circle Journal	*Personnel*
formerly *IAQC Quality*	*Production*
Circle Quarterly)	*Quality*
Industrial Week	*Training/HRD*
Iron Age	*Quality Progress*